Palgrave Studies in Sustainable Business In Association with Future Earth

Sustainability in Business is increasingly becoming the forefront issue for researchers, practitioners and companies the world over. Engaging with this immense challenge, Future Earth is a major international research platform from a range of disciplines, with a common goal to support and achieve global sustainability. This series will define a clear space for the work of Future Earth Finance and Economics Knowledge-Action Network. Publishing key research with a holistic and trans-disciplinary approach, it intends to help reinvent business and economic models for the Anthropocene, geared towards engendering sustainability and creating ecologically conscious organizations.

More information about this series at
http://www.palgrave.com/gp/series/15667

András Ócsai

Ecologically Conscious Organizations

New Business Practices Based on Ecological Commitment

palgrave
macmillan

András Ócsai
Business Ethics Center
Corvinus University of Budapest
Budapest, Hungary

ISSN 2662-1320 ISSN 2662-1339 (electronic)
Palgrave Studies in Sustainable Business In Association with Future Earth
ISBN 978-3-030-60917-7 ISBN 978-3-030-60918-4 (eBook)
https://doi.org/10.1007/978-3-030-60918-4

Cover illustration: kenkuza_shutterstock.com

This Palgrave Macmillan imprint is published by the registered company Springer Nature Switzerland AG
The registered company address is: Gewerbestrasse 11, 6330 Cham, Switzerland

Preface

In an interview in 1986, the late Erwin Chargaff, a professor of biochemistry at Columbia University, responded to the question whether there is a place for ethics in science. He claimed that there could not be. He said that while an American Indian might pray to a tree if they needed to cut it, and might also ask for forgiveness, scientists transgressed ethical boundaries in the seventeenth century when they sacrilegiously started digging into nature. For a while, due to its relative inefficiency, what we call modern science did relatively little harm. The nature of the problematic relationship between ethics and science is a question for the present times, Chargaff claimed, mainly due to the splitting of the atom, nuclear energy, and knowledge about the genetic matter of the cell nucleus. Chargaff emphasized that it was now much too late: science had lost its innocence, and science and ethics were now incompatible. He concluded that anyone who sought to be an ethical individual should study bookkeeping, or something other than science (Chargaff 1987, p. 883).[1]

Not knowing about Chargaff's suggestion, I graduated as an economist in 2002, and worked in finance, accounting, and project management for several multinational companies and in the public sector. However, I always found myself looking for something more than just an increase in salary, and further career prospects. I began asking myself, what is the noble goal of ethical, genuine, value-oriented, human behavior? Where is love and respect for nature, and for non-human beings? Can these values prevail in a business organization at all? At the end of 2009, I came across an article about Buddhist economics, which was a revelation in terms of my understanding of the importance of non-mainstream economics. I decided to study alternative economics, ranging from ecological economics to Buddhist economics, and to conduct research on value-oriented, ecologically conscious business organizations.

Unfortunately, the more than three decades that have passed since Chargaff's warning have shown that not only science but also the economy and business are in deep conflict with ethics and ecology. What can we expect from business at its best in the midst of worsening climate change and threats such as coronavirus and other hitherto unknown viral pandemics, at a time when the unpredictable consequences of what may be ecological breakdown have already significantly increased the suffering of human and non-human beings?

This book is a snapshot of the results of my decade-long search for ecological and human values in the economy and business. My intention has been to show the meaning and significance of ecological consciousness in business, and how ecologically conscious business organizations can become exemplary. In this book, I describe unusual business practices that are based on genuine ecological commitment. I hope that these examples will serve as inspiration for a more ecologically conscious way of living and functioning, and help to catalyze endeavors aimed at creatively

---

[1] Chargaff, E. (1986, November 6): *Az egyre erősödő bizonytalanság légköre* [An Atmosphere of Growing Insecurity]. Interview by Tibor Szántó. Akadémiai Értesítő / Magyar Tudomány [Academic Bulletin / Hungarian Science], Vol. 94, No. 11, pp. 877–883. http://real-j.mtak.hu/143/1/MATUD_1987.pdf. Accessed 20 July 2020 [in Hungarian].

contributing to the spiritual and material betterment of the world of business, and beyond.

Budapest, Hungary
August 2020

András Ócsai

Acknowledgments

I would hereby like to thank Paul Shrivastava and László Zsolnai, series editors of *Palgrave Studies in Sustainable Business In Association with Future Earth*, and the editorial and production team at Palgrave, particularly Jessica Harrison, Srishti Gupta, and Geetha Chockalingam, for their support and professional assistance.

I am grateful to Corvinus University of Budapest for institutional and financial support during the years it took to research and publish this book. I acknowledge the help of my colleagues at the Business Ethics Center at Corvinus University of Budapest, and that of scholars and friends from the Hungarian and international academic world, including leaders and members of the Transatlantic Doctoral Academy (TADA) on Business, Economics and Ethics, with whom I have engaged in fruitful interaction and collaboration.

I sincerely thank the interviewees involved in the empirical research for sharing details about their values, thoughts, and practices related to ecological consciousness in business. I also wish to express my thanks to my language editor, Simon Milton, for his great work improving the English of the text.

I am exceptionally grateful to László Zsolnai for selfless mentorship and continuous spiritual and intellectual support spanning more than a decade. His genuine friendship has helped me through professional and personal challenges in my life.

For their love, inspiration, support, and patience, I thank all my family members and friends, including those who have already crossed over.

András Ócsai

Praise for *Ecologically Conscious Organizations*

"As we step into the beginning of the third decade of the twenty first century the paradigm of business and management is undergoing a radical transformation that addresses such vital questions as meaning of work and purpose of life. After passing through formidable challenges and turmoils including ethical collapses that have compelled modern business organizations to engage in soul searching, conscientious business leaders worldwide have come to realize that reverence for nature and respect for all life forms is of cardinal importance in shaping the course and culture of business in future that accords primacy to ethics and human values, sustainability and spirituality. In the background of these pathfinding developments both in theory and practice for a more humane and sustainable future for the self, organization, community, society and planet this book on Ecologically Conscious Organizations by András Ócsai is a timely and valuable contribution to the existing body of literature, in this multi-disciplinary and multi-dimensional field of research. A committed academic and thinker of Business Ethics Center, Corvinus University of Budapest and also of the European SPES Forum, Professor Ócsai has not only covered the multiple strands of thought and action in the field of Business and Ecology but also elevated it to a higher level of consciousness beyond intellectual exercise by anchoring the movement on the terra firma of spiritual wisdom and experience. Coming from India, I can see and sense a palpable resonance of his work with the pioneering work of the Nobel Laureate poet and philosopher Rabindranath Tagore towards Nature-inspired education and the signal contribution of Prof. S K Chakraborty, Founder-Convener of Management Centre for Human Values, Indian Institute of Management Calcutta, in the field of Human Values and Indian Ethos in Management. I am sure the book will receive wide acceptance through creation of space for dialogue among those who would be committed to the mission of creating a humanistic, value-based and sustainable business scenario in future."

—Sanjoy Mukherjee, *Professor of business ethics and corporate social responsibility, Indian Institute of Management, Shillong, India*

"Grounded in in-depth systematic analyses of a broad array of inspiring case examples of ecologically conscious business organizations, this book is an invaluable treatise on how to achieve the harmonization of economic and deep ecological aims through a fundamental change in the existential mindset and inherent approaches of business enterprises."

—Eleanor O'Higgins, *Adjunct Associate Professor at the College of Business at UCD Dublin, Ireland, and an Associate at the London School of Economics, UK, coeditor of the Palgrave book Progressive Business Models*

"In this book Ócsai is challenging the dominating concept of business models and he gives a convincing and relevant presentation of unusual business practices that are based on genuine ecological commitment. Ócsai goes beyond ethical theory to show moral and environmental considerations and challenges in practice. This book is essential and stimulating reading for students, scholars and practitioners looking for a guide to an ecological responsible economy."

—Ove Jakobsen, *Professor and Director, Center for Ecological Economics and Ethics, Nord University, Norway*

"Bringing together knowledge and insights from a range of disciplines, this book focuses on key areas as spirituality, consciousness, nature and entrepreneurship. The major implications are considered, and the importance are highlighted. It is a beautiful book, and it will appeal to scholars and students of psychology and business, as well as business leaders wishing to gain valuable insights and inspiration into the range of issues we need to understand and act upon in the current atmosphere of bad practice, uncertainty during a pandemic and a threatening climate change."

—Knut O. J. Ims, *Professor in business ethics, Norwegian School of Economics, Bergen, Norway*

Contents

List of Figures

List of Tables

Part I

Introduction

This book addresses the topic of ecological consciousness in business organizations, with a special focus on value orientation and business models. Ecological consciousness is gaining importance today as the ecological crisis of our era, dominated by global big business, becomes increasingly evident. A large body of scientific literature has investigated the value orientations of businesses, but the topic of ecological consciousness has been much less studied in this context. Moreover, there are hardly any examples of the scrutiny of the relationship between value orientation and ecological consciousness in business.

The book goes beyond previous studies, as (i) it summarizes the literature about ecological consciousness and its appearance in business organizations; (ii) it investigates the value orientations of ecologically conscious businesses through a deeper, previously unused type of qualitative methodology; and (iii) it presents in a systematic, comparative way the value commitments and business models of selected ecologically conscious business organizations.

The following main questions come under microscope: What are the central concepts related to ecologically conscious business and an ecologically conscious economy? What are the key features of these concepts, and what is the relationship between them? What kind of value orientations do ecologically conscious business organizations have? What are the business models on which they build their operations? What are the fundamental goals and raison d'être of ecologically conscious businesses? How do they define success?

1

Ecology and Business

Why is it meaningful to examine ecologically conscious business organizations within the social science context—particularly their value background and business models? The first chapter of this book justifies the value of this goal. It also briefly presents the framework of the research that lies behind the book using a short summary of earlier studies and a discussion of related methodological issues. It then concludes with an overview of the structure of the book.

Let the Facts Speak for Themselves

Scientific research (see, among others, Carrington 2016, Waters et al. 2016) suggests that we are now living in a new era that may be called the Anthropocene[1]; a time when human activities have significantly altered

[1]Earth sciences have not yet officially recognized the Anthropocene epoch, and there is no general agreement about its beginning (some have proposed that the Neolithic Agricultural Revolution more than 12,000 years ago could be considered a fitting start date, while others

A. Ócsai, *Ecologically Conscious Organizations*, Palgrave Studies in Sustainable Business In Association with Future Earth,
https://doi.org/10.1007/978-3-030-60918-4_1

Earth's ecosystems (Crutzen and Stoermer 2000; Steffen and Broadgate et al. 2015a; Steffen and Richardson et al. 2015b). Our biosphere-transforming activities—primarily involving the globalization of societies and economies—have by now reached such an extent that they are incomparably larger and more harmful than those of other species, and are largely irreversible. It is not only our well-being, but also the very survival of our own and other species that is at stake (Pataki and Takács-Sánta 2005; Takács-Sánta 2004). To alleviate the ecological crisis affecting our planet, the spread of ecological consciousness and a praxis that focuses on restoring the natural environment is badly needed. This transformation would enable the economy to function again as a system "embedded" in nature and society (Polanyi 1944).

Owing to the work of excellent scholars and scientific communities (including Rachel Carson [1962], Club of Rome [2020], Mihajlo Mesarovic [Mesarovic and Pestel 1974], Jan Tinbergen [1977], Ernst F. Schumacher [1973], and the Stockholm Resilience Center [SRC 2020]), we have known for almost half a century that we are facing very serious ecological problems. What then, are the signs of the ecological crisis?

The main environmental problems include changes in communities of natural living beings, deforestation, and soil degradation; changes in global bio- and geochemical cycles, contamination, acid rain, smog, eutrophication, and the ozone hole; global climate change; the decline in biodiversity; food scarcity; and fresh water scarcity (Takács-Sánta 2010).

Researchers have been dealing with global climate change and the related trends since the 1970s. It is known that colder and warmer periods have periodically occurred on Earth, but climatic processes seem to have changed because of human activity. First, in 1972 the United Nations Conference on the Human Environment (held in Stockholm) addressed the phenomenon in detail (at which time the United Nations Environment Programme, UNEP, was also created). Following this, in

have traced it back to the Industrial Revolution, and others to the nuclear tests at the end of World War II). It is generally accepted, however, that the Anthropocene is dramatically different from the previous eras, and great attention should be paid to this pheonomenon because increasingly accelerating deteriorative ecological, social, and economic processes have been occurring since the 1950s (the so-called "great acceleration" [Steffen et al. 2015a]) that is transgressing planetary boundaries Steffen et al. (2015b).

1985 at the World Climate Conference in Villach, Austria, climate change was identified as a scientifically grounded fact. At conferences held in the following years (1988 in Toronto, 1990 in Geneva) participants also confirmed the need to reduce the greenhouse gasses emitted into the atmosphere. This was also due to the Brundtland Commission, which functioned from 1984 to 1987, and to the activities of the Intergovernmental Panel on Climate Change (IPCC), established in 1988 (IPCC 2020).

The IPCC examines and summarizes research findings about climate change induced by human activities. It published its *Fifth Assessment Report* in 2014, after issuing reports in 1990, 1996, 2001, and 2007. According to the former report, the terrestrial climate is obviously warming, and the rise in global average temperatures since the mid-twentieth century is due to greenhouse gas emissions of human origin. Climate change is causing global sea levels to rise steadily, the thickness of polar ice sheets to decrease, rainfall to become more intense, and drought periods to become longer. In many regions of the world, these phenomena are decreasing residents' access to safe drinking water. Particularly vulnerable regions (those affected by multiple dimensions of the crisis) are the Polar Regions, Sub-Saharan Africa, small islands, and Asian delta regions. Ecosystems facing an elevated level of danger include coral reefs, colonies of marine shellfish, tundra, coniferous forests in the taiga, as well as mountainous and Mediterranean regions. Approximately 20–30 percent of all plant and animal species are presently threatened with extinction (IPCC 2014).

In 2018, the IPCC published a special report on the impact of global warming of 1.5 °C above pre-industrial levels and related global greenhouse gas emission pathways. It concludes that human activities have already caused approximately 1.0 °C of global warming, but this is likely to reach 1.5 °C between 2030 and 2052 if the temperature increase continues at the current rate. Warming from anthropogenic emissions will persist for centuries to millennia, and will continue to cause further long-term changes in the climate system. The climate-related risks to natural and human systems depend on the magnitude and rate of warming, geographical location, level of development and vulnerability, and on the choices and implementation of adaptation and mitigation options. Limiting risks must involve societal and system transition and transformation that can be enabled by increasing adaptation—and mitigation-focused investment, policy instruments, accelerating technological innovation, and behavioral changes. Strengthening the capacity for climate action of national and sub-national authorities, civil society, the private sector, indigenous people and local communities, and greater international cooperation can support the implementation of ambitious initiatives (IPCC 2018).

The latest annual report from the World Meteorological Organization explains the impact of changing weather and climate on the socio-economic sphere, health, migration, food security, and terrestrial and aquatic life. It highlights that the past five years have been the warmest period since the systematic measurement of temperature began, and that 2010–2019 has been the warmest decade. In addition, since the 1980s each successive decade has been warmer than any preceding one. A record amount of ice has melted in both the Arctic and the Antarctic. The oceans have absorbed around 23 percent of annual CO_2 emissions, moderating the increase in the atmospheric concentration. This process, however, enhances ocean acidification. Additionally, almost every region of the World Ocean suffered at least one heat wave in 2019. This warming will continue as the amount of greenhouse gases increases. These tendencies endanger the living conditions of ocean flora and fauna. The effects of climate change are already being felt as extreme weather conditions, and their consequences are dramatically and rapidly accelerating. We are still on the wrong track regarding keeping the likely temperature change to a maximum of 1.5–2 °C above the pre-industrial level, as called for in the Paris Climate Convention. The latter report again calls on decision-makers to start taking the situation seriously, because we are slowly running out of time to act (WMO 2020).

Although the international conferences of the last three decades have generated increasingly profound results (1992 Rio de Janeiro—Agenda 21, United Nations Framework Convention on Climate Change; 1997 Kyoto Protocol; 2002 Johannesburg—World Summit on Sustainable Development; 2005 Montreal—"rulebook" for implementing the Kyoto Protocol; 2009 Copenhagen—legally non-binding Copenhagen

Accord; 2010 Cancún—Cancun Agreements, idea of setting up a Green Climate Fund and a forest protection program; 2011 Durban—Green Climate Fund; 2012 Doha—The Doha Climate Gateway; 2015 Paris—Paris Agreement; 2016 Marrakesh—call for a transformation to a low-emission global economy; 2017 Bonn—Fiji Momentum for Implementation; 2019 Madrid—The European Green New Deal), these have remained mainly diplomatic in nature so far. There are significant differences between expectations and results, so experts have repeatedly considered the series of conferences to be a failure. Considering that the definition of real and significant commitments, concrete deadlines, and sanctions has often failed—that is, no significant turnaround has happened in greenhouse gas emissions—this criticism is unfortunately valid.

Human activity, as confirmed by the *Millennium Ecosystem Assessment Report* (launched in 2000 by Kofi Annan, Secretary-General of the United Nations), is having a decisive and increasingly negative impact on Earth's ecosystems and "ecosystem services" (such as food, water, disease control, climate regulation, spiritual fulfillment, and aesthetic experience) (MEA 2005). The report summarizes the most important findings in four points: (1) in the past 50 years, humankind has changed ecosystems more rapidly and to a greater extent than ever before. This change is already threatening our ability to meet growing needs for food, drinking water, wood, fiber, and energy. We are also causing significant and increasingly irreversible losses of biodiversity. (2) The modification of ecosystems has contributed to an increase in human welfare and economic development, but at the expense of increasing the related cost—that is, the deterioration of a significant proportion of all ecosystems, a rise in the risk of non-linear change, and an increase in poverty among some groups of people. All of these factors also degrade the services that ecosystems will be able to provide to future generations. (3) The deterioration of ecosystems may significantly continue in the first half of the twenty-first century, representing a real threat to meeting the United Nations Millennium Development Goals. (4) In order to reverse the degradation of ecosystems and to meet our growing needs, significant political, institutional, and practical changes are ineluctable, but the signs of such change are not yet visible (MEA 2005).

The figures quoted in the report are astonishing: 60 percent of the ecosystems under investigation have deteriorated, or their services are being used unsustainably (drinking water, fishing, purification of air and water, regulation of regional and local climate, natural risks, and pest control). In the 30 years following 1950, more of the Earth's surface was turned into arable land than between 1700 and 1850. Today, the amount of cultivated land is equivalent to a quarter of the surface area of the Earth. In the last decades of the twentieth century, 20 percent of all coral reefs disappeared, and the condition of another 20 percent deteriorated, while 35 percent of all mangrove forests have been lost. Since 1960, the amount of water that has been collected and stored behind dams has quadrupled. The amount of water extracted from rivers and lakes has doubled. The amount of biologically reactive nitrogen introduced into terrestrial ecosystems has doubled, and the amount of phosphorus tripled. Since 1750, atmospheric concentrations of carbon dioxide have increased by 32 percent, mainly due to the burning of fossil fuels and changes in land use (60 percent of the increase is attributable to the period after 1959). By 1990, two-thirds of the area of two out of the world's 14 largest biomes (ecological communities) and half of the area of another four had been converted into land primarily for agricultural use. The rate of extinction of species has increased a thousand times over the last few hundred years (MEA 2005).

With similar goals to the Millennium Ecosystem Assessment, the Governing Council of the United Nations Environment Programme launched the Global Environment Outlook project in 1995. This is designed to help meet the reporting requirements of the Agenda 21 action plan, and also describes the state of the natural environment in regular reports. The fifth report, entitled *GEO-5*, published in 2012, confirms that human well-being and development are based on the natural environment, and that changes in the latter affect human safety, health, social relationships, and material needs. Scientific evidence supports the claim that ecosystems are operating at their biophysical boundaries, and in some cases, beyond them. Humankind is causing unprecedented changes in the state of the environment at a global and regional level. The global average temperature of the atmosphere and oceans is increasing at an accelerating rate (while the average temperature of the atmosphere in the twentieth century increased by 0.74 percent, in the twenty-first century it is expected to increase by 1.8–4 percent), while the size of polar ice sheets is decreasing and world sea-level is rising. More than two million people worldwide die prematurely each year due to air pollution. The size of the ozone hole above Antarctica is larger than ever. Land degradation caused by unsustainable land use and climate change is endangering the living conditions of approximately two billion people, mainly in developing countries. The amount of fresh water per capita is declining, and if the trend continues, by 2025 1.8 billion people will live in areas with absolute water scarcity. We continue to exploit aquatic ecosystems in a way that seriously endangers the sustainability of food production and biodiversity. The prevalence and number of individuals of a great majority of known species are steadily declining. More than 16,000 species are now at the brink of extinction, and although temperate forests expanded by 30,000 square km per year between 1990 and 2005, during the same period tropical deforestation resulted in the disappearance of 130,000 square km of rainforest per year (UNEP 2012).

The sixth *Global Environmental Outlook* was released in 2019. This reinforced the claim that the world is now not on track to meet the Sustainable Development Goals, even by 2050. The consequences of damage to the natural environment will increasingly threaten people's health and the likelihood that we can meet the goals of the Paris Agreement. Humankind must drastically scale up protective and restorative activities to improve ecological conditions. If this does not happen, by the middle of the century millions of premature deaths will occur in Africa, the Middle East, and Asia, and anti-microbially resistant pollutants in freshwater will become a major cause of death. Many pressing challenges such as the need to reduce food waste, adopt less meat-intensive diets, tackle plastic pollution in the oceans, manage water scarcity, and cope with the loss of ecosystems underline the fact that the health and prosperity of humanity is interlinked with the state of the natural environment. The report concludes that the new types of thinking involving science, technology, finance, and politics that are needed to move toward a more sustainable form of development already exist. Creating a near-zero-waste economy by 2050, green investment using two percent of countries' GDP, improved governance, land-use planning, green infrastructure, strategic investment into rural areas, the use of big data in environmental statistics, and policy interventions that address entire systems rather than individual issues are relevant examples of this. Sufficient support from public, business, and political leaders and the will to implement such policies and technologies at the right speed and scale are, however, still lacking (UNEP 2019).

The *Living Planet Report*, published by the World Wide Fund for Nature for the eleventh time in 2016, also shows a negative picture of the health of our planet, biodiversity, and the impact of human activity (WWF 2016). The most important finding of this is that the needs of humankind, calculated based on indicators from the Living Planet Index (LPI), the ecological footprint, and the water footprint of production, exceed Earth's capacity to provide them. The LPI, developed in 1997, measures the state of biodiversity on Earth by monitoring the average change in the size of vertebrate populations. Between 1970 and 2012, this global indicator declined by almost 58 percent. Thus such populations now contain, on average, fewer than 50 percent of the individuals they did fifty years ago. The ecological footprint measures the magnitude of the biologically productive land and water-covered area that can produce the renewable resources required for human activity, including the area needed for infrastructure, and for vegetation that can absorb the carbon dioxide that is being generated. The footprint had almost tripled by 2012 compared to its size in 1961, and now exceeds Earth's bio-capacity by 66 percent. This status, known as ecological overshoot, has existed since the 1970s and is primarily attributable to the magnitude of the carbon dioxide footprint, which increased from 43 percent in 1961 to 60 percent. The water footprint of production is another measure of the renewable resources that are required for human needs. This indicates that 71 countries are facing challenges in terms of the amount of water that is used but not cleaned, and the amount of water not returned to the natural cycle. The report states that if the world develops along a "business as usual scenario," by 2020 the resources generated by two Earth-like planets would be needed to meet human needs and absorb the carbon dioxide that is being generated.

The 2018 edition of the Living Planet Report restates the scientific evidence that unsustainable human activity is pushing the natural systems that support life on Earth to the edge. Economic activity depends on natural services and is estimated to be worth approximately 125 trillion USD a year. Modern human societies are ultimately built on what nature provides us with, thus are of invaluable worth in terms of our health, wealth, food, and security. Research demonstrates that human consumption is the driving force behind these unprecedented planetary changes. The still increasing demand for energy, land, and water means that the current rate of species extinction is now 100–1000 times higher than the rate it was for many millennia of Earth's history. The maintenance of biodiversity, a prerequisite for human life on the planet and the life of all species, is seriously endangered. To move beyond "business as usual," governments, business, finance, research, civil society, and individuals have to join forces and make a new global deal for nature and people. Strong leadership and the right political, financial, and consumption-related choices at every level are pivotal to sustaining humanity and nature in harmony (WWF 2018).

As our activities are driven by consumption and economic growth, we are causing significant change to our planet. Nevertheless, at this high cost, have we achieved a level of material and spiritual well-being and happiness that all humans can enjoy? A study by Colin Ash, a British economist, concludes that while economically more developed countries have become much richer over the last fifty years, the average level of happiness of people has not changed (the Easterlin Paradox), because income growth increases happiness only until a certain level of income is reached (around 20,000 USD per year in 2005 prices). Above this level, the quality and richness of interpersonal relationships contributes more to the happiness of people than rising income and consumption (Ash 2007). Angus Deaton and Daniel Kahneman, both Nobel laureates in economics from Princeton University, also raised the question whether money buys happiness. They analyzed the Gallup-Healthways Well-Being Index, a daily survey of 1000 US residents conducted by the Gallup Organization. The authors distinguished between emotional well-being (the emotional quality of an individual's everyday experience) and their life evaluation (thoughts that people have about their lives) as two aspects of subjective well-being. The authors concluded that income and education are more closely associated with life evaluation, but health, care-giving, loneliness, and smoking are relatively stronger predictors of daily emotions. Life evaluations rise continuously with level of income, but not emotional well-being. At a certain level of annual household income (around 75,000 USD) no further development in the frequency and intensity of experiences that make one's life pleasant can be observed (Kahneman and Deaton 2010). The London-based New Economics Foundation created the "Happy Planet Index" in 2006, which shows an even more complex picture. This instrument combines life expectancy, life satisfaction, and ecological footprint in a single indicator (NEF 2009). According to the 2016 data of the Happy Planet Index, which were supplemented by data about income inequality, some countries may be able to improve their aggregate score, but no single country can improve all three factors while keeping its ecological footprint below 100 percent (NEF 2016).

In 2012, the Future Earth program was launched at the United Nations Conference on Sustainable Development, or "Rio+20." It is to build on and exceed more than 30 years of research experience of the World Climate Research Programme, the International Geosphere-Biosphere Programme, DIVERSITAS, and the International Human Dimensions Programme on Global Environmental Change. The program brings together over forty thousand scientists from all over the world. It seeks answers to present challenges using a new approach to addressing the pressure on terrestrial systems and global sustainability. Compared to former attempts, it is more integrative, and solution oriented. It strives to create closer links between research programs and trends, and promotes governments, NGOs, local stakeholders, and companies that actively engage in joint work. For humankind to be able to live in a sustainable and just world, there is a need for a new kind of science that can create and operate an effective global innovation system through linking different disciplines, knowledge systems, and social partners that can help meet the United Nations Sustainable Development Goals of 2015. In addition to global research projects and research initiatives, Future Earth's strength lies in associated, so-called "Knowledge-Action Networks." Promoting active collaboration between social partners and the creation of actionable knowledge are the goals at the heart of these networks. They seek solutions to the main challenges associated with the present social and ecological crisis: emergent risks and extreme events; financial and economic reform; health; the state of the oceans; natural assets; systems of sustainable consumption and production; cities; and the water-energy-food nexus (Future Earth 2020).

In the form of a unique community presently comprised of around 100 prominent scientists, business leaders, and former politicians, the Club of Rome has addressed the critical, complex, and interconnected challenges humankind faces for more than five decades. Since its first major report, the 1972 *The Limits to Growth*, its main goal has been to alert the world to the consequences of the interaction between human systems and the health of the planet, and to actively advocate for paradigm and system shifts. Humanity must divert its path of development away from relying on the exponential consumption and population growth that jeopardizes Earth's climate and life-support systems, and address the clamant needs of impoverished billions worldwide who are suffering from increasing social and economic inequality. Through profound scientific research, holistic policy proposals, and high-level events, the Club of Rome is now concentrating on five key areas through work within five so-called impact hubs: Climate-Planetary Emergency, Reframing Economics, Rethinking Finance, Emerging New Civilization, and Youth Leadership and Intergenerational Dialogue. Human beings are inherently relational and interconnected to one another in space and time, and to nature. We thus must combine our efforts to shift to a new paradigm that can reshape our belief system and change complex economic, financial, and social systems. Such a shift can foster fundamental values that promote human dignity, respect for nature, and help protect the commons beyond current generations (Club of Rome 2020).

Indisputable signs of the ecological crisis prove that prevalent, growth-based types of economic system are unsustainable as they deplete natural resources and destroy their own prospects for survival. As American ecological economist Herman Daly writes, global economic growth, when it transgresses ecological boundaries, is associated with greater costs than benefits, thus makes us poorer, not richer. Even popular efficiency-enhancing endeavors are not appropriate solutions to this problem, because they often cause exactly the opposite effect to that we would like to achieve. Improving the efficiency of utilization of a resource increases the supply of that resource, thereby reducing its price, leading to an increase in its consumption (the so-called "Jevons paradox"), meaning that we run up against ecological limits much earlier. Moreover, through a focus on growth we cannot even achieve another goal of development: a global reduction in poverty. Growth does not serve to meet the basic needs of poorer countries, but rather serves the interests of developed ones (Daly 1999, 2008).

Predominantly, the prevailing business model of companies itself is causing and deepening the ecological crisis (Daly and Cobb 1989; Brenkert 1995; Shrivastava 1995a, 1995b; Ims et al. 2014; Capra and Jakobsen 2017; Jakobsen 2017; Shrivastava et al. 2019, 2020). Because of the pace and magnitude of ecological degradation, making small-scale adjustments is not enough. The ecological transformation of the economy, and the development and application of new and progressive business models are of vital importance. Such progressive business models involve ethical considerations, respect ecological values, and apply transdisciplinary approaches and alternative thinking. The existence of these characteristics in business is indispensable if we are to hope for fundamental change (Ims and Zsolnai 2009; Rockström 2010; Ims et al. 2014; Ims and Pedersen 2015; Storsletten and Jakobsen 2015; Zsolnai 2015; Capra and Jakobsen 2017; Jakobsen 2017; Harangozó et al. 2018; Steffen and Rockström et al. 2018; Shrivastava et al. 2019, 2020).

Social Science Context

In exploring the causes of and solutions to the ecological crisis, besides the necessary and valuable natural science approaches, there is an urgent need for the social sciences. The findings of numerous research organizations, research studies, and the reports of individual scholars and scientific communities underline the fact that without identifying and understanding the human roots and social context of ecological symptoms, we will not be able to improve deteriorating natural conditions, or even mitigate the present crisis (Daly and Cobb 1989; MEA 2005; Ims and Zsolnai 2009; Zsolnai 2015; IPCC 2018; Steffen and Rockström et al. 2018; WWF 2018; UNEP 2019; Club of Rome 2020; Future Earth 2020; WMO 2020).

The aim of this book is to explore the theory and practice of ecologically conscious businesses and to present and analyze their value orientation and business models. The book is based on social science research, and its approach is idiographic, inductive, and qualitative (Babbie 2008; Mills et al. 2010). It is idiographic because it seeks to deepen the understanding of the selected businesses cases. It is inductive as it draws conclusions based on the empirical examination of the units of observation. Finally, it is qualitative because it does not work with a representative sample nor process quantifiable data, but engages in a more detailed exploration and description of the details of each case. The results may be utilized in practice and contribute to a better understanding of the phenomenon of ecological consciousness in business and beyond.

Based on its goals, social science research can be exploratory, descriptive, and explanatory (Babbie 2008). Research can thus target several goals at the same time, which is the case here. Typical of exploratory research, the present book serves to satisfy the author's personal interest and desire for understanding, the wish for immersion in a specific social or economic phenomenon, and the desire to lay the foundations for future research. In adapting a descriptive research approach, the analysis is designed to provide a precise and careful description of the subject of the research.

From the epistemological perspective, the present research can be considered constructivist; the author accepts the foundations of scientific approaches that are rooted in the constructivist philosophy of science. These include, inter alia, questioning the idea of the independence of the external, physical world and social reality from human activity and knowledge, and also questioning the existence of a value-neutral scientific method. According to the constructivist approach, "the purpose of both lay and scientific knowledge construction is to provide useful, adequate, coherent, stable, or meaningful representation of the world in accordance with particular sets of systemic and sociolinguistic rules

Table 1.1 Summary of the basic characteristics of the research

Aspect of Classification	Basic Characteristics of the Research
Purpose:	exploratory, descriptive
Epistemology:	constructivist, interpretative
Methodology:	idiographic, qualitative, inductive
Planned utilization:	applied

Source Author's construction

and constraints in given contexts" (Maréchal 2010, p. 220). Individuals who try to understand the world that surrounds them create subjective meaning from their experiences about different things. This is also true of researchers, who accept and search for a diversity of viewpoints, construct theory during social interactions from subjective meaning determined by historical and cultural norms, and specify the patterns of such meaning. The constructivist scholar recognizes that their own philosophical assumptions, worldview, values, beliefs, and experiences influence the interpretation of meanings that are revealed, and therefore interprets the results of research through clarifying and disclosing previous assumptions and analyses (Creswell 2007) (Table 1.1).

What Does Earlier Research Say?

The value orientations of businesses have been investigated in many cases, but the topic of ecological consciousness has rarely been in the spotlight. There are hardly any examples of the study of both phenomenon together. The literature rarely addresses the issue of ecological consciousness, unlike environmental consciousness (the difference between the two concepts is discussed in the third chapter).

Susanne Kaldschmidt studied sustainability values and the impact of the personal values of top business managers on sustainability strategies. Her use of the concept "awareness" does not correspond to the notion of "consciousness," although her inspiring findings include the claim that the personal values of the executives of companies that perform better in the field of sustainability are reflected in the sustainability strategies of such companies. Kaldschmidt further emphasizes that the extent of the transfer of personal values to company strategies largely depends on what executives and managers consider their own role to be, and the role of the economy in society (Kaldschmidt 2011).

In 2008, a study of value-oriented businesses at the Business Ethics Center of Corvinus University of Budapest found that value-oriented company behavior can be implemented in Hungary's economic conditions, because—according to Robert Frank's (2004) hypothesis—the higher operating costs of the former are compensated by specific economic benefits associated with obtaining the trust and commitment of stakeholders (Zsolnai and Győri 2011).

In 2011, a piece of empirical research entitled Sustainable and Socially Responsible Business Practice was conducted by the Business Ethics Center of Corvinus University of Budapest. Within this research, progressive Hungarian businesses that incorporate ecological considerations into their business models were studied. The study reaffirmed the hypothesis of Robert Frank, demonstrating that the surveyed companies base their ecological orientation on the personal commitment and intrinsic motivation of their leaders. The motivation and definitions of success of these ecologically oriented companies are multidimensional, and the well-being of their stakeholders is just as important to them as their own financial prosperity (Győri and Ócsai 2014).

In relation to the subject of previous research, and building upon the results thereof, the research presented in this book goes beyond earlier research in the following ways: It summarizes the theoretical literature about ecological consciousness and its appearance in business enterprises. The research additionally explores the value orientations of ecologically conscious businesses through a deeper, previously unused approach to qualitative methodology; and applies a systematic, comparative method of presenting and analyzing the business models of the selected businesses that is new to this field (Chesbrough and Rosenbloom 2002).

Goals, Questions, and Methods

Due to its exploratory nature, the research required to examine the value orientation of ecologically conscious businesses requires a qualitative approach. According to the interactive model of qualitative research design, the research process should involve five levels: goals, conceptual frameworks, research questions, methods and validity, and their relationships and coherence (Maxwell 2013).

Three types of research goal can be distinguished. Personal goals are the most comprehensive, followed by the practical goals derived from these, and, ultimately, the intellectual goals underlying specific research questions.

The personal goals of the author that led to the research topic are the following:

- to do meaningful things in life, and contribute to activities and efforts aimed at improving the world;
- based on experiencing some of the problems caused by the prevailing consumption-, growth- and profit-oriented economic model, to help individuals and their business organizations recognize that in chasing only materialistic goals humankind will destroy the Earth and the biosphere that ensures their existence;
- to become a better person and a good researcher, and to pass down knowledge to help fellow human beings develop.

Practical goals are designed to help answer the following questions:

- How can we live a meaningful life while contributing to the cessation and reversal of processes destructive to nature?
- How can we develop an economy that does not destroy, but improves the conditions of nature, benefits society, and contributes to the preservation of the values of humankind?
- How can we best participate in research designed to increase understanding of the operation and underlying values of value-oriented, especially ecologically conscious, businesses?

Intellectual goals are aimed at helping explore the following questions:

What are the concepts employed in ecologically conscious businesses and the economy; what are their main characteristics and links to each other?
What values do ecologically conscious businesses hold?
What are the operating environments and contexts of these businesses like?
Why (raison d'être) and how (business model) do they work; how do such businesses implement their ethical convictions and their value orientation, and how can they cope with challenges related to the economy?
How do they define success, what are the determinants of their survival?
What are the environmentally beneficial impacts of their ecologically conscious behavior?
Do these businesses address the question of ecological transformation; do they consider it to be possible, and if so, how?
Drawing from these practical examples, may recommendations for the ecological transformation of the present economic system be made?
Is it possible to discover new theoretical concepts from an analysis of the operation of the former businesses?

A number of intellectual goals have been formulated, but the scope of the book—in order to maintain the focus of the research—is limited to examining some selected questions (the remaining research goals may be investigated in future research, as outlined in Chapter 6).

Based on the personal, practical, and intellectual goals of the author, the following research questions were developed:

1. What are the central concepts of ecologically conscious businesses and of an ecologically conscious economy? What are the key features of these concepts, and the relations among them?
2. What kind of value orientations do the ecologically conscious businesses under analysis have?

3. What are the fundamental goals and raison d'être of the studied businesses?
4. What are the definitions of success of the studied businesses?
5. Which business models do the businesses use?

The initial goal during the current phase of research into the value orientation of ecologically conscious businesses was not to create generalizable results, but to construct a deeper understanding of the selected cases that involves an exploration of related components and relationships, primarily applying a constructivist epistemological approach and less structured qualitative research methodology (Miles et al. 2014; Cassell and Symon 2004). In line with the topic, units of observation were identified from internationally well-known and Hungarian representative cases of ecologically conscious businesses. The sampling procedure was expert-based purposeful sampling. Semi-structured interviews and company documents and websites served as sources for data collection and recording. Qualitative content analysis, involving inductive logic, thematic analysis, and document analysis, was used to explore the relevant value orientations. The additional analysis of responses to further questions about value orientation were based on responses collected using a so-called Likert scale, along with the deductive analysis of answers concerning business model components, raison d'être, and the definitions of success of businesses. Prior exploration, the explication of value judgments and the assumptions of the researcher, careful documentation, clarity, consistency, triangulation of data sources and analytical methods were employed to increase the reliability and validity of the analysis. The ethical aspects of social science research were incorporated via obtaining informed consent from participants, and dealing with the latter with courtesy, respect, confidentiality, openness and honesty (Mason 2002; Krippendorff 2004; Creswell 2007; Babbie 2008; Maxwell 2013; Miles et al. 2014).

Structure of the Book

In this book we examine the theoretical concepts, value orientation, and business models of ecologically conscious businesses. To justify the topic choice, in Part I we present the external and internal drivers and goals that stimulated the implementation of the research behind the book. The research is located within the social sciences; previous studies of the topic are then outlined. In addition, besides the research questions, methodological issues are briefly summarized.

Part II reviews the basic theoretical concepts contained in the book (business enterprise and business model in Chapter 2, ecological consciousness in Chapter 3, values and value orientation in Chapter 4) and provides a comparative analysis of the main fields of the theoretical background.

Based on the results of empirical research, Part III presents working models of ecologically conscious businesses. After analyzing their value orientations, raison d'être and own definitions of success (Chapter 5), elements of their business models are portrayed in a comparative way (Chapter 6).

Part IV (Chapter 7) explores the current global context of ecologically conscious business and makes some conclusions about the future of business.

References

Ash, C. (2007). Happiness and Economics: Sustainability and Sufficiency: Economic Development in a Buddhist Perspective. *Society and Economy, 29*(2), 201–222. https://doi.org/10.1556/SocEc.29.2007.2.5.

Babbie, E. (2008). *The Basics of Social Research* (4th ed.). Belmont, CA: Thomson Wadsworth.

Brenkert, G. G. (1995). The Environment, The Moralist, The Corporation and its Culture. *Business Ethics Quarterly, 5*(4), 675–697. https://doi.org/10.2307/3857409.

Capra, F., & Jakobsen, O. D. (2017). A Conceptual Framework for Ecological Economics Based on Systemic Principles of Life. *International Journal of*

Social Economics, 44(6), 831–844. https://doi.org/10.1108/IJSE-05-2016-0136.

Carrington, D. (2016, August 29). The Anthropocene Epoch: Scientists Declare Dawn of Human-Influenced Age. *The Guardian*. https://www.theguardian.com/environment/2016/aug/29/declare-anthropocene-epoch-experts-urge-geological-congress-human-impact-earth. Accessed 23 March 2020.

Carson, R. L. (1962). *Silent Spring*. Boston, MA: Houghton Mifflin.

Cassell, C., & Symon, G. (2004). Introduction: The Context of Qualitative Organizational Research. In C. Cassell & G. Symon (Eds.), *Essential Guide to Qualitative Methods in Organizational Research* (pp. 1–10). London: Sage. https://doi.org/10.4135/9781446280119.

Chesbrough, H., & Rosenbloom, R. S. (2002). The Role of the Business Model in Capturing Value from Innovation: Evidence from Xerox Corporation's Technology Spin-Off Companies. *Industrial and Corporate Change, 11*(3), 529–555. https://doi.org/10.1093/icc/11.3.529.

Club of Rome. (2020). http://www.clubofrome.org/. Accessed 20 July 2020.

Creswell, J. W. (2007). *Qualitative Inquiry and Research Design: Choosing Among Five Approaches* (2nd ed.). Thousand Oaks, CA: Sage. https://charlesbickenheuserdotcom.files.wordpress.com/.../creswell_2007_qualitative_inquiry_and_research_design__choosing_among_five_approaches__2nd_edition.pdf. Accessed 4 March 2018.

Crutzen, P. J., & Stoermer, E. F. (2000). The Anthropocene. *IGBP Global Change Newsletter*, No. 41, pp. 17–18.

Daly, H. E. (1999). *Ecological Economics and the Ecology of Economics: Essays in Criticism*. Cheltenham and Northampton: Edward Elgar.

Daly, H. E. (2008). Frugality First. In L. Bouckaert, H. Opdebeeck, & L. Zsolnai (Eds.), *Frugality: Rebalancing Material and Spiritual Values in Economic Life* (Vol. 4, pp. 207–226). Bern: Peter Lang.

Daly, H. E., & Cobb, J. B. (1989). *For the Common Good: Redirecting the Economy toward Community, the Environment, and a Sustainable Future*. London: Green Print.

Frank, R. H. (2004). *What Price the Moral High Ground? Ethical Dilemmas in Competitive Environments*. Princeton, NJ: Princeton University Press.

Future Earth. (2020). http://www.futureearth.org/. Accessed 24 March 2020.

Győri, Zs, & Ócsai, A. (2014). Ecologically-Oriented Enterprises in Hungary. *World Review of Entrepreneurship, Management and Sustainable Development, 10*(1), 52–65. https://doi.org/10.1504/wremsd.2014.058053.

Harangozó, G., Csutora, M., & Kocsis, T. (2018). How Big is Big Enough? Toward a Sustainable Future by Examining Alternatives to the Conventional Economic Growth Paradigm. *Sustainable Development, 26,* 172–181. https://doi.org/10.1002/sd.1728.

Ims, K. J., & Pedersen, L. J. T. (Eds.). (2015). *Business and the Greater Good: Rethinking Business Ethics in an Age of Crisis.* Cheltenham and Northampton: Edward Elgar.

Ims, K. J., & Zsolnai, L. (2009). Holistic Problem Solving. In L. Zsolnai & A. Tencati (Eds.), *The Future International Manager* (pp. 116–129). London: Palgrave Macmillan. https://doi.org/10.1057/9780230274068_7.

Ims, K. J., Pedersen, L. J. T., & Zsolnai, L. (2014). How Economic Incentives May Destroy Social, Ecological and Existential Values: The Case of Executive Compensation. *Journal of Business Ethics, 123,* 353–360. https://doi.org/10.1007/s10551-013-1844-6.

Intergovernmental Panel on Climate Change (IPCC). (2014). *Climate Change 2014: Synthesis Report.* Contribution of Working Groups I, II and III to the Fifth Assessment Report of the Intergovernmental Panel on Climate Change. IPCC, Geneva, 151. https://www.ipcc.ch/site/assets/uploads/2018/02/SYR_AR5_FINAL_full.pdf. Accessed 8 March 2020.

Intergovernmental Panel on Climate Change (IPCC). (2018). *Global Warming of 1.5°C.* An IPCC Special Report on the Impacts of Global Warming of 1.5°C Above Pre-Industrial Levels and Related Global Greenhouse Gas Emission Pathways, in the Context of Strengthening the Global Response to the Threat of Climate Change, Sustainable Development, and Efforts to Eradicate Poverty. In Press. https://www.ipcc.ch/site/assets/uploads/sites/2/2019/06/SR15_Full_Report_High_Res.pdf. Accessed 8 March 2020.

Intergovernmental Panel on Climate Change (IPCC). (2020). http://www.ipcc.ch/. Accessed 8 March 2020.

Jakobsen, O. (2017). *Transformative Ecological Economics: Process Philosophy, Ideology and Utopia.* London and New York, NY: Routledge. https://doi.org/10.4324/9781315205434.

Kaldschmidt, S. (2011). *The Values of Sustainability: The Influence of Leaders' Personal Values on Sustainability Strategies.* Dissertation of the University of St. Gallen, School of Management, Economics, Law, Social Sciences and International Affairs.

Kahneman, D., & Deaton, A. (2010). High Income Improves Evaluation of Life but not Emotional Well-Being. *Proceedings of the National Academy of Sciences September, 107* (38), 16489–16493. https://doi.org/10.1073/pnas.1011492107.

Krippendorff, K (2004). *Content Analysis: An Introduction to its Methodology* (2nd ed.). Thousand Oaks, CA: Sage.

Maréchal, G. (2010). Constructivism. In A. J. Mills, G. Eurepos, & E. Wiebe (Eds.), *Encyclopedia of Case Study Research* (pp. 220–225). Thousand Oaks, CA: Sage. https://doi.org/10.4135/9781412957397.

Mason, J. (2002). *Qualitative Researching* (2nd ed.). London: Sage. www.sxf.uevora.pt/wp-content/uploads/2013/03/Mason_2002.pdf. Accessed 12 April 2020.

Maxwell, J. A. (2013). *Qualitative Research Design: An Interactive Approach* (3rd ed.). London: Sage.

Millennium Ecosystem Assessment (MEA). (2005). *Millennium Ecosystem Assessment: Ecosystems and Human Well-being: Synthesis*. Washington, DC: Island Press.

Mesarovic, M., & Pestel, E. (1974). *Mankind at the Turning Point: The Second Report to the Club of Rome*. New York, NY: Dutton.

Miles, M. B., Huberman, A. M., & Saldana, J. (2014). *Qualitative Data Analysis: A Methods Sourcebook* (3rd ed.). Thousand Oaks, CA: Sage.

Mills, A. J., Eurepos, G., & Wiebe, E. (Eds.) (2010). *Encyclopedia of Case Study Research*. Thousand Oaks, CA: Sage. https://doi.org/10.4135/9781412957397.

New Economics Foundation (NEF). (2009). *The Happy Planet Index 2.0: Why Good Lives Don't have to Cost the Earth*. http://happyplanetindex.org/s/2009-Happy-Planet-Index-report.pdf. Accessed 17 March 2020.

New Economics Foundation (NEF). (2016). *The Happy Planet Index 2016: A Global Index of Sustainable Wellbeing*. http://happyplanetindex.org/s/Briefing-paper-HPI-2016.pdf. Accessed 17 March 2020.

Pataki, Gy., & Takács-Sánta, A. (Eds.) (2005). *Természet és gazdaság: Ökológiai közgazdaságtan szöveggyűjtemény* [Nature and Economy: Key Texts of Ecological Economics]. Budapest: Typotex Kiadó. [in Hungarian].

Polanyi, K. (1944). *The Great Transformation: The political and Economic Origins of Our Time*. Boston, MA: Beacon Press.

Rockström, J. (2010). *Let the Environment Guide Our Development.* http://www.ted.com/talks/johan_rockstrom_let_the_environment_guide_our_development. Accessed 15 March 2020.

Schumacher, E. F. (1973). *Small is Beautiful: A Study of Economics As If People Mattered*. New York, NY: Harper and Row.

Shrivastava, P. (1995a). Ecocentric Management for a Risk Society. *The Academy of Management Review, 20*(1), 118–137. https://doi.org/10.5465/amr.1995.9503271996.

Shrivastava, P. (1995b). Environmental Technologies and Competitive Advantage. *Strategic Management Journal, 16*(Special Issue Summer), 183–200. https://doi.org/10.1002/smj.4250160923.

Shrivastava, P., Zsolnai, L., Wasieleski, D., Stafford-Smith, M., Walker, T., Weber, O., et al. (2019). Finance and Management for the Anthropocene. *Organization & Environment, 32*(1), 26–40. https://doi.org/10.1177/1086026619831451.

Shrivastava, P., Stafford Smith, M., O'Brien, K., & Zsolnai, L. (2020). Perspective: Transforming Sustainability Science to Generative Positive Social and Environmental Change Globally. *One Earth, 2*(4), 329–340. https://doi.org/10.1016/j.oneear.2020.04.010.

Steffen, W., Broadgate, W., Deutsch, L., Gaffney, O., & Ludwig, C. (2015a). The Trajectory of the Anthropocene: The Great Acceleration. *The Anthropocene Review, 2,* 81–98. https://doi.org/10.1177/2053019614564785.

Steffen, W., Richardson, K., Rockström, J., Cornell, S. E., Fetzer, I., Bennett, E. M., Biggs, R., Carpenter, S. R., de Vries, W., de Wit, C. A., Folke, C., Gerten, D., Heinke, J., Mace, G. M., Persson, L. M., Ramanathan, V., Reyers, B., Sörlin, S. (2015b). Planetary Boundaries: Guiding Human Development on a Changing Planet. *Science, 347*(6223), 1259855. https://doi.org/10.1126/science.1259855.

Steffen, W., Rockström, J., Richardson, K., Lenton, T. M., Folke, C., Liverman, D., Summerhayes, C. P., Barnosky, A. D., Cornell, S. E., Crucifix, M., Donges, J. F., Fetzer, I., Lade, S. J., Scheffer, M., Winkelmann, R., Schellnhuber, H. J. (2018). Trajectories of the Earth System in the Anthropocene. *Proceedings of the National Academy of Sciences, 115*(33), 8252–8259. https://doi.org/10.1073/pnas.1810141115.

Stockholm Resilience Center. (2020). https://www.stockholmresilience.org/. Accessed 16 March 2020.

Storsletten, V. M. L., & Jakobsen, O. D. (2015). Development of Leadership Theory in the Perspective of Kierkegaard's Philosophy. *Journal of Business Ethics, 128,* 337–349. https://doi.org/10.1007/s10551-014-2106-y.

Takács-Sánta, A. (2004). The Major Transitions in the History of Human Transformation of the Biosphere. *Human Ecology Review, 11*(1), 51–66. http://www.humanecologyreview.org/pastissues/her111/111takacssanta.pdf. Accessed 3 April 2020.

Takács-Sánta, A. (2010). *Rapa Nui or Tikopia?* Notes of the 2010/2011 Course on Human Ecology Titled "Ecological Crisis and Ways Out". Budapest. [in Hungarian].

Tinbergen, J. (1977). *RIO, Reshaping the International Order: A Report to the Club of Rome*. New York, NY: New American Library.

United Nations Environment Programme (UNEP). (2012). *GEO5 Global Environment Outlook: Environment for the Future We Want*. Nairobi: United Nations Environment Programme. https://wedocs.unep.org/bitstream/handle/20.500.11822/8021/GEO5_report_full_en.pdf?sequence=5&isAllowed=y. Accessed 22 March 2020.

United Nations Environment Programme (UNEP). (2019). GEO6 Global Environment Outlook: Healty Planet, Healthy People. Cambridge, UK: Cambridge University Press. https://wedocs.unep.org/bitstream/handle/20.500.11822/27539/GEO6_2019.pdf?sequence=1&isAllowed=y. Accessed 22 March 2020.

Waters, C. N., Zalasiewicz, J., Summerhayes, C., Barnosky, A. D., Poirier, C., Gałuszka, A., Cearreta, A., Edgeworth, M., Ellis, E. C., Ellis, M., Jeandel, C., Leinfelder, R., McNeill, J. R., deB. Richter, D., Steffen, W., Syvitski, J., Vidas, D., Wagreich, M., Williams, M., Zhisheng, A., Grinevald, J., Odada, E., Oreskes, N., Wolfe, A. P. (2016). The Anthropocene is Functionally and Stratigraphically Distinct from the Holocene. *Science, 351*(6269), aad2622. https://doi.org/10.1126/science.aad2622.

World Meteorological Organization (WMO). (2020). *WMO Statement on the State of the Global Climate in 2019* (WMO-No.1248). Geneva: WMO. https://librarywmo.int/doc_num.php?explnum_id=10211. Accessed 25 March 2020.

World Wide Fund for Nature (WWF). (2016). *Living Planet Report 2016: Risk and Resilience in a New Era*. Gland, Switzerland: WWF International. http://awsassets.panda.org/downloads/lpr_living_planet_report_2016.pdf. Accessed 22 March 2020.

World Wide Fund for Nature (WWF). (2018). *Living Planet Report 2018: Aiming Higher*. In M. Grooten & R. E. A. Almond (Eds.). Gland: WWF. https://s3.amazonaws.com/wwfassets/downloads/lpr2018_full_report_spreads.pdf. Accessed 22 March 2020.

Zsolnai, L. (2015). *Post-Materialistic Business: Spiritual Value-Orientation in Renewing Management*. Houndmills: Palgrave Macmillan.

Zsolnai, L., & Győri, Zs. (2011, September 15–17). *Can Ethics Survive in Competitive Environments?* Empirical Evidence from Values-Driven Businesses, European Business Ethics Network 24th Annual Conference.

Part II

Ecological Consciousness in a Business Context

This part of the book first describes the importance of business models and defines the concepts of "business enterprise" and "business model." It then shows how ecological consciousness differs from environmental consciousness, and what the related approaches—such as deep ecology and ecological economics—are. It also discusses the ethical and spiritual aspects of ecological consciousness, and how these are relevant in the real world. The final chapter of this part of the book investigates how business organizations can implement ecologically conscious ways of functioning, and what the underlying values are that can guide them.

2

The Importance of Business Models

In this book, the term "business" is used to refer to business organizations or business enterprises. In the business and management literature there are no standard, widely accepted definitions for the latter terms, but being motivated primarily by profit appears to be an essential part of them. However, ethical, social, and ecological considerations can also be components of a genuine business enterprise. In fact, business practices can only be justified when they are good for society, and do no harm to nature.

Research into business models has expanded over the past few years. After reviewing the most relevant concepts related to innovative and sustainable business models, this chapter highlights the definition and six key dimensions of business models promoted by Chesbrough and Rosenbloom (2002) as a shared framework for the comparative analysis of ecologically conscious business organizations presented in Part III.

A. Ócsai, *Ecologically Conscious Organizations*, Palgrave Studies in Sustainable Business In Association with Future Earth,
https://doi.org/10.1007/978-3-030-60918-4_2

Business Enterprise

In this book, the term "business" is used to mean business enterprise, although in the literature there are no standardized definitions of "business" and "enterprise." The Business Dictionary defines a business as an organization or economic system in which goods and services are exchanged for each other, or for money. Every business needs some investment and a sufficient number of buyers to whom their products or services can be sold on an ongoing basis for a profit. Businesses may be privately or publicly owned. There are also nonprofit businesses (Business Dictionary 2020a).

In examining the concept of "enterprise" we find that it is defined as a company or an entrepreneurial activity that is particularly characterized by initiative and ingenuity (Business Dictionary 2020b). A "business enterprise" especially is usually defined as an endeavor, the main purpose of which is to make a profit, not just to employ the entrepreneur or others (Business Dictionary 2020c). OECD similarly defines a business enterprise as a business project or venture that is launched in the hope of making a profit. The term usually refers to a business entity that engages in business, and is therefore used as a synonym for the words "company" and "firm" (OECD 1993).

Based on such general definitions, the priority of being motivated by profit appears to be a defining characteristic of a business enterprise. Shane and Venkataraman (2000), who believe that entrepreneurial activity involves finding and exploiting profitable opportunities, support this view. Due to the logic of market competition, enterprises are forced to create market value; that is, to survive they are forced to produce and sell their products and services to their market partners (Bruni and Zamagni 2007). Veblen (1904) also emphasizes the relevance of financial gain as the main goal of business, the usual result of which is the accumulation of wealth. As a critique of capitalism, Veblen also adds that business owners and managers tend to hinder the operation of the industrial system by limiting production to maximize profit, which activity can be identified as the cause of many social problems (for instance, high levels of unemployment) (Veblen 1904).

The functioning of the modern economy is based on a materialistic conception of human activity. According to this perspective, human beings are self-interested individuals who have only materialistic desires and sources of motivation. In economics and business, this understanding is called the "homo oeconomicus" model of man. According to this model, individuals seek to maximize their self-interest and are only interested in material value as expressed in monetary terms. Based on this concept, the materialistic leadership model assumes the presence of an external, monetary source of motivation, and measures success in terms of profit (Zsolnai 2015).

Entrepreneurs who create and maintain businesses, however, look for business opportunities, take risks, and create or reorganize their organizations not only to reap financial success, but also in the hope of achieving professional, market, social, and individual success (Vecsenyi 2003). A business enterprise is "a human activity whose primary purpose, its raison d'être[,] is to satisfy consumer needs by [generating] profit" (Chikán 1997, p. 16). A profit orientation is only one of the necessary conditions (besides independence, risk-taking, and operating in a real market) which mark out an organization as a business enterprise. A desire for profit making is therefore a basic requirement, but this is not enough to explain the functioning of a business enterprise: satisfying consumer needs, meeting the organization's mission, and the specific means of achieving basic goals are the starting point for this (Chikán 1997). Some also consider social enterprises to be business enterprises, the mission of which—achieving social goals—takes priority over profit. Profit that is generated by such organizations cannot be distributed among owners, but is used to meet further targets and support communities (Petheő 2009). Hisrich et al. (2013) draw attention to the importance of factors beyond financial profit, pointing out that an enterprise is a value-creating process that takes risks using time and resources to achieve a financial return and increase independence and personal contentment.

According to Drucker (1954), business can only be justified when it is good for society. In his opinion, the prevailing economic theory of business enterprises and behavior, the principle of maximizing profit—which is just a more complicated way of saying "buying cheap, selling dear"—only explains how business enterprises have worked so far, but cannot explain how they *should* work. The concept of profit maximization in this regard is thus meaningless (Drucker 1973). In fact, it may be claimed that profit is not the cause and goal but the outcome of a successful business operation (Drucker 1973; Kay 2010).

Ethical considerations are an integral part of the concept and operation of business enterprises. There is no business which can avoid producing at least some benefit to society, even if it is primarily interested in maximizing profit. However, a profit motive cannot be the sole target of a business, because this does not provide any guidance about which business enterprises should be set up, nor how, or how to operate them. The existence and activities of business enterprises are actually determined by which social needs they meet with their products and services (Allinson 1998).

Business Model

The literature on business models has expanded significantly over the past decade. Zilahy (2016) provides a good overview of the general definitions and features of business models, especially innovative and sustainable ones. In this section we present the main concepts which are the most relevant to the research topic.

According to Joan Magretta (2002), a business model is basically a story that summarizes answers to the following main questions that confront business: who are the customers, what does value mean to them, how can a profit be made by the business, and based on which economic factors can value be created for customers at a reasonable cost? When creating a new business model, a new story is written, but such new stories are in fact iterations of earlier ones, involving revisions and the reuse of universal human experiences. That is, all new business models are based on the general value chain concept that is the basis of all businesses. The value chain has two main parts: first, the design and production of a product or a service; and second, delivering the product or service to the customer and collecting the reward. A business model can generate novelty by creating a new product or service, or improve a process in a preexisting value chain.

Casadesus-Masanell and Ricart (2011), instead of predefining the elements of the ideal business model—which can hamper the creation of revolutionary business models through fixed assumptions—rather focus on the decisions and choices of the leaders who create the business models. Management decisions about how a company should work are all pervasive and include decisions about remuneration practices, procurement contracts, the location of sites, the degree of vertical integration, and sales and marketing initiatives. These decisions have consequences that affect the value creation logic of the company, and thus stakeholders and the company itself, so when defining the business model such consequences must be taken into account: Companies can make three types of decisions when designing business models. (1) Choices regarding operational policies determine the activities of the company. (2) Asset choices affect what resources and tangible assets the company employs and uses. (3) Governance choices involve the allocation of power and decision-making rights, and establish how to make decisions involving the previous two forms of choices. The consequences of these choices can be flexible. For example, price increases can quickly lead to a drop in sales. However, they can be rigid, too. The characteristics of company culture change only over a longer period of time. Differentiating between the consequences of the latter choices is useful, because they have different impacts on the competitiveness of a company. The outcomes of flexible choices can easily be copied, while those of rigid choices are difficult or take a longer time to implement, so they can generate competitive advantage.

The definition given by Chesbrough and Rosenbloom (2002) understands the business model as a coherent framework that transforms technological features and opportunities as inputs into economic outputs through customers and markets. The former authors define six main elements of the business model.

1. Value propositions: what values the company creates for customers based on the technology they use.
2. Market segment: which customers benefit, and for what purpose, from the given technology, and how the company generates revenue from this.

3. Cost structure and profit potential: taking into account the given value propositions and the structure of the value chain, at what cost and with which expectations about profit may value be captured.
4. Structure of the value chain: what the structure of the value creation process is, and what resources are required for its operation.
5. Position within the value network: what place does the company occupy within the network that links suppliers to customers, and who are its competitors and partners.
6. Competitive strategy: with what strategy can the company build and maintain its competitive advantage.

Together, these six components serve, in addition to creating value for customers, to generate a return on financial investment that enables a business model to be implemented and a business to further develop.

References

Allinson, R. E. (1998). Ethical Values as Part of the Definition of Business Enterprise and Part of the Internal Structure of the Business Organization. *Journal of Business Ethics, 17,* 1015–1028. https://doi.org/10.1023/A:1006063114697.

Bruni, L., & Zamagni, S. (2007). *Civil Economy: Efficiency, Equity, Public Happiness*. Bern: Peter Lang. https://doi.org/10.1108/17465680810907323.

Business Dictionary. (2020a). *Business*. http://www.businessdictionary.com/definition/business.html. Accessed 26 March 2020.

Business Dictionary. (2020b). *Enterprise*. http://www.businessdictionary.com/definition/enterprise.html. Accessed 26 March 2020.

Business Dictionary. (2020c). *Business Enterprise*. http://www.businessdictionary.com/definition/business-enterprise.html. Accessed 26 March 2020.

Casadesus-Masanell, R., & Ricart, J. E. (2011). How to Design a Winning Business Model. *Harvard Business Review, 89*(1/2), 100–107. https://hbr.org/2011/01/how-to-design-a-winning-business-model#. Accessed 26 March 2020.

Chesbrough, H., & Rosenbloom, R. S. (2002). The Role of the Business Model in Capturing Value from Innovation: Evidence from Xerox Corporation's

Technology Spin-Off Companies. *Industrial and Corporate Change, 11*(3), 529–555. https://doi.org/10.1093/icc/11.3.529.
Chikán, A. (1997). *Vállalatgazdaságtan* [*Business Economics*]. Budapest: Aula Kiadó [in Hungarian].
Drucker, P. F. (1954). *The Practice of Management*. New York: Harper.
Drucker, P. F. (1973). *Management: Tasks, Responsibilities, Practices*. New York: Harper – Row.
Hisrich, R. D., Peters, M. P., & Shepherd, D. A. (2013). *Entrepreneurship* (9th ed.). New York: McGraw-Hill/Irwin.
Kay, J. A. (2010). *Obliquity: Why Our Goals Are Best Achieved Indirectly*. London: Profile Books.
Magretta, J. (2002). Why Business Models Matter. *Harvard Business Review, 80*(5), 86–92. https://hbr.org/2002/05/why-business-models-matter#. Accessed 26 March 2020.
OECD – Organization for Economic Co-operation and Development. (1993). *Business enterprise in Glossary of Industrial Organisation Economics and Competition Law*. Compiled by R. S. Khemani & D. M. Shapiro, commissioned by the Directorate for Financial, Fiscal and Enterprise Affairs, OECD. https://stats.oecd.org/glossary/detail.asp?ID=3207. Accessed 26 March 2020.
Petheő, A. I. (2009). *A vállalati társadalmi felelősségen túl: A szociális vállalkozás* [*Beyond Corporate Social Responsibility: The Social Enterprise*]. Ph.D. dissertation, Small Business Development Center, Corvinus University of Budapest, Budapest [in Hungarian].
Shane, S., & Venkataraman, S. (2000). The Promise of Entrepreneurship as a Field of Research. *The Academy of Management Review, 25*(1), 217–226. https://doi.org/10.5465/amr.2000.2791611.
Veblen, T. (1904). *The Theory of Business Enterprise*. New York: Charles Scribner's Sons. www.businessbuildersbanquet.com/software/veblen2.pdf. Accessed 26 March 2020.
Vecsenyi, J. (2003). *Vállalkozás – Az ötlettől az újrakezdésig* [*Business—From Idea to Start Over*]. Budapest: Aula Kiadó [in Hungarian].
Zilahy, G. (2016). Sustainable Business Models—What Do Management Theories Say? *Vezetéstudomány* [*Budapest Management Review*], *XLVII*(10), 62–72. http://unipub.lib.uni-corvinus.hu/2497/1/VT2016n10p62.pdf. Accessed 26 March 2020.
Zsolnai, L. (2015). *Post-Materialistic Business: Spiritual Value-Orientation in Renewing Management*. Houndmills: Palgrave Macmillan. https://doi.org/10.1057/9781137525987.

3

Beyond Environmental Consciousness

This chapter first examines the concepts of "ecology" and "human ecology" as types of the transdisciplinary study of man-made environmental problems. It then presents the evolution of the study of and different approaches to "consciousness" in Eastern and Western traditions. The chapter shows how "ecological consciousness" began to be distinguished from "environmental consciousness" from the late 1960s onwards. Environmental consciousness understands environmental problems too narrowly, seeing them mainly as technical problems, and thus does not recognize the root causes of the environmental crisis.

Ecological problems can only be solved if the relationship between nature, society, and individuals is well understood, and if we recognize that environmental problems are the inevitable consequence of false

Based on the permission of the publisher, some parts of this chapter are revisions of one of the author's journal articles formerly published in Hungarian: Ócsai, A. (2018). A vállalkozások ökológiai tudatossága [Ecological Consciousness of Businesses]. *Vezetéstudomány* [Budapest Management Review], *XLIX* (9), 2–19. https://doi.org/10.14267/veztud.2018.09.01.

A. Ócsai, *Ecologically Conscious Organizations*, Palgrave Studies in Sustainable Business In Association with Future Earth,
https://doi.org/10.1007/978-3-030-60918-4_3

ontological and epistemological assumptions and the instrumental rationality embodied in the social and cultural institutions of modernity (modern capitalism, industrial technology, individualism, and mechanistic science). The chapter ends with a summary of further relevant concepts related to the topic (inter alia, deep ecology and ecosophy, ecological economics, and the circular economy), different ethical and spiritual ideas (ecological conscience, land ethics, Gaian ethics, moral disengagement strategies, and the principle of responsibility), and comments on the relevance of some selected worldviews (Christianity, Gandhi's philosophy, and Buddhist economics).

Defining Ecology

The origins of ecology as a science can be traced back to the beginnings of natural science (Benson 2000; Egerton 2001). The term "ecology" was used as early as in 1858 in a letter by Henry David Thoreau (Harding and Bode 1958), but with no explanation of its content. The first definition is attributed to Ernst Haeckel, who in 1866 defined ecology as a comprehensive science that involves examining the relationships between living organisms and their external environment and the organic and inorganic living conditions of organisms (Friederichs 1958). In the science that further developed following the turn of the twentieth century, ecology was defined by Charles Elton (1927) as scientific natural history, while Odum (1963) considered it to be the study of the structures and functions of nature. According to McNaughton and Wolf (1973), ecology is the scientific study of the interactions between organisms and their environment. Whittaker (1975) states that ecology is the examination of living systems and their environmental relationships. Krebs (2001) writes about ecology as the "science of interactions" that determines the distribution and mass of organisms. Such definitions are not uniform, and the different trends involve differences in methodology. Hungarian ecologist Pál Juhász-Nagy has primarily been concerned with clarifying the theoretical foundation of the concept and field of ecology with scientific precision, and the development of mathematical modeling as the study methodology (Juhász-Nagy 1984, 1986, 1993; Pásztor and Oborny 2007; Hahn 2014).

In this book, we understand ecology as "synbiology," which involves examination of the level of organization located above the individual. The supraindividual levels include populations, communities/associations, biomes, and the biosphere. Ecologists study the regularity and types of interaction between organisms and their environment, between populations of living organisms (and systems of populations) and the environment, and the conditions limiting or supporting their existence, and effects on their productivity (Hortobágyi and Simon 2000).

"Human ecology" can be considered the transdisciplinary study of man-made environmental problems. The basic questions human ecology addresses, which overlap with many classical disciplines in the natural and social sciences, are what changes human activities cause in nature; what the social causes and consequences of these changes are; and how it is possible to mitigate ecological changes and adapt to them (Takács-Sánta 2009).

Western and Eastern Approach to Consciousness

According to the Merriam-Webster online dictionary (2020), consciousness is: (1) (a) the state or quality of consciousness, especially being conscious of something within oneself; (b) being conscious of an external object, state, or fact; (c) concern, attention to a social, political cause; (2) the state of being characterized by sensation, emotion, will and thought; (3) the totality of conscious states of an individual; (4) the normal state of conscious life; (5) the higher level of mental life when the individual is conscious, as opposed to unconscious processes.

It is clear from the complexity of the word that no uniform definition of the concept of consciousness has yet emerged. Consciousness is also approached in different ways in the Eastern and Western traditions (Velmans 2009). In the following, we briefly summarize the historical evolution of consciousness in Western thinking, and some approaches to consciousness in the Eastern traditions.

In Western philosophy, the issue of consciousness has been a subject of interest since ancient times. Plato dealt with questions concerning human nature, the soul, and mind, and Aristotle examined the nature of perception and consciousness. In the early modern times, the focus of René Descartes and his followers was the relationship between mind and body. The claim they made was that the mind can be distinguished from the body, and that all mental states can be considered a form of thinking, which requires consciousness. At the end of the seventeenth century, John Locke had similar views about the relationship between thinking and consciousness, but Gottfried Leibniz recognized the existence of unconscious perceptions and distinguished between external consciousness (perception) and self-consciousness (apperception). A century later, the decisive work of Immanuel Kant proved that understanding consciousness requires the acceptance of the existence and study of the mental structures and unconscious mental states and mechanisms that are prerequisites for conscious experience. Since the end of the nineteenth century, consciousness research has taken many directions. The examination of consciousness through introspective methods was pursued in psychology, and the work of Sigmund Freud increased the general acceptance of the existence of unconscious mental states and processes. In philosophy, phenomenology deals with the issue of consciousness, primarily through the work of Edmund Husserl and Martin Heidegger. With the development of brain research, neuropsychology, and neuroscience in the 1980s, interdisciplinary interest in consciousness research strengthened, and dedicated journals, book series, and conferences emerged to generate a deeper understanding of it (Gennaro, n. d.).

Modern medical and psychological research, through psychological experiments and the analysis of cases of altered states of consciousness, examines whether human and animal consciousness is objectively measurable, and seeks to understand its underlying neurological and psychological mechanisms (Koch 2004). "Integrated information theory" aims to scientifically explain consciousness and examine whether specific physical systems are conscious, and, if so, what degree of consciousness they have. The theory states that consciousness is present to varying degrees in biological organizations, ranging from the simplest organisms through non-mammalian species to the human fetus, to premature babies and patients with cerebral cortex injury. Digital computers and forms of artificial intelligence, however, are not conscious (Tononi and Koch 2015).

The Mind and Life Institute, established by the fourteenth Dalai Lama, neuroscientist Francisco Varela, and lawyer and entrepreneur Adam Engle, aims at bridging Western scientific thinking and the contemplative practices inspired by Buddhism. Over the past thirty years, dozens of scientific studies, journal articles, and conferences have pointed out—based on objective observation and analysis—that modern science needs to be complemented by analytical methods based on contemplative practices and self-observation to generate truly "humane" results that can reduce human suffering (Mind and Life Institute 2020).

Contemplative science examines the cognitive, neurological, physiological, behavioral, and social manifestations of the mind in contemplative consciousness. It is inspired by Buddhist values, but its main purpose is to combine science, philosophy, and religion through empirical methods without religious bias (Wallace 2007).

Buddhist philosophy tells us that there is no constant, unchanging soul or ego, and consciousness cannot exist independently of matter, detection, perception, and aspiration. Moreover, they do not exist independently, but only exist, they are formed according to our senses and objects (form, sound, fragrance, taste, tactile things, and thoughts) (Rahula 1974). Thus, our consciousness is made up of seeds that were sown by our own past actions and those of our family and society. In our consciousness, our thoughts, words, and actions arise every moment and create our bodies, minds, and our world, so it is up to us how we shape our consciousness (Nhat Hanh 2008). The fourteenth Dalai Lama also draws attention to the importance of causal relationships in the Buddhist conception of consciousness (2005, quoted by Marques 2012). He also states that consciousness is one of the prominent elements of spiritual development, and that during our lifetime we are capable of spiritual development, having a higher level of experience, and achieving the ultimate state of omniscience through increasing the continuity of our consciousness (identified as the Buddha nature found in every human being) (Dalai Lama 1995 quoted by Marques 2012).

According to the Upanishads, the ancient Indian teachings, consciousness is the essence of an immanent being, the Atman, which can actually be identified with Brahman; with the pure, transcendent, free consciousness that allows nature and man to exist (Sen 2008 quoted by Velmans 2009). Consciousness is described in the Vedas as a principle that is present in matter, in life, and in the mind from the outset after it has crystallized from a finer, universal, and infinite state into a coarser form (Chakraborty 1995). Consciousness is present in every being, is constant, independent from space and time, and is the source of all physical and social reality. Its highest physical manifestation, however, is embodied in humanity, whose members are capable of self-reflection and self-realization; that is, of attaining unity with all other beings, individual consciousness, and the source of all, Universal Consciousness (Pruzan 2016). Moreover, for humans, grasping the power of individual consciousness and attaining the original state of Consciousness is not just an opportunity, but a task that should be accomplished (Chakraborty 1995).

Ecological Consciousness and Its Ethical Aspects

In this section, we examine the topic of ecological consciousness in detail, starting from the origin of the concept, through its appearance in the literature, to a presentation of its ethical implications.

From Ecological Consciousness to the Circular Economy

The origin of ecological consciousness as a phenomenon can be traced back to Paleolithic gatherer-hunter-fisher societies. Archeological and comparative ethnographic studies confirm that the psychological representation of the "natural" state of the human soul was approximately the same on every continent. In such ancient societies, ecological consciousness included the identification of the "self" with nature and respect for life. The universe was considered a holy being, and humans a part of the great unity of nature and dependent on it, not dominant over it. Every being was seen as part of a greater whole; and humankind interconnected with every animate and inanimate being. Ecological consciousness was also characteristic of early agricultural societies and thus part of the mindset of the first great civilizations. In Ancient Greece, the Pythagoreans believed that humans were a microcosm of the universe; the body of a human was made up of the same elements as the universe, and their soul was derived from its soul. Plato and the Stoics also considered the cosmos to be a living creature, together with all living beings, and by nature similar to them. The universe lived and had a soul and consciousness, from which the human soul and intellect originated. In the East, the teachings of Hinduism and Taoism about humanity were similar (Hughes 1991). However, as the biosphere-transforming activity of humankind went through six major leaps (the use of fire, the appearance of language, the development of agriculture, the emergence of civilizations, the European conquests, and the technical-scientific-energetic revolution; Takács-Sánta 2004), each increasingly extensive, humans gradually became physically, psychologically, and spiritually separated from non-human nature. Ecological consciousness weakened at the community level, and the state of the natural environment deteriorated (Hughes 1991).

Since the 1980s, there has been increasing interest in ecological consciousness. The concept began to be distinguished from environmental consciousness at the end of the 1960s by environmental activists and philosophers, who believed that conventional nature conservation movements were interpreting environmental problems too narrowly. This philosophical viewpoint, initially proclaimed by few, has since become the perspective adopted by environmental movements over the last few decades, and has led to profound changes in society, cultural, political and economic institutions by redefining the concepts of individual, society, and nature (Christopher 1999).

In the formulation of Christopher (1999), ecological consciousness is concern for environmental problems fueled by the knowledge and experience of the degradation of nature. Ecological consciousness also implies that modern thinking is based on false ontological and epistemological presuppositions that prevent modern people from correctly perceiving and responding to environmental problems.

According to ecologist thinkers, conventional environmental consciousness degrades environmental problems into technical problems; it is therefore unable to help with understanding their root causes. Environmental problems can only be solved if concern for the devastation of nature is accompanied by an "ecological" understanding of the relationship between nature, society, and the individual (Christopher 1999: p. 358). At the center of ecological consciousness is the belief that environmental problems are the inevitable consequence of an instrumental rationality embodied in the social and cultural institutions of modernity (modern capitalism, industrial technology, individualism, and mechanistic science); thus without new social and cultural institutions based on a new rationality, global disaster is unavoidable (Christopher 1999: p. 361).

Beyond feeling the increasing ecological threat and experiencing related anxiety, ecological consciousness also implies that by formulating a new metaphysical framework of rationality and a new understanding of the nature of the self and its place in the universe we can give meaning to the threat. The steps of this process are the following. (1) Replacing the atomistic concept of the self with a holistic approach (understanding that nature and the individual exist together in ecosystems). (2) Developing an ethical system that allows escape from anthropocentrism in line with the new ontological framework. (3) Recognizing that the realization of an extended self-understanding is possible through a pre-rational process involving changes in individuals' feelings and relationships to the world. (4) Searching for an ecological rationality: combining the previous steps, thereby creating a viable way to re-rationalize the sociocultural relations that support the actualization and empowerment of ecological consciousness (Christopher 1999: pp. 362–363).

According to Hamilton (2010), the development of ecological consciousness depends on the appearance of a new kind of sense of self and a new relationship of man to the natural environment. In the case of rich, consumption-based societies, one must understand how the personal identity of individuals is created by consumption and the institutions that serve it, and how people act when influenced by these factors. Instead of confronting consumers with information about environmental degradation, it may be more effective to show them whether a consumer lifestyle can really make them happy.

Deep ecology, developed by Norwegian philosopher Arne Naess, can be considered both a philosophical and an operative approach (Naess 1989). Naess criticizes environmental thinking, which focuses on short-term problems (i.e. "shallow" ecology), because it assumes that environmental pollution and resource depletion can be solved through technology. In contrast, Naess believes that deep ecology, which involves exploring the roots of problems, is needed, along with a redefinition of predominantly reductionist, anthropocentric ideology, and, within it, the individual. This should involve reconstructing our own self-image, and radically changing our mindset. Based on the teachings of many prominent spiritual predecessors (Aristotle, Buddha, Saint Francis, Spinoza, Thoreau, Aldo Leopold, and Heidegger), the approach seeks to address fundamental questions such as how can we cope with today's ideological struggles, what is the place of man in nature, and how can we care for future generations. Solutions may be found by applying the pluralistic view of ecophilosophy, which involves the consideration of ecological principles (complexity, diversity, symbiosis, and unity) and a personal approach called "ecosophy." On this basis—by viewing the ecology and the economy as of equal importance—every human being must be able to develop their individual worldviews, values, and norms, to act upon them, and take responsibility (Ims 2015).

White (2011) derives the concept of ecological consciousness from the work of researchers who deal with deep ecology and ecosophy. The concept has been addressed—often using different terms, including "ecological self," "ideal state of being," "self-realization," and "ecological sensibility"—by different scholars since its appearance in the 1970s (Beck 1995; Bragg 1996; Christopher 1999; Devall 1988; Devall and Sessions 1985; Drengson 1989, Hill et al. 2004; Leff 1978; Milbraith 1989; Morris 2002; O'Sullivan and Taylor 2004; Uhl 2004). In summarizing the results, White defines ecological consciousness as deep awareness of individuals' biological, ecological, emotional, and spiritual relationships with non-human beings. It is one's personal identification with non-human nature, respect for the intrinsic value of non-human nature, and deep concern for the destruction of our natural environment—and handling this through rational understanding and an active, emotional, psycho-spiritual attitude. It is the intention of "self-realization," which includes commitment to non-human beings. It is the understanding that the global environmental crisis is caused by the prevailing state of—globalized, industrial, consumer—modernity, and a disconnected consciousness. It is the motivation to cope with global and personal concerns, and to understand concepts that are beyond humanity through experientially and emotionally connecting to the natural environment (White 2011: p. 42).

Ecological economics is related to ecological consciousness. This discipline, formed by the thoughts of Karl Polanyi (1944), Kenneth Boulding (1966), Nicholas Georgescu-Roegen (1971), Ernst F. Schumacher (1973), Herman Daly (Daly 1999; Daly and Farley 2004), and Robert Costanza (Costanza et al. 1997), characteristically differs from environmental economics, which is part of mainstream economics. According to ecological economics, the economy is part of the ecosystem, not the other way around. Nature, society, and economy are interconnected in dynamic unity. In ecological economics, a holistic, transdisciplinary, and organic perspective, intergenerational equity, a long time horizon for natural processes, the carrying capacity of the Earth, and the issue of sustainable development play an important role (Daly and Farley 2004; Capra and Jakobsen 2017; Jakobsen 2017). Ecological economics must reinforce its ethical background by relying on Hans Jonas's imperative of responsibility. The main elements of this are that humans are members, not masters of the community of life on Earth. Moreover, that the Earth and its living systems are not merely natural resources, but beings intrinsically worthy of respect and care. Careful use and the fair sharing of low-entropy sources and sink capacities that support living conditions are required (Brown and Timmermann 2015).

A new kind of economics that is capable of dealing with the current challenges of the world should be based on an organic worldview that relies on the unity of economy, nature, and society. A shift from the competition-based, mainstream economic paradigm with its mechanistic, instrumental and reductionist worldview is required that involves change at structural and individual levels so that consumption and lifestyle habits and values can become supportive of solidarity and sustainability. This requires circularity, respect for pluralistic values, and transparent cooperation based on communication (Ims and Jakobsen 2006; Ingebrigtsen and Jakobsen 2007; Jakobsen 2017). This mindset is the basis of the circular economy, in which production, distribution, consumption, and recycling take place in much closer unity through cycles. Instead of one-off consumption events, the goal is to increase the lifetime of products, reduce the amount of waste, and increase commodity efficiency (for example, through repair, reuse, and recycling). In addition to global and national processes, local solutions and local currencies will play a key role in this (Ingebirgsten and Jakobsen 2007; European Commission 2015, 2018; Jakobsen 2017).

Ethical Aspects of Ecological Consciousness

Nobel laureate poet and artist Rabindranath Tagore always had deep respect for the natural environment. He was particularly concerned about deforestation, and probably the first person in India to initiate a festival for tree planting. This occurred at the end of the 1920s (Sen 1997). His desire to sustain nature stems from a central preoccupation with a harmony of relationships based on care and concern. With a perspective rooted in traditional Indian ethical values, non-dualism, oneness, and the interconnection of all beings, Tagore highlighted the importance of ecological stability and the sustainable development of the whole universe (Sarin 2014).

Tagore argued that civilization has become dissociated from the context of the cosmos and that dehumanizing, mainstream materialistic attitudes have caused humanity to lose their harmony and identification with nature. The internal causes of ecological imbalance are basic vices such as greed, jealousy, lust, and pride manifested in commercialism, consumerism, and unbridled competition. Tagore holds that the cosmic unity between man and nature is attainable through developing a deep kinship with natural entities. The latter should not be considered mere physical objects, but God-given gifts that complete us and provide us with sources of bliss and peace that lead to the emergence of our best values. Tagore regards the world as the expression of beauty, which he shows us in many of his creative masterpieces, such as in a poem entitled "When I See the World as a Song." Tagore states that beauty creates harmony in relationships that lead to soul consciousness, and the expansion of aesthetic, moral, and spiritual consciousness. One's whole existence is interlinked, thus through identification with nature we can rise above our narrow ego and realize oneness within our soul, where the key to cosmic consciousness is (Sarin 2014; Mukherjee 2018).

In an essay entitled "The Ecological Conscience," American naturalist Aldo Leopold writes that the conservation of nature must arise from what is ethically and aesthetically correct. Only those things are right that preserve the integrity, stability, and beauty of a natural community, including soil, water, flora and fauna (Leopold 1949).

If we accept the need for an ecological conscience, economic gains cannot be an excuse for "unsocial land use" or ecological "atrocities." It is advisable to encourage proper land use through social rewards that are proportionate to the importance to society of the former (Leopold 1949). The basis of preservation must be "land ethics," which perceives humanity as a part of ecosystems, and expands the scope of ethics to the Earth. This new kind of ecological consciousness means that humans must become members of the ecological community through transforming themselves from masters of "life's commonwealth" into equals with other species (Feng Lin and Fyles 2015).

Experiencing the ecological destruction caused by the economic, industrial, and military activities of the twentieth century and the enormous damage to the natural and human life of the Vietnam War, American Trappist monk and philosopher Thomas Merton agreed with Aldo Leopold that there is a need to strengthen ecological conscience. Without this, the ruthless and mindless exploitation of nature and man will continue. Behind the ecological tragedies caused by business and wars, we find aggression, fear, and the desire for domination of the modern Western man cloaked in clichés, hidden behind the mask of individuals as "defenders of freedom and democracy." The psychological roots of this are dehumanization and alienation. Man confuses the value of objects and abstractions (commodities, money, and property) with life itself, and appreciates immediate profit more than anything else. Developing an ecological conscience requires that we recognize our responsibilities to other members of the terrestrial community, and respect all forms of life (Merton 1968).

A very important representative of ecological consciousness is the English geochemist-ecologist James Lovelock. Based on the experience of research into global ecological change triggered by human activity and a program that searched for Martian life that was launched in the 1960s, Lovelock developed, with the American biologist Lynn Margulis, so-called Gaia theory. According to this theory, terrestrial animate and inanimate systems are closely related and form a self-regulating (homeostatic) system. Named after the Greek goddess Mother Earth, "Gaia" refers to the complex, self-regulating system of Earth's biosphere, atmosphere, water, and land that create the optimal physical-chemical environment for life on earth (Lovelock 2009). In light of this, Gaian ethics requires that economic activities do not undermine "the intactness and integrity of the global patterns and mechanisms of the Earth" (refraining from species extermination, greenhouse gas emissions, and the carbon dioxide emissions that cause global warming) (Zsolnai 2001).

According to Stanford psychologist Albert Bandura (2007), if we really want to be responsible caretakers for nature and preserve it for future generations, then we have to make it harder to apply moral disengagement strategies to those who commit ecologically destructive activities. With the help of psychological strategies, one can disassociate one's conscience in order to continue to undertake activities harmful to nature and avoid facing their negative consequences. Activities that cause global ecological and human damage (such as deforestation, desertification, global warming, melting ice sheets, rising sea levels, extreme weather conditions, soil degradation, biodiversity loss, etc.) are often "justified" by reference to a higher social, national, or economic purpose. Morally disengaged actors may attempt to prove the acceptability of their own practices with "exonerative comparisons," and activities can be hidden behind "euphemistic language." People also can reduce their accountability through the "displacement and diffusion of responsibility"; disregard, minimize, or dispute the harmful effects they cause; dehumanize and disparage victims; or discredit the "messengers of harmful effects." These psychosocial mechanisms work on an individual and social level, so it is particularly important that we reduce or eliminate the factors inhibiting the conservation of the natural environment and the future, and activate our ecological conscience.

Having experienced the dramatic change in the nature, spatial, and temporal scope of human activity, German-American philosopher Hans Jonas drew attention to the need for a new kind of ethics, and to the importance of the principle of responsibility. Humans are causing cumulative and irreversible damage to living nature, thus it is an ethical requirement to care and behave responsibly toward natural beings, which all have intrinsic value. We must live and act so that we do not endanger the future of life on Earth. It is a duty of humanity to adopt a caring attitude based on a non-reciprocal attitude toward future generations and nature. Human responsibility to preserve the living conditions of future generations and natural beings is of a substantive nature (Jonas 1984; Zsolnai 2014a). Economic decision-makers also have an ethical responsibility toward their stakeholders, depending on whether they are linked contractually (suppliers, employees, and consumers) or naturally (local communities, natural environment, and future generations) (Zsolnai 2000).

On the basis of his extensive anthropological, biological, linguistic, psychological, cybernetic, ecological, and philosophical research, British-American biologist Gregory Bateson concluded that the duality found in modern philosophical and scientific thinking (mind–body, man–nature, society–ecology, biological–emotional, God–nature) is basically false. The world is made up of systems involving individuals, societies, and ecosystems, which are part of a supreme, comprehensive system. Many call this God; Bateson refers to it as "Mind." Consciousness is the bridge between the individual, society, and ecology, but the limited consciousness developed through Western epistemology is not compatible with the universal Mind. The reason for this is that Western thinking is too purpose-driven, and thus narrows attention, perception, and the receptiveness of consciousness. It reinforces the misconception that humanity can control all systems and customize them to suit its own needs, thereby unbalancing natural systems and destroying self-correcting mechanisms. As a solution, Bateson proposes the practice of humility and the acceptance of natural cybernetic (self-controlled) systems. Thinking and cognition has to be developed into a more complete form of consciousness that synthesizes emotions and subconscious factors. To achieve this, the following factors are needed: extending love from individuals to societies and ecosystems; practicing arts, poetry, and music to expand the capacity of the mind; developing the relationship between humans and animals and nature; and religious practice, or spirituality. A healthy ecology of human civilization involves a unified system of nature and human civilization, in which civilization is as flexible as nature, and is open even to slow changes in its basic characteristics (Bateson 1972).

Ecological Consciousness and Spirituality

We have seen above how often the subject of spirituality appears in the study of ecological consciousness. Now, let us look at the topic of ecological consciousness through the lenses of spirituality and see how some worldviews approach ecological consciousness.

Spirituality: The Search for the Meaning of Life

Modern economic activity that focuses on maximizing profit and growth is threatening the integrity and diversity of natural ecosystems, along with the autonomy and culture of local communities and the living conditions of future generations. To preserve nature and meet real human needs, a moderate and careful economy is needed. This requires the internal motivation of economic actors to serve the public good, and to measure their success in other categories of value besides money. The background and motivational basis for this can be spirituality, because, without this, ethical business initiatives and environmental measures can become ineffective and often lead to the opposite outcomes to those which were intended (Zsolnai 2015).

The well-being of human communities, natural ecosystems, and future generations, therefore, requires dedicated, genuine care, which can come from an experience of unity with other beings and the universal source of creation. Spiritual experiences can play a prominent role in the development of the personality and ethical behavior of decision-makers, and contribute to a deeper understanding of different decision-making situations and systems, thereby helping create new categories, and overcome existing paradigms (Zsolnai 2014b). Spirituality can be a significant factor in sustainable lifestyles, as spiritually inspired people may pursue more pro-environmental activities and live a happier and more satisfied life than other individuals (Csutora and Zsóka 2014).

Spirituality has long been linked exclusively to religion, but today it clearly exceeds the framework of institutionalized religions. It consists of the following main components: connection to the inner "I"; the search for universal values that help the individual transcend their self-centered aspirations; deep compassion for all living beings; and connecting with the source of life (Bouckaert and Zsolnai 2012). According to the definition developed by the European SPES Institute (2020), spirituality is the search for the meaning of life—in various sociocultural forms—that connects people with every living being and with God or Ultimate Reality.

The Economic Application of Spirituality

Spiritual-based leadership can play a key role in the economic application of spirituality. Spirituality can help guide leaders as an internal source in their search for meaning, purpose, and fulfillment both in the business world and in the world of their consciousness and conscience. Their external action and internal reflection support each other. Rationality and spirituality become reinforcing viewpoints (Pruzan 2011). However, it is not enough to transform managerial education and management practices. The mindset and consciousness of managers must be changed, and their internal guidance and conscience strengthened (Pruzan 2015a).

Coming to know the essence of being, the experience of the true Self, is possible for all leaders. This will then be reflected in the leader's decisions in the external business world. However, the acceptance, development, and promotion of the concept and practice of spiritual-based leadership depend first and foremost on to what extent leaders become conscious of their own spirituality—their inborn divine nature and state of perfection (Pruzan 2015b).

According to Luk Bouckaert, spiritual-based leadership can be considered a kind of transformative leadership. The purpose of transformative leadership is to support the development of individuals and organizations in the following ways: increasing development of a common vision and values, cooperation, open communication, trust, intrinsic motivation, empowerment, and charismatic-, serving- and value-driven management. The four main types of transformative leadership can be displayed in Table 3.1 consisting of a vertical and a horizontal axis. The two extreme values of the vertical axis are market-driven leadership (M) and spirit-centered leadership (S). On the horizontal axis, there are hierarchical (H) and democratic (D) versions of leadership. In the table divided into four parts by the two axes (Market leadership [M + H], CSR Leadership [M + D], Aristocratic leadership [S + H], Spiritual-based leadership [S + D]) leaders can be practically described as being of mixed types, but some features are characteristically predominant. The main characteristics of

Table 3.1 Types of transformative leadership

Market

	Hierarchy	Democracy
Market	Market leadership (M + H)	CSR leadership (M + D)
Spirit	Aristocratic leadership (S + H)	Spiritual-based leadership (S + D)

Spirit

Source Author's construction based on Bouckaert (2016)

spiritual-based leadership are that every human being has the ability to lead and follow, so the operation of an organization and leadership are based on co-creativity and co-responsibility. Spiritual-based leadership empowers participants and supports social relationships based on trust, reciprocity, and interconnectedness (Bouckaert 2016).

Lozano and Ribera (2004) find that spirituality and leadership practice interact. Spirituality manifests itself in leadership when it is developed by leaders through effort and vigilance. Leaders then receive feedback during their exercise of leadership that influences their own conception of life, human characteristics, and spirituality. Spirituality can thus lead to a qualitative change in leaders, and through them also in organizations, which can ultimately affect every member of the organization. In a spiritually based organization containing spiritually driven individuals, the following positive effects can be observed: The personal values and abilities of the members of the organization develop, and professional and ethical responsibility strengthens. Relationships among members, the quality of products, and organizational processes improve. The expression of, development of, and experience of values are enhanced. Relations with internal and external stakeholders are also strengthened (Lozano and Ribera 2004).

During the last few decades, many scholars have argued that a paradigm shift in mainstream management thinking and education is necessary. New insights from the humanities (including the arts, literature, and music) and spirituality have been used to call for the establishment of a better connection between management-type learning and life for the comprehensive and integral development of the individual. Rabindranath Tagore's alternative higher education system at his university Visva Bharati in Santiniketan, West Bengal, India, could serve as an example of how to transform our organizations and ourselves for the better. Based on Tagore's call and practice of humanism, openness and otherness, and learning in an ambience of nature, the university aims at promoting holistic human development and the natural expression of students' full potential. Inspired by Tagore's conception, the integration of liberal arts into management education may also increase the potential of managers by emphasizing the importance of wisdom and character. A liberal arts education can strengthen personal values and interdisciplinary and cross-cultural perspectives, adaptive learning, critical thinking, creativity, human caring, respect for nature and all creation, and reverence for life. Such an approach can help executives to create value for all stakeholders, to aspire to non-materialistic goals, and to live a meaningful and soulful life that is sensitive toward nature and the spirit (Mukherjee 2018).

Worldviews and Ecological Consciousness

In this section, we will examine how ecological consciousness appears in some of the important worldviews and systems of thought of our time: Christianity, Gandhi's philosophy, and Buddhist economics.

Inspired by the teachings of Saint Francis of Assisi, the patron saint of ecology, Pope Francis's encyclical "Praise be to you" (*Laudato si'*) presents the ecological position of the Roman Catholic Church. Pope Francis calls attention to the significance of the ecological crisis and connects it with the imperative of social justice. The encyclical describes the ecological and social crisis of today (environmental pollution, climate change, drinking water scarcity, loss of biodiversity, a decline in human quality of life and the degradation of societies, and global inequality) with scientific precision, and presents the teachings of Saint Francis of Assisi as inspiration for finding solutions. Concern for vulnerable people and natural beings, peace, joy, selflessness, a feeling of openness toward ourselves and the world, and material renunciation that fosters spiritual wealth are the most important components of what is called "integral ecology."

Integral ecology is a transdisciplinary approach that respects both nature and humanity, and is oriented by humane values. Ecology and the economy, the natural and social sciences, the arts and education must work together to replace utilitarian (individualist, endless-growth-based, competition-, consumption- and unregulated market-based) modern thinking with the ideal of "ecological citizenship" based on equity, justice, moderate consumption, recognition of the intrinsic value of nature, and a holistic worldview. The basis of individual and community ecological transformation should be ecological spirituality, in which humanity recognizes, through generous care, sensitivity, gratitude, and self-sacrificing work, that they are not separate from the world but live in a universal community with all other creatures (Pope Francis 2015).

To put these ideals into practice and to address economic challenges, starting with the thoughts and economic activities of young scholars and activists, Pope Francis convened in Autumn 2020 the international meeting "The Economy of Francesco. Young people, a pact, the future and Assisi 2020" (after discussion with the Bishop of Assisi, Domenico Sorrentino, and the economist Luigino Bruni). Lead by genuine concern for the pathological state of the world and care for the poor, the former invited young economists and entrepreneurs to develop and implement a new economic model based on communion, gratitude, and reciprocity that would promote an alternative to the dominant capitalist lifestyle (The Economy of Francesco 2020).

Gandhi‘s philosophy was based on the teachings of Hinduism, Jainism, and Buddhism, and was inspired by writing by John Ruskin, entitled *Unto This Last*. The ancient ethical principle of non-harming (*ahimsa*) became Gandhi's creed. Non-harming was a central element of his pursuit of Truth as the ultimate reality of existence. Gandhi showed a personal example of this when he achieved his political goals not by force but by passive resistance to the oppressive power of Britain.

Gandhi used non-harming in all aspects of his life—in his work, politics, and in economic, religious, ethical, and ecological issues. His main objective was to alleviate Indian poverty, which he intended to do with the help of self-sufficient, small-scale, decentralized, ecologically sustainable farms that could locally meet basic human needs. He was not the enemy of economic development, capital, machinery, or the market, but he stood against unlimited industrialization, profit-making companies, and the market distribution of resources (Kovács and Ócsai 2015). His ecological views were also based on non-harming: he claimed that animals also have rights; that we can realize the purpose of our lives, understanding ourselves only if we consider that we are one with all beings; and that selfless service leads to the understanding that God is present in all beings (Timmerman 2015).

Gandhi's conception had a great influence on the English economist Ernst Friedrich Schumacher, who developed the concept of Buddhist economics in the 1970s (Kovács and Ócsai 2015). The earliest teachings of Buddhism do not deal specifically with nature, because environmental pollution was not a problem in around the fifth century BC. The main issue was how to eliminate human suffering. The environmental attitude of Buddhism can be considered ecological because it advocates for the development of environmental virtues (non-harming, compassion, preferring the small scale, gratitude, contentment, simplicity, wisdom, and consciousness) that sensitize us to ecological problems. The main purpose of a Buddhist lifestyle and strategy is to eliminate suffering, which can be achieved by following the Noble Eightfold Path (Kovács 2015). This contrasts with the principles of modern Western economics (profit maximization, the satisfaction of desires and introduction of markets, the instrumental use of the world, and ethics based on self-interest). The main elements of Buddhist economics are the minimization of suffering, the simplification of desires, the practice of non-harming, and genuine care and generosity through which production and consumption can be transformed more sustainable (Zsolnai 2014c).

References

Bandura, A. (2007). Impeding Ecological Sustainability through Selective Moral Disengagement. *International Journal of Innovation and Sustainable Development, 2*(1), 8–35. https://doi.org/10.1504/ijisd.2007.016056.

Bateson, G. (1972). *Steps to an Ecology of Mind: Collected Essays in Anthropology, Psychiatry, Evolution, and Epistemology*. London: Jason Aronson Inc. nomadicartsfestival.com/wp.../02/Gregory-Bateson-Ecology-of-Mind.pdf. Accessed 28 March 2020.

Beck, U. (1995). *Ecological politics in an Age of Risk*. Cambridge: Polity Press.

Benson, K. R. (2000). The Emergence of Ecology from Natural History. *Endeavour, 24*(2), 59–62. https://doi.org/10.1016/s0160-9327(99)01260-0.

Bouckaert, L. (2016). Why do we Need a Spiritual-Based Theory of Leadership? In M. Chatterji & L. Zsolnai (Eds.), *Ethical Leadership: Indian and European Spiritual Approaches* (pp. 17–33). London: Palgrave Macmillan. https://doi.org/10.1057/978-1-137-60194-0_2

Bouckaert, L., & Zsolnai, L. (2012). Spirituality and Business: An Interdisciplinary Overview. *Society and Economy, 34*(3), 489–514. https://doi.org/10.1556/socec.34.2012.3.8.

Boulding, K. E. (1966). The Economics of the Coming Spaceship Earth. In H. Jarrett (Ed.), *Environmental Quality in a Growing Economy* (pp. 3–14). Baltimore, MD: Resources for the Future/Johns Hopkins University Press.

Bragg, E. (1996). Towards Ecological Self: Deep Ecology Meets Constructionist Self-Theory. *Journal of Environmental Psychology, 16,* 93–108. https://doi.org/10.1006/jevp.1996.0008.

Brown, P. G., & Timmermann, P. (Eds.) (2015). *Ecological Economics for the Anthropocene: An Emerging Paradigm.* New York, NY: Columbia University Press. https://doi.org/10.7312/brow17342.

Capra, F., & Jakobsen, O. D. (2017). A Conceptual Framework for Ecological Economics Based on Systemic Principles of Life. *International Journal of Social Economics, 44*(6), 831–844. https://doi.org/10.1108/IJSE-05-2016-0136.

Chakraborty, S. K. (1995). *Ethics in Management: Vedantic Perspectives.* Oxford: Oxford University Press.

Christopher, M. (1999). An Exploration of the "Reflex" in Reflexive Modernity: The Rational and Prerational Social Causes of the Affinity for Ecological Consciousness. *Organization & Environment, 12*(4), 357–400. https://doi.org/10.1177/1086026699124001.

Costanza, R., Perrings, C., & Cleveland, C. J. (Eds.) (1997). *The Development of Ecological Economics.* Cheltenham: Elgar.

Csutora, M., & Zsóka, Á. (2014). May Spirituality Lead to Reduced Ecological Footprint? Conceptual Framework and Empirical Analysis. *World Review of Entrepreneurship, Management and Sustainable Development, 10*(1), 88–105. https://doi.org/10.1504/wremsd.2014.058056.

Dalai Lama, H. H. (1995). *The World of Tibetan Buddhism.* Boston, MA: Wisdom Publications.

Dalai Lama, H. H. (2005). *The Universe in a Single Atom: The Convergence of Science and Spirituality.* New York, NY: Broadway Books.

Daly, H. E. (1999). *Ecological Economics and the Ecology of Economics: Essays in Criticism.* Cheltenham and Northampton: Edward Elgar.

Daly, H. E., & Farley, J. (2004). *Ecological Economics: Principles and Applications.* London: Island Press.

Devall, B. (1988). *Simple in Means, Rich in Ends: Practicing Deep Ecology.* Layton, UT: Gibbs M. Smith.

Devall, B., & Sessions, G. (1985). *Deep Ecology: Living as if Nature Mattered*. Layton, UT: Gibbs M. Smith.

Drengson, A. (1989). *Beyond Environmental Crisis: From Technocrat to Planetary Person*. New York, NY: Peter Lang.

Egerton, F. N. (2001). A History of the Ecological Sciences: Early Greek Origins. *Bulletin of the Ecological Society of America, 82*(1), 93–97. http://esapubs.org/bulletin/current/history_list/history_part1.pdf Accessed 26 March 2020.

Elton, C. S. (1927). *Animal Ecology*. London: Sidgwick and Jackson.

European Commission. (2015). *Closing the Loop: Commission Adopts Ambitious New Circular Economy Package to Boost Competitiveness, Create Jobs and Generate Sustainable Growth*. Press release, Brussels, 2 December 2015, http://europa.eu/rapid/press-release_IP-15–6203_en.htm. Accessed 27 March 2020.

European Commission. (2018). *Circular Economy: Implementation of the Circular Economy Action Plan*. 2018 Circular Economy Package. http://ec.europa.eu/environment/circular-economy/index_en.htm.Accessed 27 March 2020.

European SPES Institute. (2020). *Definition of Spirituality*. http://www.eurospes.org/content/our-mission-spiritual-based-humanism. Accessed 28 February 2020.

Feng Lin, Q., & Fyles, J. W. (2015). Following in Aldo Leopold's Footsteps. Humans-in-Ecosystem and Implications for Ecosystem Health. In P. G. Brown & P. Timmermann (Eds.), *Ecological Economics for the Anthropocene: An Emerging Paradigm* (pp. 208–232). New York, NY: Columbia University Press. https://doi.org/10.7312/brow17342-008.

Friederichs, K. (1958). A Definition of Ecology and Some Thoughts About Basic Concepts. *Ecology, 39*(1), 154–159. https://doi.org/10.2307/1929981.

Georgescu-Roegen, N. (1971). *The Entropy Law and the Economic Process*. Cambridge: Harvard University Press.

Gennaro, R. J. (n.d). *Consciousness: The Internet Encyclopedia of Philosophy*. ISSN 2161–0002. http://www.iep.utm.edu/consciou/ Accessed 27 March 2020.

Hahn, I. (2014). *Növényökológia* [Plant Ecology]. Department of Plant Taxology, Ecology and Theoretical Biology, Eötvös Loránd University, Budapest, Projected Slides of the 2014 Lecture on Plant Ecology. http://ramet.elte.hu/~ramet/oktatas/Novenyokol_kornyezettan/2014_novenyokologia.pdf. Accessed 26 March 2020. [in Hungarian].

Hamilton, C. (2010). Consumerism, Self-creation and Prospects for a New Ecological Consciousness. *Journal of Cleaner Production, 18*(6), 571–575. https://doi.org/10.1016/j.jclepro.2009.09.013.

Harding, W., & Bode, C. (Eds.) (1958). *The Correspondence of Henry David Thoreau*. New York, NY: New York University Press. https://www.walden.org/wp-content/uploads/2016//Correspondence.pdf. Accessed 2 April 2020.

Hill, S., Wilson, S., & Watson, K. (2004). Learning Ecology: A New Approach to Learning and Transforming Ecological Consciousness. In E. O'Sullivan & M. Taylor (Eds.), *Learning Toward an Ecological Consciousness: Selected Transformative Practices* (pp. 47–64). New York, NY: Palgrave Macmillan. https://doi.org/10.1007/-1-349-73178-7_4.

Hortobágyi, T., & Simon, T. (Eds.) (2000). *Növényföldrajz, Társuléstan és Ökológia* [Plant Geography, Synbiology and Ecology]. Budapest: Tankönyvkiadó. [in Hungarian].

Hughes, J. D. (1991). The Psychology of Environmentalism Healing Self and Nature. *Trumpeter, 8*(3). http://trumpeter.athabascau.ca/index.php/trumpet/article/view/458/759. Accessed 27 March 2020.

Ims, K. J. (2015). Deep Ecology and Personal Responsibility. In L. Zsolnai (Ed.), *The Spiritual Dimension of Business Ethics and Sustainability Management* (pp. 47–56). New York, NY: Springer. https://doi.org/10.1007/978-3-319-11677-8_5.

Ims, K. J., & Jakobsen, O. D. (2006). Cooperation and Competition in the Context of Organic and Mechanic Worldviews—A Theoretical and Case based Discussion. *Journal of Business Ethics, 66*(1), 19–32. https://doi.org/10.1007/s10551-006-9055-z.

Ingebrigtsen, S., & Jakobsen, O. (2007). *Circulation Economics: Theory and Practice*. Bern: Peter Lang.

Jakobsen, O. (2017). *Transformative Ecological Economics: Process Philosophy, Ideology and Utopia*. London and New York, NY: Routledge. https://doi.org//9781315205434.

Jonas, H. (1984). *The Imperative of Responsibility: In Search of an Ethics for the Technological Age*. Chicago, IL: The University of Chicago Press.

Juhász-Nagy, P. (1984). *Beszélgetések az ökológiáról* [Conversations about Ecology]. Budapest: Mezőgazdasági Kiadó. [in Hungarian].

Juhász-Nagy, P. (1986). *Egy operatív ökológia hiánya, szükséglete és feladatai* [The Lack, the Need and the Tasks of an Operative Ecology]. Budapest: Akadémiai Kiadó. [in Hungarian].

Juhász-Nagy, P. (1993). *Az eltűnő sokféleség* [Biological Diversity in Destruction]. Budapest: Scientia Kiadó. [in Hungarian].

Koch, C. (2004). *The Quest for Consciousness: A Neurobiological Approach*. Englewood, CO: Roberts and Company.

Kovács, G. (2015). Buddhist Spiritual Orientation to Nature and Sustainability. In L. Zsolnai (Ed.), The *Spiritual Dimension of Business Ethics and Sustainability Management* (pp. 57–67). New York, NY: Springer. https://doi.org/10.1007/978-3-319-11677-8_6.

Kovács, G., & Ócsai, A. (2015). The Spirit of Non-violene and Peace in Business. In L. Bouckaert & M. Chatterji (Eds.), *Business, Ethics and Peace* (pp. 231–245). Bingley: Emerald Group Publishing. https://doi.org/10.1108/s1572-832320150000024014.

Krebs, C. J. (2001). *Ecology: The Experimental Analysis of Distribution and Abundance*. San Francisco, CA: Benjamin Cummings.

Leff, H. (1978). *Experience, Environment, and Human Potentials*. New York, NY: Oxford University Press.

Leopold, A. (1949). The Ecological Conscience. In A. Leopold (Ed.), *A Sand County Almanach*. Oxford: Oxford University Press. http://www.public.iastate.edu/~fridolph/leopold.html. Accessed 2 April 2020

Lovelock, J. (2009). *The Vanishing Face of Gaia: A Final Warning*. London: Allen Lane.

Lozano, J. M., & Ribera, R. (2004). A New Chance for Management, A New Challenge for Spirituality. In L. Zsolnai (Ed.), *Spirituality and Ethics in Management* (pp. 175–185). Boston, MA, Dordrecht and London: Kluwer Academic Publishers. https://doi.org/10.1007/1-4020-2365-0_15.

Marques, J. (2012). Consciousness at Work: A Review of Some Important Values, Discussed from a Buddhist Perspective. *Journal of Business Ethics, 105*(1), 27–40. https://doi.org/10.1007/s10551-011-0932-8.

McNaughton, S. J., & Wolf, L. L. (1973). *General Ecology*. New York, NY: Holt, Rinehart and Winston.

Merriam-Webster Dictionary and Thesaurus (2020). *Consciousness*. https://www.merriam-webster.com/dictionary/consciousness. Accessed 27 March 2020.

Merton, T. (1968). *The Ecological Conscience*. (kivonat) The Catholic Worker. June 1968. http://www.democraticunderground.com/discuss/duboard.php?az=view_all&address=115x180150. Accessed 2 April 2020.

Milbraith, L. (1989). *Envisioning a Sustainable Society*. Albany, NY: State of New York Press.

Mind & Life Institute. (2020). *Mission*. https://www.mindandlife.org/mission. Accessed 27 March 2020.

Morris, M. (2002). Ecological Consciousness and Curriculum. *Journal of Curriculum Studies, 34*(5), 571–587. https://doi.org/10.1080/0108187.
Mukherjee, S. (2018). Management and Liberal Arts: A Transformational Odyssey with Rabindranath Tagore. In L. Bouckaert, K. J. Ims, & P. Rona (Eds.), *Art, Spirituality and Economy: Virtues and Economics 2* (pp. 139–156). Cham: Springer. https://doi.org/10.1007/978-3-319-75064-4_13.
Naess, A. (1989). *Ecology, Community and Lifestyle: Outline of an Ecosophy.* Cambridge: Cambridge University Press. https://doi.org/10.1017/cbo9780511525599.
Nhat Hanh, T. (2008). *The Heart of the Buddha's Teaching. Transforming Suffering into Peace, Joy, and Liberation.* E-book. London: Random House. https://terebess.hu/zen/mesterek/Thich%20Nhat%20Hanh%20-%20The%20Heart%20of%20Buddha%27s%20Teaching.pdf. Accessed 2 April 2020.
Odum, E. P. (1963). *Ecology*. New York, NY: Holt, Rinehart and Winston.
O'Sullivan, E. V., & Taylor, M. M. (Eds.) (2004). *Learning toward an Ecological Consciousness: Selected Transformative Practices*. New York, NY: Palgrave Macmillan. https://doi.org/10.1007/978-1-349-73178-7.
Pásztor, E., & Oborny, B. (Eds.) (2007). *Ökológia* [Ecology]. Budapest: Nemzeti Tankönyvkiadó. [in Hungarian].
Polanyi, K. (1944). *The Great Transformation: The Political and Economic Origins of Our Time*. Boston, MA: Beacon Press.
Pope Francis. (2015). *Encyclical letter Laudato Si':On Care for our Common Home.* http://w2.vatican.va/content/dam/francesco/pdf/encyclicals/documents/papa-francesco_20150524_enciclica-laudato-si_en.pdf. Accessed 3 April 2020.
Pruzan, P. (2011). Spirituality as the Basis for Leadership. In L. Bouckaert & L. Zsolnai (Eds.), *The Palgrave Handbook of Spirituality and Business* (pp. 287–295). London: Palgrave. https://doi.org/10.1057/9780230321458_35.
Pruzan, P. (2015a). Spiritual-Based Leadership: A Paradox of Pragmatism. In L. Zsolnai (Ed.), *The Spiritual Dimension of Business Ethics and Sustainability Management* (pp. 169–172). New York, NY: Springer. https://doi.org/10.1007/978-3-319-11677-8_14.
Pruzan, P. (2015b). Further Reflections on Spirituality and Spiritual-based Leadership. In L. Zsolnai (Ed.), *The Spiritual Dimension of Business Ethics and Sustainability Management* (pp. 191–198). New York, NY: Springer. https://doi.org/10/978-3-319-11677-8_19.
Pruzan, P. (2016). Science and Spirituality. In P. Pruzan, (Ed.), *Research Methodology: The Aims, Practices and Ethics of Science*. Switzerland: Springer. Unpublished Chapter.

Rahula, W. (1974). What the Buddha Taught (2nd and enlarged ed.). New York, NY: Grove Press. https://web.ics.purdue.edu/~buddhism/docs/Bhante_Walpola_Rahula-What_the_Buddha_Taught.pdf. Accessed 4 April 2020.

Sarin, I. (2014). Artistic Disclosure of Nature. Heidegger and Tagore. *Existenz: An International Journal in Philosophy, Religion, Politics, and the Arts, 9*(1), 45–52. https://existenz.us/images/read-pdf.gif. Accessed 2 April 2020.

Schumacher, E. F. (1973). *Small is Beautiful: A Study of Economics As if People Mattered*. New York, NY: Harper and Row.

Sen, A. (1997). Tagore and His India. *The New York Review of Books, 44*(11), 55–63. https://www.nybooks.com/articles/1997/06/26/tagore-and-his-india/. Accessed 10 April 2020.

Sen, S. (2008). The Vedic-Upanisadic concept of Brahman (The Highest God). In A. Eshleman (Ed.), *Readings in Philosophy of Religion: East Meets West* (pp. 43–51). Malden, MA: Blackwell.

Takács-Sánta, A. (2004). The Major Transitions in the History of Human Transformation of the Biosphere. *Human Ecology Review, 11*(1), 51–66. http://www.humanecologyreview.org/pastissues/her111/111takacssanta.pdf. Accessed 3 April 2020.

Takács-Sánta, A. (2009). *Környezeti problémák: A generalisták és a társadalmi dimenzió hiánya* [Environmental Problems: Lack of Generalists and The Social Dimension]. Magyar Tudomány [Hungarian Science]. 2009/1. pp. 62-66. [in Hungarian]

The Economy of Francesco. (2020). https://francescoeconomy.org/who-we-are/. Accessed 3 April 2020.

Timmerman, P. (2015). The Ethics of Re-Embedding Economics in the Real: Case Studies. In P. G. Brown & P. Timmermann (Eds.), *Ecological Economics for the Anthropocene: An Emerging Paradigm* (pp. 21–65). New York, NY: Columbia University Press. https://doi.org/10.7312/brow17342-002.

Tononi, G., & Koch, C. (2015). Consciousness: Here, There and Everywhere? Philosophical Transactions of the Royal Society. *Biological Sciences, 370*(1668), 20140167. https://doi.org/10.1098/rstb.2014.0167.

Uhl, C. (2004). *Developing Ecological Consciousness: Path to a Sustainable World*. Lanham, MD: Rowman & Littlefield Publishers.

Velmans, M. (2009). How to Define Consciousness-and How Not to Define Consciousness. *Journal of Consciousness Studies, 6*(5), 139–156. cogprints.org/6453/1/How_to_define_consciousness.pdf. Accessed 1 April 2020.

Wallace, B. A. (2007). Principles of Contemplative Science. In B. A. Wallace (Ed.), *Contemplative Science: Where Buddhism and Neuroscience Converge*. New York, NY: Columbia University Press.

White, P. R. (2011). A Phenomenological Self-Inquiry into Ecological Consciousness. *Ecopsychology.*, *3*(1), 41–50. https://doi.org/10.1089/eco.201 00054.

Whittaker, R. H. (1975). *Communities and Ecosystems*. New York, NY: Macmillan.

Zsolnai, L. (2000). *A döntéshozatal etikája* [Ethics of Decision Making]. Budapest: Kossuth Kiadó. [in Hungarian].

Zsolnai, L. (2001). *Ökológia, gazdaság, etika* [Ecology, Economy, Ethics]. Budapest: Helikon Kiadó. [in Hungarian].

Zsolnai, L. (2014a). Ethical Decision Making. In L. Zsolnai (Ed.), *Beyond Self: Ethical and Spiritual Dimensions of Economics* (pp. 45–64). Bern: Peter Lang. https://doi.org/10.3726/978-3-0353-0596-8/17.

Zsolnai, L. (2014b). Ethics Needs Spirituality. In L. Zsolnai (Ed.), *Beyond Self: Ethical and Spiritual Dimensions of Economics* (pp. 79–83). Bern: Peter Lang. https://doi.org/10.3726/978-3-0353-0596-8/20.

Zsolnai, L. (2014c). Buddhist Economic Strategy. In L. Zsolnai (Ed.), *Beyond Self. Ethical and Spiritual Dimensions of Economics* (pp. 119–138). Bern: Peter Lang. https://doi.org/10.3726/978-3-0353-0596-8/23.

Zsolnai, L. (2015). Spirituality, Ethics and Sustainability. In L. Zsolnai (Ed.), *The Spiritual Dimension of Business Ethics and Sustainability Management* (pp. 3–11). New York, NY: Springer. https://doi.org/10.1007/978-3-319-11677-8_1.

4

Ecological Consciousness and Value Orientations in Business

This chapter presents different concepts concerning how business organizations may implement ecologically conscious ways of functioning. It covers, inter alia, the "moralist model" of companies, the "ecological worldview," "sustainability-driven businesses," "true business sustainability," "entrepreneurship inspired by nature," "environmental commitment," the "really responsible company," "ecological entrepreneurship," and "ecologically sustainable business." The book suggests considering those business organizations as ecologically conscious which are willing to put ecological aspects at the center of their functioning, and which are able to operate in an alternative way to prevailing materialistic, one-dimensional, and profit-maximizing businesses.

According to business ethicist George Brenkert, the business world operates according to a special "ethics" that is related to the free market system and the nature of business organizations. Based on this, the economy is not able to function in an environmentally responsible way because its primary goal within the framework defined by society and the government is to maximize profits. This is the "economic model" of companies, in contrast to which, according to the "moralist model,"

A. Ócsai, *Ecologically Conscious Organizations*, Palgrave Studies in Sustainable Business In Association with Future Earth,
https://doi.org/10.1007/978-3-030-60918-4_4

companies are moral actors, which—beyond complying with laws—must act morally, socially, and in an environmentally responsible way; that is, minimize damage, and solve environmental problems. To this end, companies should take an approach based on biocentric environmental ethics (Hoffman 1991 quoted by Brenkert 1995). Further, global consciousness that evolves from the environmental conscience of individual companies is needed (Goodpaster 1990 quoted by Brenkert 1995). However, the parameters of the economy and companies (i.e., attitudes and values necessary for a free market enterprise such as bureaucratic business structures, short-term profit-interest, growth constraints, resource utilization, specialization, and price competition) make it difficult for economic actors to behave ethically, and their moral consciousness becomes fragmented. A fundamental change to the economic system and business organizations is therefore needed (strengthening accountability, expanding rationality, democratization, openness, environmental protection, and sustainable development) so that companies and their employees can act morally, and their environmental responsibility can be strengthened (Brenkert 1995).

In terms of environmental problems, the industrial and ecological worldviews are sharply different. As claimed by environmental thinker Timothy O'Riordan, in the case of the ecological worldview, the goal is harmony with nature. Nature is not just a resource, because every species is equal, and natural beings have intrinsic value. The Earth's resources are finite and thus define limits for economic growth. Science and technological development cannot solve all problems; technology has to adapt to nature and man. Instead of striving to satisfy unbounded consumer desires, the emphasis must be on meeting human needs, in line with the idea that people are able and willing to moderate their needs by following a consciously simple lifestyle. The distribution of power should be decentralized and take into account the rights of nature and people (O'Riordan and Cameron 1994 quoted by Zsolnai 2001).

Businesses and Sustainability

Many pieces of research discuss how businesses should support ecological and social processes rather than destroy them. However, most of these studies consider economic actors to be self-interested and profit-maximizing entities that strive to incorporate sustainable development principles into existing business strategies. This limited framework can be widened by reversing the perspective in order to reveal the organizational factors through which entrepreneurs motivated by sustainability-related values can achieve the latter most effectively in competitive market conditions. The qualitative analysis of case studies of successful sustainable enterprises of different sizes and business models operating in four different sectors and continents leads to the conclusion that there are five categories in which the former can be compared with conventional business enterprises: (i) The objective and reason d'être of successful sustainable enterprises is to preserve and strengthen the quality of human and natural resources over the longest possible time; (ii) Sustainable enterprises strive to increase the benefits and synergies of every activity, rather than solely pursuing a strategy of cost-effectiveness; (iii) Sustainable enterprises harmonize their objectives, seeking satisfactory results from multiple goals simultaneously, and do not just aim to maximize the value of a single dimension of their set of goals; (iv) The expected qualitative aspects of the results serve as decision criteria; and (v) They distribute benefits based on merit and non-power relations (Parrish 2010, p. 517).

The values adopted and promoted by sustainability-driven businesses may create balance among individuals, other people, and nature, but can cause tension within the organization. Successful entrepreneurs are distinguished from others by the fact that, besides having a proper value orientation, they can manage emerging organizational tensions by successfully achieving the objectives listed above (Parrish 2010).

Sustainability management is becoming increasingly widespread in large companies, but the impact of such aspirations does not appear to have triggered an overall improvement in the ecological state of our planet. In looking for the reasons for the "big disconnect" between micro-development and macro-degradation, a four-item typology can support the analysis of the sustainability of business models. The starting point is Milton Friedman's concept of today's business attitude of "business-as-usual." Refined shareholder value management models that deal exclusively with ecological and social issues that pose an economic risk or opportunity without changing their core business strategy follow this strategy. At the third level, some business models take into account economic, social, and environmental considerations. This is the "triple bottom line" concept. At the highest level, "truly sustainable business models" extend the scope from making an effort to minimize negative impacts to understanding how to maximize positive impact on critical social and ecological issues. Such enterprises forge their solutions to the most pressing sustainability challenges into business opportunities. They try to exert influence not only at the company level, but also throughout their entire sector and in other sectors. This is done through increasing their transparency, sharing examples of good practice, establishing shared self-regulation practices and standards, building cooperation with non-economic actors, and striving to change the rules of the game. Changing perspective this way is a huge challenge, requiring a fundamentally different strategic attitude from business entities, while a number of very significant barriers—such as the strong value orientation of shareholders toward financial markets and demands for short-term returns—make it very difficult to achieve (Dyllick and Muff 2015).

From Environmental Responsibility to Businesses Inspired by Nature

In the current situation, beyond improving environmental performance, the meaning of which is, unfortunately, not uniformly and comprehensively understood, only new conceptions of ethics and social and environmental responsibility can help ensure environmental protection. This presupposes meeting environmental requirements in the absence of state regulation or norms. The commitment of enterprises to social and environmental issues is evolving from a focus on compliance and from minimizing impact toward making a positive contribution to the ecology of the planet. The basis for such environmental commitment can be social standards (for instance, stakeholder expectations, or state regulations); technological opportunities (successful types of innovation, the nature of relationships within the supply chain); as well as the cognitive and behavioral characteristics of business leaders (environmental commitment, morality, and presuppositions) (Csutora and Kerekes 2004; Kerekes and Wetzker 2007).

Standard environmental management and corporate social responsibility tools aimed at the conservation of natural resources and the reduction of pollution and risk include cleaner production, energy rationalization, eco-efficiency, environmentally friendly products, product life cycle analysis, environmental product labeling, environmental performance assessment, environmental reports, industrial ecology, ecological accounting, environmental management systems, ethical codes, corporate governance standards, sustainability reports, product certificates, and socially responsible investment. Such operational approaches and instruments are necessary but not sufficient for fostering sustainable development. Sustainable development is a strategic issue for the economy and for humankind. "Truly Responsible Companies" can contribute to creating solutions in five key areas: (i) minimizing transport and preferring local markets; (ii) strengthening justice and fairness; (iii) avoiding an excessive focus on profit generation; (iv) achieving and maintaining an optimal size; and (v) supplying products that meet real needs. Such businesses can evolve (modeled as rising up through pyramid-like categories) starting from "normal local businesses" through "value-based organizations" and "entrepreneurs for something else [than just financial return]" into "companies serving their communities." It is also important that individuals (company owners and managers) take responsibility for implementing these radical changes. Even a complete redesign of basic products and strategies or the founding of new companies may be necessary, and much more "real action" than simply communicating about the former is needed (Tóth 2007).

The majority of economic enterprises in modern societies exploit nature and destroy ecosystems because they view them as simple economic resources. Capital and labor are usually considered to be more important factors of production than nature, so business strategies tend to be built on the former. However, nature-inspired, sustainable businesses have a different worldview and innovate products and services that help regenerate natural services, re-connecting people with nature ("regenerative eco-innovation"). The basis of this worldview is a kind of environmental wisdom that recognizes that humankind is a part of nature, and very much depends on it. Nature exists for all species, so limited resources should not be used to satisfy only human needs. Sustainable businesses need to be eco-efficient. They should solve real ecological problems, in parallel with meeting human needs and generating economic value. They should also be eco-effective: i.e., produce products and services that actually serve human needs and improve quality of life (Hofstra 2015).

In order for an entrepreneur inspired by nature to be successful, they should adhere to five principles: (i) predict unexpected threats caused by changes in relation to natural resources and transform these into business opportunities, recognizing the role of nature as teacher and mentor; (ii) take into account the different interests of business, society, and nature; (iii) achieve long-term economic efficiency combined with ethical perspectives and ecological effectiveness; (iv) discover and not exploit nature; and (v) generate business value in a broad sense, including economic, ecological, moral, social, and spiritual value (Hofstra 2015).

Ecological Entrepreneurship

The research area of ecologically sustainable business has been fragmented despite its development since the mid-1990s. There is no uniform definition of ecological entrepreneurship, although many variants of the term are widely used. The most common of these include sustainable entrepreneurship, ecopreneurship, environmental entrepreneurship, and green entrepreneurship. Ecologically sustainable business is the process of identifying, evaluating, and implementing business opportunities that minimize the environmental impact of an enterprise, and thus operating for the benefit of local communities and society as a whole (Gast et al. 2017).

Six main factors characterize the existence and operation of ecologically sustainable enterprises. (1) The drivers of engaging in ecologically sustainable entrepreneurship are opportunity, necessity, and personal values. (2) The drivers of conducting business in an ecologically sustainable way are values, the market, and compliance. For these first two factors, the role of intrinsic motivation, personal values, and volunteering is of paramount importance in the commitment to sustainability. Such enterprises do not primarily pursue economic goals, but seek to change people's mindset and society as a whole, and to create value for the environment and society. The latter outputs refer to Factor (3); that is, the micro-, meso-, and macro-level results of ecologically sustainable businesses. (4) The means of operating in an ecologically sustainable way involve redesigning business practices and networking. The role of networks and cooperating with stakeholders is extremely important, as individual enterprises alone have little chance of influencing public policies, or (5) fully meeting financial and market challenges. Factor (6) is support for ecologically sustainable businesses, of which the role of business schools, universities, and other educational institutions is outstanding. Nowadays, the role of these institutions is changing, and their curricula of business subjects need to be transformed in order to truly fulfill their responsibilities and increase the sustainability knowledge of businesses in relation to setting up ecologically sustainable businesses and making existing ones more sustainable (Gast et al. 2017).

It is an essential goal of societies and economies that humankind creates well-being in a sustainable way. Sustainable development is necessary for mitigating the ecological crisis, which requires social and environmental initiatives that take into account ecological, human, social, and economic factors. The well-being these create should be distributed in a balanced way between meeting current consumption needs and the need for reinvesting into the long-term future. An ecological enterprise is a form of business that meets these requirements, and whose actors develop new practices that create economic assets for local communities while remaining committed to preserving cultural, ecological, and environmental integrity. For their successful operation it is essential to correctly identify the potentially high-value traditional products and practices of local communities and to properly apply legal and regulatory instruments (such as logos and trademarks) that can shape and protect their niche markets. For the survival and development of ecological businesses, it is crucial to be able to successfully involve and mobilize external stakeholders within value networks, through whom more and more links between producers and consumers can be established (Marsden and Smith 2005).

Based on the former paragraphs, those businesses can be considered ecologically conscious which are capable of and willing to operate in alternative ways, and to put ecological considerations at the center of their operations.

Values and Value Orientation

This section presents the most important theories and concepts concerning value, analyzes the issue of value orientation, and discusses the findings of relevant studies.

Values and Value Theories

A number of disciplines—including anthropology, moral philosophy, political science, sociology, theology, social psychology, economic ethics, behavioral economics, management science, and corporate governance—deal with the philosophical, ethical, ideological, social, and aesthetic aspects of value and value orientation. Accordingly, several different definitions of value exist that have evolved over time.

Values are important and lasting beliefs; ideas accepted by members of a society about what is good, what is wrong, what is desirable, and what should be avoided. Values significantly influence the behavior and attitudes of individuals, and serve as comprehensive guidelines for them in different situations (Business Dictionary 2020).

The concept of value has been used since the eighteenth century primarily to express the "value of something"; that is, in the economic sense (for example, in Adam Smith's writings on political economy). Then, in the nineteenth century, as more and more philosophers (including Rudolf Hermann Lotze, Wilhelm Windelband, Friedrich Nietsche, Eduard von Hartmann, Hugo Münsterberg, and Wilbur Marshall Urban) became interested in the problematic of value, the interpretation became increasingly broad. In his book *General Theory of Value*, Ralph Barton Perry considered value as "any object of any interest." He later identified eight areas of importance for values: morality, religion, art, science, economics, politics, law, and custom (Encyclopaedia Britannica 2020).

Several disciplines investigate values (Kaldschmidt 2011). Coherent value theories (for instance, Rokeach 1979; Schwartz 1992) study the nature of values and value systems. In recent decades, various pieces of research have focused on the impact of values on national culture (Kluckhohn and Strodtbeck 1961; Schwartz and Bilsky 1987; Inglehart and Baker 2000; Hofstede and Hofstede 2005; Sagiv and Schwartz 2007) or company culture (Hofstede and Hofstede 2005; Schein 2010). Research has also been conducted on the effects of values on leadership behavior (Agle et al. 1999; Krishnan 2001; Lord and Brown 2001; Klenke 2005; Byrne and Bradley 2007; Resick et al. 2011), on the ethical organizational climate (Grojean et al. 2004), and on ethical decision making (Ford and Richardson 1994; Nonis and Swift 2001; Eberhardt-Toth and Wasieleski 2013; Marsh 2013). The role of values in the operation of social and ecological enterprises (Hemingway and Maclagan 2004; Hemingway 2005; Dixon and Clifford 2007) and environmentally oriented behavior (Karp 1996; Bansal 2003) has also been examined.

There are many differences between value concepts and definitions, and a lack of synthesis (Rohan 2000; Hitlin and Piliavin 2004). Let us review how important value theories define values.

American anthropologist Clyde Kluckhohn called values individual- or group-specific facts that determine human action by defining a combination of tools, goals, and methods (Kluckhohn 1951).

According to social psychologist Milton Rokeach, values are long-lasting beliefs based on whether certain behaviors (instrumental values) or end-states of existence (terminal values) are individually or socially preferred to those which are different from or opposed to them. The emphasis is thus shifted from action to motivation (Rokeach 1973).

Another social psychologist, Shalom Schwartz, suggests that basic values are the goals that we want to achieve in the form of principles that guide our lives. Values are also beliefs that directly affect us, and which overarch our various actions and situations. Values are evaluation criteria that determine how we judge actions, procedures, situations, and people. Differently from norms and attitudes, values can be arranged in a hierarchy. They influence activities on the basis of their relative importance, depending on a given situation (Schwartz 2006).

Geert Hofstede studied people's personal values, researching how each culture influences the cultural values that its members hold dear. Initially four, then six cultural dimensions were differentiated to illustrate the relationship between national and organizational culture: individualism–collectivism; uncertainty avoidance (from weak to strong); power distance (from small to large); masculinity (goal orientation)–femininity (relationship orientation); future orientation (short-term – long-term); and indulgence–restraint (Hofstede and Hofstede 2005).

Edgar Schein's model distinguishes three levels of organizational culture: (1) the level of artifacts and behaviors, which can be identified from outside the organization; (2) the level of declared values and beliefs; and, (3) common underlying assumptions, which are often based on participants' unconscious values or convictions. Thus, the primary sources of organizational culture are the values, convictions, and basic assumptions of the founders, thus the most important task of managers is to recognize and understand these so as to be able to adapt to unavoidable organizational change and meet challenges (Schein 2010).

Value Orientation

Value orientations identify desirable and avoidable goals for individuals, communities, and societies, thereby defining and controlling human behavior (Rokeach 1973).

Anthropologist Florence Kluckhohn and psychologist Fred Strodtbeck studied the phenomenon of value orientation with the aim of fostering understanding of the differences between human societies and their communication with each other. According to value orientation theory, societies face some universal problems, in response to which each culture selects its own solution from a limited number of value-based solutions according to their own preferences and values (Hills 2002). The five basic problems and categories of responses to them are the following: Which aspect of time the latter focus on (past, present, and future); the relation of humans to their natural environment (domination, harmony, and humility); the relationship between individuals (super- and subordination, equality, and individualism); the main motivation for behavior (existence, change, and performance); and what the basic nature of humans is (bad, neutral, good, and mixed) (Kluckhohn and Strodtbeck 1961 quoted by Hills 2002). A sixth value dimension (space: here, there, far) has been proposed but not elaborated in detail, so it has not become part of the theory. Value orientation theory has weaknesses. It is more general than specific, thus it is not well suited to predicting expected behavior in a given situation. It is simplistic, since most behavior cannot be classified into a category. Because of the use of rankings, it is difficult to analyze statistically. Its undisputed merit, however, is that it brings us closer to understanding values. It has inspired many subsequent pieces of research and laid the foundations for the important results of universal value surveys (Rokeach 1979; Schwartz 1992; Hofstede and Hofstede 2005) (Hills 2002). The psychological research of values is also important because it helps us to evaluate the full spectrum of human life, not just the positive and negative aspects of attitudes. In addition, the examination of values is also essential for understanding human thinking, feelings, and behavior, and for undertaking comparative analyses between cultures and groups, and within groups (Hills 2002).

Schwartz (2006) examined the value orientation of national cultures. Culture has been defined as a complex of meanings, beliefs, practices, symbols, norms, and values that are common among members of a society, the most important characteristics of which are prevailing values. The emphasis awarded values expresses the ideals of a given culture; the shared ideas of individuals about what is good and desirable. Values that serve as ideals are therefore the main elements of the cultural value orientation which strengthens the coherence of a given culture. Value orientations gradually adapt to changing external circumstances and internal processes. In every case, their examination focuses on the emphasis on values in deep layers of culture. According to Schwartz's research results, the cultural value orientation of societies can be distinguished according to three main dimensions (the corresponding values are given in parentheses):

(1) the autonomy of the individual (intellectual: broadmindedness, curiosity, or affective: pleasure)—and their embeddedness in society (social order, obedience, respect for tradition);
(2) egalitarianism (social justice, equality)—hierarchy (authority, humility);
(3) harmony with the world (unity with nature, world at peace)—mastery (ambition, daring).

Based on these, Schwartz was able to identify seven transnational cultural groups with specific characteristics differentiable along bipolar dimensions: West European, English-speaking, Latin American, East European, South Asian, Confucian, African, and Middle Eastern.

An Analysis of Ecological Consciousness and the Value Orientation of Businesses

Ecological consciousness and the value orientation of businesses are individually addressed in various ways in the literature, although publications typically do not examine the relationship between them. The following section summarizes how the personal values of individuals and the characteristics of decision making can affect the ethicality of decisions, and what attributes and conditions seem to be needed for corporate social responsibility and value-oriented, ecologically conscious business functioning.

(1) Multiple articles argue that the personal characteristics and values of individual decision makers do affect the ethicality of business decisions.

The value commitments of leaders can be decisive in terms of the corporate social responsibility of a company. The question then arises, is the term "corporate" social responsibility meaningful at all (Hemingway and Maclagan 2004)? The characteristics of individual decision makers include nationality, religion, gender, age, education, occupation, and type of personality. Of these, the impact of personal characteristics (gender, age, nationality, and religion), education and occupation, and the direction of the variable associations is variable. Among individual values, the impact of Machiavellism seems to be the strongest (Ford and Richardson 1994). Important individual factors that determine ethical decision making include individual moral philosophy, gender, age, education, occupation, nationality, and religion. Individual values, indeed, have a positive impact on professional ethics, but length of employment does not necessarily affect the ethical profile of individuals (Loe et al. 2000).

The moral beliefs, attitudes, and values of individuals form personal moral philosophies based on two dimensions: concern for morality, and practical consequences. Situationists strive for the "best" possible outcomes regardless of moral principles. Subjectivists base their judgments on personal values and practical concerns. Absolutists consider actions to be morally acceptable as long as they have positive consequences and comply with ethical rules. Exceptionists follow moral guidelines, albeit allowing some exceptions for practical reasons. Individuals can apply a variety of different personal moral philosophies, so business decisions cannot be uniformly evaluated. Therefore, the latter should not be the aim, but rather examining them from the (former) four perspectives, along with promoting the open discussion of ethical questions, and reaching a deeper understanding of business practices (Forsyth 1992).

The concept of "ethical leadership" varies from one culture to another. There are significant differences, which can be traced back to the different core values of different cultures. However, apart from such differences, the character of leaders, respect for others, following self-interest, and the abuse of power are prominent issues in all cultures, the handling of which requires virtuous behavior and credibility (Resick et al. 2011). Some of the important values for ethical leadership are consciousness, commitment, credibility, and perseverance. The environmental factors involved in decisions are embedded in the value of consciousness (Marsh 2013).

Leaders of large companies perceive stakeholder attributes involving power, legitimacy, and urgency as being of key importance, which affects the degree to which managers prioritize competing stakeholder voices (Agle et al. 1999). Stakeholder attributes considered relevant by sustainability-driven entrepreneurs may consist of legitimacy, philosophy, and impact. The former entrepreneurs tend to work with stakeholders who comply with legitimate societal rules, who share their philosophy and basic values, and who have significant potential impact in terms of generating change in ecological and social areas of the economy (Schlange 2006). The personal values of managers and entrepreneurs do influence the operating- and decision-related processes of companies, which can increase social and environmental performance (Agle et al. 1999; Schlange 2006).

The evaluation of sustainability issues depends on the moral maturity of decision makers and the extent to which they consider sustainability issues to be moral issues. An individual with strong sustainability values is intrinsically motivated to consider sustainability issues as important company strategic issues, and to even act accordingly. The sustainability-related values of an individual determine how morally important they consider sustainable-development-related issues to be (Eberhardt-Toth and Wasieleski 2013).

However, based on the social cognitive theory of self-regulation (Bandura 1991), it is not only values but also personal agency that influence the decisions and actions of managers and entrepreneurs. Even if they have pro-environmental values, they can assess business opportunities that cause harm to the natural environment as attractive and appropriate for exploitation. Decision-makers' cognitive disengagement and violation of their own values seem to be stronger when the former have high entrepreneurial self-efficacy and perceive a state of industry munificence, but resource abundance as low (Shepherd et al. 2013).

Some consider ethical decision making to be no different from other types of decision making. The reason is that decision makers themselves tend not to differentiate in relation to whether they are making ethical or other types of decisions (Elm and Radin 2012). Based on shareholder theory, ethical company behavior toward stakeholders may be possible. The well-being of non-shareholder stakeholders is also compatible with the ethical values described in shareholder theory based on Kantian "duties of rights." To put this into practice, the principles of corporate governance need to be well established, and shareholders should take greater responsibility for the activities of their companies (Mansell 2013).

(2) The characteristics of decision making also affect the ethicality of decisions.

Features of decision-making situations may include reference groups, reward and punishment, codes of conduct, types of ethical problems, organizations, industries, and business competitiveness. Moreover, individuals typically consider themselves to be more ethical than other reference persons. They increasingly identify themselves with the top management's belief system, as they are encouraged by the company reward system. Codes of conduct and an ethical corporate culture have a positive effect on the ethics of individual behavior, but larger company size and higher position have unfavorable effects. Interestingly, the ethicality of the industry overall does not really affect individual decision making, but competitiveness does (Ford and Richardson 1994).

Important organizational factors that influence ethical decision making are codes of ethics, remuneration systems, and corporate culture. A code of ethics mostly expresses the values of top management. The marketing orientation and marketing performance of the company is also an important aspect of ethical decision making (Loe et al. 2000).

(3) What are the characteristics of and conditions required for corporate social responsibility and value-oriented, ecologically conscious functioning?

There are different approaches to corporate social responsibility, such as instrumental, political, integrative, and ethical. These can be distinguished along four dimensions: financial gain, political performance, social needs, and ethical values. The ethical theories that best take into account the natural environment and ecology are stakeholder theory, theories of universal rights, sustainable development, and the public good (Garriga and Melé 2004). Managers' personal value commitments and the changes they make can stimulate corporate social responsibility, not only those corporate policies and business and strategic considerations (image, reputation, stakeholder management, integration into the local community) which are important for the company as a whole (Hemingway and Maclagan 2004).

The strategic, business, and instrumental use of the corporate social responsibility concept does not make it truly sustainable. It is necessary to rethink companies, governance, and organizations, and to reestablish them, therein ensuring the economic system does not destroy, but preserves and restores the natural environment, reestablishes the true meaning of work, and supports valuable innovation and well-being that respects natural boundaries (Milton 2010).

Ecopreneurship is a new approach to creating environmentally and socially responsible and economically viable businesses. Business models based on linking entrepreneurialism and environmentalism may need reciprocal relationships with corporate, community, social, and governmental partners to promote and maintain economic sustainability (Dixon and Clifford 2007). Sustainability-driven entrepreneurs strive to balance the requirements of the triple bottom line and create sustainable values in the most general sense. They can be characterized as having an all-embracing perception that involves integrating the perspectives of their stakeholders, as identified in a comprehensive and future-oriented way (Schlange 2006).

Respect for the natural environment does not appear or is not emphasized in numerous articles. The lack of consideration of the natural environment (which appears indirectly, involving a narrow or short-term focus), is identified in a paper by Resick and co-authors (2011). It is worth examining why ecology is of such little importance to leaders. In Ford and Richardson (1994), Loe et al. (2000), Hemingway and Maclagan (2004), and Marsh (2013), the natural environment and ecology are not identified as particularly prominent parts of ethical action, leadership, and responsible company behavior. Forsyth (1992) describes the constraints imposed by the social environment on the economic system, which should be supplemented by examining the constraints that result from the vulnerability and finite nature of the natural environment. Reflecting on research by Kopfer-Rácz et al. (2013) about the socio-cultural elements of Hungarian SMEs, it is interesting to consider how much the orientation on the short-term material success of Hungarian small enterprises is compatible with the long term, ecological mindset necessary for operating in an ecologically conscious way.

Further examination of the four types of moral beliefs (situationist, subjectivist, absolutist, and exceptionist) that underlie business decisions are needed to more deeply explore the characteristics of ethical decision making and, on the basis of this, generate a better understanding of economic decisions from several perspectives (Forsyth 1992). According to Ford and Richardson (1994), the number of empirical studies about the factors that influence ethical decision making is low (especially in terms of the variables education, age, duration of employment, and income), and some factors have not been studied at all so far (for instance, family status, number of children, and type of career). In addition to studying demographic characteristics, it would be advisable to supplement the previous results with some attitude-related research (i.e., involving work or organizational commitment), decision-making characteristics (in terms of the existence of external regulations, the economic environment, and industry competitiveness), and values at the deep level of company cultures. It may also be useful to develop clearer terminology (such as what ethical behavior means), and to further test existing models. Loe, Ferrell, and Mansfield (2000) suggest that the study of ethical issues related to decision making should be extended to other research areas (such as marketing orientation, quality, and performance); and that longitudinal studies are required to monitor temporal changes, while understanding the broader responses of industry may increase analytical validity and applicability. Further research about the components of intentions and moral character of decision makers also seems to be indispensable.

Based on Mansell's (2013) conclusions, it remains an open question how much the practical design and operation of ethical company policies depend on the moral character and experience of employees; and what the impact of the interests, well-being, and happiness of stakeholders means in practice. In connection with moral character, Eberhardt-Toth and Wasieleski (2013) examined the moral judgment of French financial professionals but not their actual actions. There is no clear correlation between these factors, and the authors consider it to be worth further research. Hemingway and Maclagan (2004) suggest the further study of to what extent individual characteristics (for example, insight, and influence) contribute to the social responsibility of organizations. It is also a methodological question how to separate individual and company values, and how to empirically collect data about interactions between individuals, and individuals and companies.

Elm and Radin's (2012) initial qualitative examination that involved research with decision makers of more value-oriented and profit-oriented businesses helps confirm whether ethical and other types of decision making are actually different. The outcome is also related to the size of the sample, but the fact that the investigated leaders were not selected through representative but purposeful or expert sampling limits the generalizability of Marsh's (2013) study.

Bárth-Fehér (2012), Győri (2012), and Szegedi (2012) are not concerned about how to evaluate the instrumental use of ethics and ethical systems. Milton (2010) leaves open the question how the concept of corporate social responsibility can translate into genuine value commitment. On the topic of corporate social responsibility, Garriga and Melé (2004) propose a more detailed examination of the four dimensions of corporate social responsibility theories (instrumental, political, integrative, and value-based), and possibly the development of a new theory that exceeds the latter in scope.

Finally, based on experience, a strong value orientation is typically found to exist in small businesses, so it may be interesting to compare the value commitments of value-oriented companies with the average socio-cultural attitudes of micro, small-, and medium-sized enterprises (Kopfer-Rácz et al. 2013).

Values and the Value Orientation of Businesses

According to Peter French (1979), companies themselves have a moral personality, while Kenneth Goodpaster (1990, quoted by Brenkert, 1995) draws attention to the existence of their environmental conscience. Patricia Werhane (1985) also views companies as moral actors because their actions are based on the intentions of morally responsible natural persons; that is, the moral inputs of their constituents.

In this book, we identify the values and value orientations of businesses with values revealed during case analyses and personal interviews with the official representatives of such businesses. The results of previous studies (Kaldschmidt 2011; Zsolnai and Győri 2011; Győri and Ócsai 2014) and several pieces of literature (Ford and Richardson 1994; Meglino and Ravlin 1998; Agle et al. 1999; Loe et al. 2000; Grojean et al. 2004; Hemingway and Maclagan 2004; Hemingway 2005; Schlange 2006; Shepherd et al. 2013) support the suitability of this method. These studies confirm that the personal values of founders, owners, and managers of companies have a decisive influence on the values and value orientation of their businesses. However, in order to broaden the focus of the topic, among future research directions it may be interesting to flesh out the values and value orientations of businesses by examining the values and value orientations of other organizational actors, including employees.

References

Agle, B. R., Mitchell, R. K., & Sonnenfeld, J. A. (1999). Who Matters to CEOs? An Investigation of Stakeholder Attributes and Salience, Corporate Performance, and CEO Values. *Academy of Management Journal, 42*(5), 507–525. https://doi.org/10.5465/256973.

Bandura, A. (1991). Social Cognitive Theory of Self-regulation. *Organizational Behavior and Human Decision Processes, 50*(2), 248–287. https://doi.org/10.1016/0749-5978(91)90022-L.

Bansal, P. (2003). From Issues to Actions: The Importance of Individual Concerns and Organizational Values in Responding to Natural Environmental Issues. *Organization Science, 14*(5), 510–527. https://doi.org/10.1287/orsc.14.5.510.16765.

Bárth-Fehér, Sz. (2012). Fenntarthatóság a hazai vállalati gyakorlatban [Sustainability in the practice of Hungarian firms], Vezetéstudomány [Budapest Management Review], Vol. *XLIII, no., 10,* 44–54. [in Hungarian].

Brenkert, G. G. (1995). The Environment, The Moralist, The Corporation and Its Culture. *Business Ethics Quarterly, 5*(4), 675–697. https://doi.org/10.2307/3857409.

Business Dictionary. (2020). Values. http://www.businessdictionary.com/definition/values.html. Accessed 31 March 2020.

Byrne, G. J., & Bradley, F. (2007). Culture's Influence on Leadership Efficiency: How Personal and National Cultures Affect Leadership Style. *Journal of Business Research, 60*(2), 168–175. https://doi.org/10.1016/j.jbusres.2006.10.015

Csutora, M., & Kerekes, S. (2004). A környezetbarát vállalatirányítás eszközei [Instruments of Environmentally Friendly Corporate Governance]. KJK Kerszöv, Budapest [in Hungarian].

Dixon, S. E. A., & Clifford, A. (2007). Ecopreneurship—A New Approach to Managing the Triple Bottom Line. *Journal of Organizational Change Management, 20*(3), 326–345. https://doi.org/10.1108/09534810710740164.

Dyllick, T., & Muff, K. (2015). Clarifying the Meaning of Sustainable Business: Introducing a Typology from Business-as-Usual to True Business Sustainability. *Organization & Environment, 29*(2), 156–174. https://doi.org/10.1177/1086026615575176.

Eberhardt-Toth, E., & Wasieleski, D. M. (2013). A Cognitive Elaboration Model of Sustainability Decision Making: Investigating Financial Managers' Orientation Toward Environmental Issues. *Journal of Business Ethics, 117*(4), 735–751. https://doi.org/10.1007/s10551-013-1715-1.

Elm, D. R., & Radin, T. J. (2012). Ethical Decision Making: Special or No Different? *Journal of Business Ethicsv, 107*(3), 313–329. https://doi.org/10.1007/s10551-011-1041-4.

Encyclopaedia Britannica. (2020). Axiology. https://www.britannica.com/topic/axiology. Accessed 2 April 2020.

Ford, R. C., & Richardson, W. D. (1994). Ethical Decision Making: A Review of the Empirical Literature. *Journal of Business Ethics, 13*(3), 205–221. https://doi.org/10.1007/bf02074820.

Forsyth, D. R. (1992). Judging the Morality of Business Practices: The Influence of Personal Moral Philosophies. *Journal of Business Ethics, 11*(5–6), 461–470. https://doi.org/10.1007/bf00870557.

French, P. A. (1979). The Corporation as a Moral Person. *American Philosophical Quarterly, 16*(3), 207–215. https://www.jstor.org/stable/pdf/20009760.pdf. Accessed 12 April 2020.

Garriga, E., & Melé, D. (2004). Corporate Social Responsibility Theories: Mapping the Territory. *Journal of Business Ethics, 53*(1–2), 51–71. https://doi.org/10.1023/b:busi.0000039399.90587.34.

Gast, J., Gundolf, K., & Cesinger, B. (2017). Doing Business in a Green Way: A Systemic Review of the Ecological Sustainability Entrepreneurship Literature and Future Research Directions. *Journal of Cleaner Production, 147,* 44–56. https://doi.org/10.1016/j.jclepro.2017.01.065.

Goodpaster, K. E. (1990). Can a Corporation Have an Environmental Conscience? In W. M. Hoffman, R. Frederick, & E. S. Petry (Eds.), *Business, Ethics, and the Environment*. New York: Quorum Books.

Grojean, M. W., Resick, C. J., Dickson, M. W., & Smith, D. B. (2004). Leaders, Values, and Organizational Climate: Examining Leadership Strategies for Establishing an Organizational Climate Regarding Ethics. *Journal of Business Ethics, 55*(3), 223–241. https://doi.org/10.1007/s10551-004-1275-5.

Győri, Zs. (2012). Első- és másodfajú etikai kudarcok [First Kind and Second Kind Ethical Failures]. Vezetéstudomány [Budapest Management Review]. Vol. XLIII, No. 10, pp. 56–62. http://unipub.lib.uni-corvinus.hu/945/1/vt_2012n10p56.pdf. Accessed 2 April 2020. [in Hungarian].

Győri, Zs., & Ócsai, A. (2014). Ecologically-oriented Enterprises in Hungary. World Review of Entrepreneurship, Management and Sustainable Development, Vol. 10, No. 1. pp. 52–65. https://doi.org/10.1504/wremsd.2014.058053.

Hemingway, C. A. (2005). Personal Values as a Catalyst for Corporate Social Entrepreneurship. *Journal of Business Ethics, 60*(3), 233–249. https://doi.org/10.1007/s10551-005-0132-5.

Hemingway, C. A., & Maclagan, P. W. (2004). Managers' Personal Values as Drivers of Corporate Social Responsibility. *Journal of Business Ethics, 50*(1), 33–44. https://doi.org/10.1023/b:busi.0000020964.80208.c9.

Hills, M. D. (2002). Kluckhohn and Strodtbeck's Values Orientation Theory. *Online Readings in Psychology and Culture, 4*(4). https://doi.org/10.9707/2307-0919.1040.

Hitlin, S., & Piliavin, J. A. (2004). Values: Reviving a Dormant Concept. *Annual Review of Sociology, 30*(1), 359–393. https://doi.org/10.1146/annurev.soc.30.012703.110640.

Hoffman, W. M. (1991). Business and Environmental Ethics. *Business Ethics Quarterly, 1*(2), 169–184. https://doi.org/10.2307/3857261.

Hofstede, G., Hofstede, G. J. (2005). *Cultures and Organizations: Software of the Mind: Intercultural cooperation and its importance for survival*. McGraw-Hill, New York.

Hofstra, N. (2015). Entrepreneurship Inspired by Nature. In L. Zsolnai (Ed.), *The Spiritual Dimension of Business Ethics and Sustainability Management* (pp. 159–166). New York: Springer. https://doi.org/10.1007/978-3-319-11677-8_13.

Inglehart, R., & Baker, W. E. (2000). Modernization, Cultural Change, and the Persistence of Traditional Values. *American Sociological Review, 65*, 19–51. https://doi.org/10.2307/2657288.

Kaldschmidt, S. (2011). The Values of Sustainability: The Influence of Leaders' Personal Values on Sustainability Strategies. Dissertation of the University of St. Gallen, School of Management, Economics, Law, Social Sciences and International Affairs.

Karp, D. G. (1996). Values and Their Effect on Pro-environmental Behavior. *Environment and Behavior, 28*(1), 111–133. https://doi.org/10.1177/0013916596281006.

Kerekes, S., & Wetzker, K. (2007). Keletre tart a "társadalmilag felelős vállalat" koncepció [The Concept of a "Socially Responsible Company" is Heading East], Harvard Business Manager: Korszerű menedzsment elmélet és megvalósítás [Advanced Management Theory and Implementation] Vol. 9, No. 4, pp. 37–47. [in Hungarian].

Klenke, K. (2005). Corporate Values as Multi-level, Multi-domain Antecedents of Leader Behaviors. *International Journal of Manpower, 26*(1), 50–66. https://doi.org/10.1108/01437720510587271.

Kluckhohn, C. (1951). Values and Value-orientations in the Theory of Action. In T. Parson & E. A. Shils (Eds.) (2013): Toward a General Theory of Action. Harvard Univesrity Press, Cambridge. https://doi.org/10.4159/harvard.9780674863507.c8.

Kluckhohn, F. R., & Strodtbeck, F. L. (1961). *Variations in Value Orientations.* Evanston: Row, Peterson.

Kopfer-Rácz, K., Hofmeister-Tóth, Á., & Sas, D. (2013). A hazai kis- és közepes vállalatok szociokulturális beállítódása a Hofstede-dimenziók mentén [The Socio-cultural Attitudes of the Hungarian Small and Medium

Enterprises along the Hofstede Dimensions], Vezetéstudomány [Budapest Management Review], Vol. XLIV, No. 10, pp. 2–11. http://unipub.lib.uni-corvinus.hu/1353/1/vt_2013n10p2.pdf. Accessed 12 April 2020 [in Hungarian].

Krishnan, V. R. (2001). Values Systems of Transformational Leaders. *Leadership and Organizational Development Journal, 22*(3), 126–132. https://doi.org/10.1108/01437730110389274.

Loe, T. W., Ferrell, L., & Mansfield, P. (2000). A Review of Empirical Studies Assessing Ethical Decision Making in Business. *Journal of Business Ethics, 25*(3), 185–204. https://doi.org/10.1023/a:1006083612239.

Lord, R. G., & Brown, D. J. (2001). Leadership, Values, and Subordinate Self-concepts. *Leadership Quarterly, 12*(2), 133–152. https://doi.org/10.1016/s1048-9843(01)00072-8.

Mansell, S. (2013). Shareholder Theory and Kant's 'Duty of Beneficence'. *Journal of Business Ethics, 117*(3), 583–599. https://doi.org/10.1007/s10551-012-1542-9.

Marsden, T., & Smith, E. (2005). Ecological Entrepreneurship: Sustainable Development in Local Communities Through Quality Food Production and Local Branding. *Geoforum, 36*(4), 440–451. https://doi.org/10.1016/j.geoforum.2004.07.008.

Marsh, C. (2013). Business Executives' Perceptions of Ethical Leadership and Its Development. *Journal of Business Ethics, 114*(3), 565–582. https://doi.org/10.1007/s10551-012-1366-7.

Meglino, B. M., & Ravlin, E. C. (1998). Individual Values in Organizations: Concepts, Controversies, and Research. *Journal of Management, 24,* 351–389. https://doi.org/10.1177/014920639802400304.

Milton, S. (2010). Some Observation on CSR and Strategic Management, Vezetéstudomány [Budapest Management Review]. Vol. XLI, No. 2, pp. 59–67. http://unipub.lib.uni-corvinus.hu/2697/1/vt2010n2p59-67.pdf. Accessed 2 April 2020.

Nonis, S., & Swift, C. O. (2001). Personal Value Profiles and Ethical Business Decisions. *Journal of Education for Business, 76*(5), 251–256. https://doi.org/10.1080/08832320109599644.

O'Riordan, T., & Cameron, J. (1994). The History and Contemporary Significance of the Precautionary Principle. In T. O'Riordan & J. Cameron (Eds.), *Interpreting the Precautionary Principle* (pp. 1–30). London: Earthscan.

Parrish, B. D. (2010). Sustainability-driven Entrepreneurship: Principles of Organization Design. *Journal of Business Venturing, 25*(5), 510–523. https://doi.org/10.1016/j.jbusvent.2009.05.005.

Resick, C. J., Martin, G. S., Keating, M. A., Dickson, M. W., Kwong Kwan, H., & Peng, C. (2011). What Ethical Leadership Means to Me: Asian, American, and European Perspectives. *Journal of Business Ethics, 101*(3), 435–457. https://doi.org/10.1007/s10551-010-0730-8.

Rohan, M. J. (2000). A Rose by Any Name? The Value Construct. *Personality and Social Psychology Review, 4*(3), 255–277. https://doi.org/10.1207/s15327957pspr0403_4.

Rokeach, M. (1973). *The Nature of Human Values*. New York: The Free Press.

Rokeach, M. (1979). *Understanding Human Values: Individual and Societal*. New York: The Free Press.

Sagiv, L., & Schwartz, S. H. (2007). Cultural Values in Organizations: Insights for Europe. *European Journal of International Management, 1*(3), 176–190. https://doi.org/10.1504/ejim.2007.014692.

Schein, E. H. (2010). *Organizational Culture and Leadership*. San Francisco: Jossey-Bass.

Schlange, L. E. (2006). Stakeholder Identification in Sustainability Entrepreneurship: The Role of Managerial and Organisational Cognition. *Greener Management International, 55*(13), 13–32. www.jstor.org/stable/greemanainte.55.13. Accessed 18 April 2020.

Schwartz, S. H. (1992). Universals in the Content and Structure of Values: Theoretical Advances and Empirical Tests in 20 Countries. In M. Zanna (Ed.), *Advances in Experimental Social Psychology* (Vol. 25, pp. 1–65). New York: Academic Press. https://doi.org/10.1016/S0065-2601(08)60281-6.

Schwartz, S. H. (2006). A Theory of Cultural Value Orientations: Explication and Applications. *Comparative Sociology, 5*(2–3), 137–182. https://doi.org/10.1163/156913306778667357.

Schwartz, S. H., & Bilsky, W. (1987). Toward a Universal Psychological Structure of Human Values. *Journal of Personality and Social Psychology, 53*(3), 550–562. https://doi.org/10.1037//0022-3514.53.3.550.

Shepherd, D. A., Patzelt, H., & Baron, R. A. (2013). "I Care About Nature, but…": Disengaging Values in Assessing Opportunities That Cause Harm. *Academy of Management Journal, 56*(5), 1251–1273. https://doi.org/10.5465/amj.2011.0776.

Szegedi, K. (2012). Hazai nagyvállalati etikai kódexek tartalmi elemzése [Content Analysis of Code of Ethics of Hungarian Large Companies]. Vezetéstudomány [Budapest Management Review]. Vol. XLIII, No. 1, pp. 47–55. http://unipub.lib.uni-corvinus.hu/2548/1/vt2012n1ksz-47.pdf. Accessed 3 April 2020 [in Hungarian].

Tóth, G. (2007). A Valóban Felelős Vállalat. A fenntarthatatlan fejlődésről, a vállalatok társadalmi felelősségének (CSR) eszközeiről és a mélyebb stratégiai megközelítésről [The Truly Responsible Company. On Unsustainable Development, Corporate Social Responsibility (CSR) Tools and a Deeper Strategic Approach], KÖVET, Budapest [in Hungarian].

Werhane, P. H. (1985). *Persons, Rights, and Corporations*. New York: Prentice Hall, Englewood Cliffs.

Zsolnai, L. (2001). *Ökológia, gazdaság, etika [Ecology, Economy, Ethics]*. Budapest: Helikon Kiadó. [in Hungarian].

Zsolnai, L., & Győri, Zs. (2011). Can Ethics Survive in Competitive Environments? Empirical Evidence from Values-Driven Businesses, European Business Ethics Network 24th Annual Conference. 15–17 September 2011.

Part III

Working Models of Ecologically Conscious Businesses

This part of the book first introduces the main characteristics of the empirical research and two samples of ecologically conscious business organizations. It then presents and analyzes the value orientations of the selected enterprises, and reveals how they define their raison d'être and what they mean by success. The second chapter in this section reviews the elements of their business models.

5

Ecologically Conscious Business Organizations and Their Value Orientations

The ancient philosophers Plato, Aristotle, and Confucius perceived the essence of human existence as creation; that is—in economic terminology—production, not consumption. However, production may be associated not only with material goods, but also with the creation of higher values (Allinson 2009, 2011). In light of this perspective, how can we relate to the consumer society of today, the "values" it conveys, growth-oriented economies, and the profit-oriented businesses that serve them? Can we create a state of general human well-being and ecological sustainability, in which we can achieve the individual goals that make human existence worthwhile, based on a materialistic conception of the economy? This is hardly possible using the materialistic and mainstream economic and business models with which we have almost completely ruined the biosphere (Zsolnai 2001; Pataki and Takács-Sánta 2005; Magnuson 2007).

What can we do to avoid and even restore the devastation of Earth? We need to make sure that economic activity does not occur for its own sake, but exists to serve people. It should contribute to the creation of real, positive values for society and help reduce and eliminate negative impacts. For this to happen, financial profit and growth should not

A. Ócsai, *Ecologically Conscious Organizations*, Palgrave Studies in Sustainable Business In Association with Future Earth,
https://doi.org/10.1007/978-3-030-60918-4_5

be considered goals, but only means (Allinson 2009). In addition, to preserve the Human-Earth system an ecologically sensitive economy is needed that recognizes the integrity of natural beings and the dignity of their existence. However, this can only be imagined through an ecological turn by which humans become reconciled with themselves and reestablish a covenant with nature (Zsolnai 2001). The necessary ecological turn can be fostered if modern man's distorted attitude and behavior incompatible with sustainability is replaced by a spiritual value orientation that represents unity, compassion, and a demeanor of self-discipline (Lázár 2011).

Earlier research has shown that a positive relationship between a genuine value orientation and economically successful business operations that pay special attention to environmental impacts does exist. Continuing in this direction, this chapter examines the value orientations of some ecologically conscious business organizations to reveal the core values behind their functioning. These businesses, which make ecological considerations the center of their operations, can thus be considered ecologically conscious and capable of and willing to operate in alternative ways to the organizations that currently prevail in our materialistic economic system.

This chapter introduces the main methodological features of the empirical research underlying this book, and presents two samples of ecologically conscious business organizations. One sample consists of eight internationally well-known ecologically conscious enterprises from all over the world, while the other sample contains fourteen well-known ecologically conscious businesses based in Hungary. They are briefly described to familiarize readers with this special set of business organizations.

On Empirical Investigation

In the current phase of research of the value orientations of ecologically conscious businesses, the generalization of results is not the primary goal, but obtaining a deeper understanding of the selected cases. We can examine the characteristics of the chosen businesses and the factors that influence their operations primarily through a constructivist epistemological approach (Creswell 2007; Maréchal 2010) and by applying so-called "less structured qualitative research" methodology (Cassell and Symon 2004; Miles et al. 2014). Further methodological issues in the empirical research process involve the units of observation, the sampling procedure, data collection and analysis, the reliability and validity of the analysis, and ethical questions (Kvale 1994; Hunyadi et al. 1997; Mason 2002; Patton 2002; Krippendorff 2004; Creswell 2007; Babbie 2008; Maxwell 2013; Miles et al. 2014).

The book focuses on the population of ecologically conscious business organizations, of which two samples are examined. The reason for selecting and analyzing two samples is the hypothetical difference between the two subsets, and the (partly) different methods of data collection and analysis that were used. One sample consists of eight internationally well-known ecologically conscious companies from around the world. In these cases, the enterprises were selected as the units of observation. A list of the businesses in the international sample and related data is provided in Table 5.1.

Table 5.1 Main characteristics of ecologically conscious businesses in the international sample

Company name	Seat (country)	Main product/service	Year of foundation
Green Monday	Hong Kong	Plant-based foods, lifestyle	2012
Houdini Sportsware	Sweden	Functional outdoor clothing	1993
Interface	USA	Modular carpet	1973
Natura	Brazil	Natural cosmetics, direct marketing	1969
Organic India	India	Organic teas, herbal products	1997
Patagonia	USA	Outdoor clothing, apparel	1973
Scott Bader	Great Britain	Composites, adhesives, polymers	1921
TerraCycle	USA	Waste collection, recycling	2001

Source Author's construction

The other sample contains fourteen well-known ecologically conscious business organizations based in Hungary. In the case of these companies, the official representatives (owners and/or managers) were the units of observation as we undertook personal interviews with them. A list of the businesses in the Hungarian sample and related data are included in Table 5.2.

Due to the specific nature of the topic, requiring special knowledge, samples were selected through expert or purposeful sampling (Hunyadi et al. 1997; Babbie 2008). They were built up based on personal- and e-mail discussions with distinguished scholars and practitioners from

Table 5.2 Main characteristics of ecologically conscious businesses in the Hungarian sample

Company name	Seat (city in Hungary)	Main product/service	Year of foundation
Skanska Hungary	Budapest	Construction	1987
Nekedterem Hungary	Budapest	Home delivery of local food	2012
Réthy Fashion	Szigetszentmiklós	Fashion design from recycled jeans	2012
Bio-Drog-Berta	Kalocsa	Organic spices, food products	1995
Ecoizm/Zöldbolt	Veszprém	Trade in organic household products	2007
ALTEO Energy	Budapest	Alternative energy production	2008
Hajtás Pajtás	Budapest	Bike courier	1999
Pannonhalmi Abbey Winery	Pannonhalma	Wine and herbal products	2002
NES Shoes	Budapest	Ecological footwear design	2008
Béres Pharmaceuticals	Budapest	Alternative medicine	1993
Kör Architect Studio	Budapest	Architectural design	1989
Pipacs Bakery	Budapest	Organic bread	2014
Pendits Vineyards and Winery	Abaújszántó	Biodynamic wine	1991
MagNet Bank	Budapest	Banking	1995

Source Author's construction

the field (including individuals from the University of Hong Kong; the Norwegian School of Economics, Bergen, Norway; the University of Victoria, Canada; and Corvinus University of Budapest, Eötvös Loránd University, and the University of Pannonia, the latter three from Hungary).

Because of the different characteristics of the companies in the two samples and the availability of the representatives of the Hungary-based enterprises, the two samples were processed using different methods. In the case of the internationally well-known ecologically conscious businesses, the main goal was to depict the value profiles of each company based on publicly available information. With the Hungary-based enterprises, personal contacts were established, and through personal interviews more detailed data sets could be collected and deeply analyzed.

Two types of data collection methods were applied. On the one hand, company websites, publicly available official data, company documents, financial statements, corporate social responsibility or sustainability reports, codes of ethics and conduct, annual reports, information from external sources (media, authorities, customers, and industry peers) were gathered about all the companies in both samples. Semi-structured personal interviews with the owners and managers of the Hungary-based ecologically conscious businesses and one of the international cases (personal conversation with Tom Szaky, founding owner of TerraCycle at a company presentation at the Corvinus University of Budapest, Hungary in 2016) were also conducted (Kvale 1996, 2006; Mason 2002; King 2004; Barlow 2010).

A questionnaire with strictly predefined content and closed questions was not used in the interviews with Hungarian companies, but rather an interview guide (Appendix 1). The related questions were formulated based on the literature related to the research topic, preliminary discussions with experts from the field, and the author's previous knowledge and research experience. The six main topics of the questions were: (1) the characteristics of the business; (2) the interpretation and value orientation of the former regarding ecological consciousness; (3) ecological aspects of the operation of the business; (4) the relationship between competition and ecology; (5) the company's assessment of the potential benefits of ecological consciousness; and (6) business perspectives about ecological consciousness in the Hungarian economy. When a Likert scale was used by an interviewee to answer a question, they were also asked to give a detailed explanation of their response. Thus through the combined use of techniques typical of semi-structured and structured interviews, the advantages of the richness of detail of a qualitative approach could be preserved, but, bearing in mind the limitations of Likert-scale based surveys,[1] answers also became—at least partially—formally comparable and depictable (Barlow 2010; Robbins and Heiberger 2011).

Research into the value orientations of the Hungary-based ecologically conscious businesses was carried out using both deductive and inductive approaches. Analysis of the importance of ecological values[2] followed a deductive logic, as the latter were identified from the theory. Identification of elements of business models and definitions of the business raison d'être and success were similar to a deductive approach because they were designed to map the emergence of preexisting categories. However, transcripts of the interviews, field notes, and documents used as secondary data sources were analyzed using inductive logic through qualitative content analysis (Patton 2002; Krippendorff 2004; Hsieh and Shannon 2005; Bowen 2009; Stan 2010) and thematic analysis (Boyatzis 1998; Fereday and Muir-Cochrane 2006; Lapadat 2010). During the content analysis, starting with texts, patterns that could be used to characterize the value background, motivation, culture, and mindset of the enterprises were sought out. Thirty-six patterns were identified, and aggregate clusters were formed from those patterns more similar to each other.

[1]The limitations of measuring using a Likert scale include, but are not limited to, the following:

1. The Likert scale is an ordinal scale, thus data obtained with the instrument can not be used to perform mathematical-statistical operations (e.g., calculation of arithmetic and geometric means and standard deviations) that can be applied to higher levels of measurement such as interval scales or ratio scales (Hunyadi et al. 1997; Jamieson 2004);
2. Answers to questions may suffer from multiple distortions, such as social desirability, acquiescence, and a centralizing tendency (Cassell and Symon 2004; Babbie 2008; McLeod 2008; Mills et al. 2010).

[2]Thirteen ecological values were predefined through a theoretical literature review. These encompass humility, biodiversity, non-possession, trust, responsibility, holistic approach, temperance, respect for ecosystems, reciprocity, love, natural embeddedness, intrinsic value of natural beings, and openness to mystery.

Qualitative research strives for the greatest possible objectivity, reliability, and validity. In order to increase objectivity, the author's value judgments, assumptions, and goals were explored and presented, and the research process was documented in detail. Data recording and storage were based on the precautionary principle, so that the entire process could be verified and replicated. To increase reliability, different types of triangulation (data source triangulation, and inter-researcher triangulation) were employed. In order to enhance the validity of the research findings, quotations taken from texts of documents and interviews that supported the findings were added, and data analysis was conducted according to both a deductive and inductive approach (Krippendorff 2004; Miles et al. 2014). This qualitative research, which used only two smaller samples, was not designed to be representative, but rather to help with exploring and synthesizing the details of the selected cases. This research strategy can produce new insights of use in further research, and lead to suggestions for business practices.

Consideration of ethical issues was not a separate factor, but a key aspect that was taken into account during every part of the research design and implementation (Maxwell 2013). Interviewees received all the necessary information in time and in sufficient detail to enable them to make a decision about their participation in the research (i.e., to give their informed consent). During the organization and conduct of interviews, interruption of the work of interviewees was minimized. All the information we received was treated confidentially. Throughout the research process, open and honest communication was maintained, and potential information and power asymmetry were carefully considered and avoided (Kvale 2006; Creswell 2007).

The findings of this book should be seen in the light of some of the limitations of the empirical research that underlie them. To answer the research questions, two small samples were used, meaning that it is not possible to consider the research results representative of the total population of ecologically conscious organizations. However, the initial goal during the current phase of research was not to create generalizable results, but to construct a deeper understanding of the selected cases, their components, and relationships. This is why an exploratory research design and a qualitative approach were applied. Capacity and time constraints did not permit the application of longitudinal research, which could have further refined the results of the study. In addition, sampling bias must be acknowledged, as in the international sample only world-renowned companies were studied, but because of local knowledge, even very small businesses were examined in the Hungarian sample. Some of the differences between the ecologically conscious businesses in the international and the Hungarian sample may be explained through this sampling distortion.

Value Orientations of Ecologically Conscious Business Organizations in the International Sample

This section presents the value orientations of ecologically conscious businesses in the international sample using the same structure in each case. A short introduction is followed by a summary of the history of the organization and its core values.

Green Monday

Green Monday is a social start-up group dedicated to tackling climate change and global food security. David Yeung and Francis Ngai founded it on Earth Day in 2012. Two years later, Fast Company Magazine selected it as one of China's 50 Most Innovative Companies. It promotes low-carbon, sustainable lifestyles and works to make the former simple, easy to implement, and disseminate. It functions as a platform that brings together the efforts of companies, restaurants, schools, and members of the public to promote social and environmental responsibility. As Asia's first plant-based grocery store, its Green Common initiative aims to provide its customer community with food that is produced and marketed in a sustainable, innovative, healthy, and ethical way (Green Monday 2020).

History: The basic idea of Green Monday is the recognition that the current system of food production contributes as much to global warming and the degradation of the natural environment as heavy industry, transport, or fossil fuel-based electricity generation (Green Monday 2020). According to a 2006 report by the Food and Agriculture Organization of the United Nations, meat-based food production is responsible for 18 per cent of the world's annual total greenhouse gas emissions (mainly carbon dioxide, methane, and nitrous oxide). This is more than the combined emissions of cars, rail, and aviation (FAO 2006). Accordingly, eating a vegetarian meal is less harmful to the environment, and even having a meat-free day once a week can significantly reduce one's carbon footprint. Green Monday achieved significant success even in its founding year by developing vegetarian menus for Hong Kong's number one fast-food network. In cooperation with twenty leading food service providers, it has launched a school food program for 600,000 students in more than 800 public and higher education institutions. In 2013, it also started offering its services at the University of Hong Kong and Hong Kong International Airport. In 2014, a Green LUCK food aid program was launched, and nearly a quarter of all college students at Columbia University chose the Green Monday menu. In 2015, the food the organization offers became available at Washington University (St. Louis), University of California, Los Angeles (UCLA), a German and an English university, HSBC, a number of restaurant chains, and more than 300,000 students at 39 schools in Albania. It also opened several grocery stores as part of the Green Common business project. During 2016, additional stores were opened, sales channels expanded, and own-brand products were launched. Green Monday also participated in organizing the Earth Day Forum and first TV show on vegetarianism in the US program, while the Green Monday Ventures business services initiative also commenced (Green Monday 2020).

Core values: Green Monday's vision is to be a global player in relation to sustainable public good. Its mission as an innovative and multifaceted social business platform is to guide individuals, communities, and companies to lead a more sustainable, healthy, and conscious lifestyle that supports the fight against climate change, and promotes food safety, health, and animal welfare. Green Monday emphasizes the beneficial effects of vegetarianism, but does not expect people to make a sudden and drastic dietary transition (Green Monday 2020). One reason for this is that the founder, David Yeung, as a practicing Buddhist, seeks to reduce suffering. He encourages people not to strive to fully give up eating meat, but only to start to reduce the amount they consume (Zimberoff 2017). Green Monday sets an example, and is constantly informing its customers and the public that eating meat-free meals on one day a week is an easy and effective way to reduce their carbon footprint and improve their health. The name of the company expresses the fact that Monday, the first day of the working week, fills the body and mind with new energy, giving new impetus to a new beginning. The color green draws attention to the benefits of sustainable living and eating, love of the Earth, and the importance of finding harmony. It also inspires people to practice these principles (Green Monday 2020).

Green Monday's motto is "Make change happen, make green common." The three pillars of its approach are simplicity, ease of implementation, and dissemination. While the issues of climate change and animal welfare are complex, the solutions need to be simple. The message of the relevance of having a meat-free meal once a week is crystal clear, yet it can lead to great results in terms of the health of the planet and people. Green Monday believes that knowledge alone is not enough for successful change, but through influencing people's emotions, a fashionable, viral trend should be created. Using its branding, marketing, and PR experience, Green Monday has managed to build its rapidly growing brand so that customers can perceive its everyday meals as contributing to the mission of a movement that successfully works for the common good. The concept of becoming sustainable ("Go Green") is already supported by most people, but channels and frameworks for joint action are often lacking. For ease of implementation, Green Monday has developed a social business approach that supports a green lifestyle both in terms of demand (e.g., by providing information and conducting awareness-raising campaigns for consumers and partner companies) and the supply side (active market participation in food retail, corporate consulting, and venture capital investment) (Green Monday 2020).

Houdini Sportsware

Houdini Sportsware AB is a Swedish outdoor clothing company founded by Lotta Giornofelice in 1993. Its headquarters is in Nacka, an eastern suburb of Stockholm. It produces and markets a full range of functional clothing in an ethical and sustainable manner. With an annual turnover of almost seventeen million EUR in 2019 and 45 employees, the main goal is to serve its customers who are seeking to actively protect the Earth. Houdini also strives to eliminate all adverse environmental impacts, and achieve a state of sustainability and functionality even from the stage of product design. Its products are now directly available in eighteen countries on three continents (Houdini 2020; Largest Companies 2020).

History: The company's history can be traced back to an idea about a new raw material (stretch wool) that was still unknown in the early 1990s. It was thought up during a New Zealand ski and mountaineering tour. Building on this novelty, the company first started producing functional underwear on a small scale. Houdini's products soon became very popular among climbers. However, the company also attracted attention because it was founded (and is still run by) women, in a male-dominated clothing industry (the current managing director is Eva Karlsson). In the early 2000s, Houdini introduced another innovation: it started to produce underwear and insulated clothing that, in contrast to the norms of the time, was fashionable as well as functional. Despite some negative feedback from other industrial players, customers welcomed the innovation positively. In 2007, Houdini made great strides in sustainability: after years of ongoing consultation with its suppliers, it started manufacturing its first recycled polyester products. Today, it continues to organize its activities around sustainability and in recent years has launched a number of new environmental projects. These include producing clothing from residual fabrics in 2010, second-hand clothing sales and the rental of outerwear since 2012, and the climate-neutral design of its Gothenburg store in 2014, which is bicycle-friendly and promotes sustainability through its operations (the building has been awarded a Green Building Certification called Leadership in Energy and Environmental Design) (Houdini 2020).

Core values: Houdini's core values, sources of motivation, and goals were published in a statement at the end of 2017 called The Houdini Manifesto. The main driving force behind its activities is a deep love of nature and the experiences this provides. Houdini recognizes that nature is of intrinsic value, regardless of human needs, and that human activity has created an unsustainable situation on Earth, in which companies have a significant role to play and therefore a major responsibility. The current system of producing, using, and then degrading products into waste at an accelerating rate is not working. Houdini, therefore, considers its mission to transform its operations into a circular system to be in harmony with natural principles, and it is inspired by nature. The requisite change depends simultaneously on interrelated and closely intertwined natural, social, and economic factors. Houdini fights against overconsumption, for the development and application of sustainable technologies, and for working together with others and sharing knowledge. Houdini constantly monitors its own operations, striving for fuller transparency and continuous improvement in order to meet challenges that arise. Other values include free thinking, encouraging individuality, passion, uncompromising creativity, the desire to explore the world, the importance of communities of friends, joy, long-term commitment, taking into account the interests of future generations, and minimizing the ecological footprint, and having an overall positive impact on the world (Houdini 2018, 2020).

Interface

Atlanta-based Interface, one of the world's largest manufacturers of office and household modular carpet, floor mat, and office fabric, was founded by Ray C. Anderson in 1973. The company manufactures its products on four continents, sells them in more than 100 countries, employs 4100 people, and made a profit after tax of almost 80 million USD in 2019, with sales of more than 1.3 billion USD. The company, which faithfully represents its late founder's commitment to industrial ecology and sustainability, is associated with a number of significant industry innovations, several valuable brands, outstanding performance, and a customer-centric company culture. For more than two decades, Interface has been among the most well-recognized companies in terms of striving for sustainability, along with Unilever and Patagonia, among others. Through its Mission Zero® and Climate Take Back™ programs and attempts to climb up its own "Mount Sustainability" (associated with the goal of sending zero waste to landfill, reducing fossil fuel energy use to zero, as well as eliminating process water use and emitting zero greenhouse gasses), Interface seeks to completely eliminate the negative effects of its operations, reverse negative ecological processes, and maintain its leadership in implementing these changes (GlobeScan 2019; Interface 2019, 2020).

History: Ray Anderson graduated as an industrial and systems engineer in 1956. After a decade and a half of experience in the carpet trade, recognizing the growing demand for free lay carpet tiles, he founded Interface in collaboration with a British company, Carpets International Plc., and American investors. The company, which originally had 15 employees, successfully rose to the challenge of managing steeply rising raw material costs thanks to the use of advanced technology. It has grown rapidly due to its popular products, and had annual sales of 80 million USD at the time of listing in 1983. Interface has expanded internationally over the years and has become an industry leader after numerous product and technological innovations, opening up to newer markets (households, luxury vinyl floors), and having made more than 50 acquisitions (Interface 2020). The deep commitment to sustainability, inspired by Paul Hawken's book *The Ecology of Commerce* (Hawken 1993), has mainly been felt since the mid-1990s. Inspired by the book, Anderson wrote his own book on the environmental impact of Interface production and its business model (Anderson 1998). The next significant step in the unfolding transformation was the Mission Zero® program that was announced in 2006 that had the goal of eliminating all of the company's negative environmental impacts by 2020. The founder's death in 2011 did not change the mission of Interface, which continued to be implemented until 2017 under the leadership of Dan Hendrix and then Jay Gould, and was even strengthened by joining the fight against global warming through the Climate Take Back initiative (Interface 2020).

Core Values: Interface sees itself as a "purpose-driven" company, and its core values are consciousness, compassion, action, and a passionate team that wants to "do things right" in parallel with "doing the right things." Its five value commitments are: (1) to plan better things; (2) to be original and generous; (3) to inspire others; (4) to create unity, and (5) a better future. (1) Interface is a revolutionary and entrepreneurial organization. It is a pioneer in the carpet industry that is working on the renewal of the industrial system by researching unknown, unusual, and unlikely solutions. Its organizational culture is based on discovery, innovation, and experimentation, which can lead to progress, success, and a more livable world. (2) Interface is also a community based on trust, deep relationships, and inclusion, and includes a network of supporters and collaborators. (3) It is determined to stand up boldly, with the help of its innovative products and by setting an example, to make the industrial world realize that it is possible to act for the greatest good, and to encourage companies to change. (4) Interconnectedness is a central element of its activities. Just as a harmonious, functional floor covering is made up of interconnected modules, Interface is also part of a larger whole consisting of interdependent elements, whereby partnerships and collaborations can achieve more together than separately. (5) According to the intellectual heritage of the founder, and in the hope of a livable future, it is understood that the relationship between man and nature must be fundamentally reshaped through the business world. This requires long-term planning, persistent action, and the adoption of guidelines based on natural principles (Interface 2020).

Natura

Founded in 1969, Natura is Brazil's largest cosmetics manufacturer and leader in direct marketing. With the Australian brand Aesop and the English brand The Body Shop, it has been part of a global cosmetics group headquartered in Sao Paulo under the name Natura & Co. since 2017. To this group the iconic American beauty brand Avon joined in January 2020, making it the world's fourth largest pure-play beauty group. Natura has been guided by sustainable development guidelines from the outset, and its customer relations are of paramount importance, so its basic trading strategy has been direct sales. Currently, 1.8 million consulting partners are conveying Natura's values and products to customers in ten countries on three continents. Innovation is at the heart of Natura's sustainable development: the company spent 2.4 per cent of its annual net revenue of over 2.2 billion USD in 2019 on product development, and has continuously launched new products on its main markets. Complemented by similarly committed and strong brands for social and environmental sustainability, Natura & Co. data (which indicate that the brands serve 200 million consumers in more than 100 countries on five continents, have 40,000 employees and 6.3 million consultants and representatives, along with 10 billion USD gross revenue) show that one of Brazil's most emblematic companies has become a truly global organization (Natura 2020a, b; Natura & Co. 2020).

History: The founder of Natura, Antonio Luiz de Cunha Seabra, an economist, worked early in his career on the production of typewriters and calculators before turning to the creation of beauty care products in a small family-owned laboratory in Sao Paulo in the 1960s. Natura was founded in 1969 under the name Natura Cosméticos, and the company's products were sold through a small shop. Remaining in direct contact with his customers, the founder developed his philosophy of beauty care: to connect beauty with well-being and skin care with self-esteem through the production and distribution of skin-care products made of natural ingredients. The by-now well-recognized floral logo of Natura was created in 1970 to symbolize the unity of nature and beauty. By 1977, Natura already had 40 products, and the Natura Brasil magazine was then launched. In 1984, Natura was the first beauty care company in the world to start selling its products in refillable form. In 1995, as a first major step toward social responsibility and recognition of the utmost importance of education for social development, the entire profit of the company's newly launched Crer Para Ver product line was donated to the French organization Entraide Scolaire Amical, which supports schoolchildren. In 2000, the Ekos brand was introduced, whose products stem from Brazil's rich natural treasures. In 2001, Natura inaugurated its headquarters in Cajamar, with the creed of not just dreaming of a better world, but implementing it. In the following years, this idea was gradually put into practice. An ISO 14001 environmental management certificate was obtained in 2004. The testing of products on animals stopped in 2006. In 2007, Natura received a carbon-neutral certificate for its entire production chain. In 2010, Natura became the first Brazilian company to join the WWF Climate Defenders initiative. The Amazonia program of Natura (aimed at preserving the environmental and social values of rainforests) was launched in 2011. In 2013, Natura acquired the Australian brand Aesop, which adheres to similar sustainability principles. In 2014, Natura was the first publicly traded company in the world to attain B Corporation sustainability certification, in line with which the accomplishment of social and environmental goals is a formal and mandatory element of the company's business model. In 2017, The Body Shop, and in 2020, Avon, joined Natura. The company has grown steadily over the decades, from becoming a listed company in Sao Paulo in 2004, starting its expansion in France in 2005, and building a second production facility in Benevides, northern Brazil, in 2012 (Balch 2013; Natura 2020a, b).

Core values: Natura's motto is *Bem Estar Bem* ("well-being well"), which indicates a state in which one feels at harmony and can thus establish an empathetic, successful, and joyful relationship with other people, nature, and wholeness. This is the starting point and the basic philosophy that inspires Natura to be a key player in social progress and to build clear, transparent relationships with all its stakeholders, and to produce and market products and services that help implement these principles. Underlying these goals are six main value commitments. (1) Relation: life is a chain of relationships, everything in the universe is interconnected, and the proper evaluation of relationships is the foundation of human development for peace and solidarity. (2) Improvement: striving for the continuous development of individuals, organizations, and society. (3) Truth: improving the quality of relationships is based on a commitment to truth. (4) Diversity: the diversity of people and perspectives is the source of prosperity and the existence of all beings. (5) Freedom: striving for beauty, people's inner goals must be free from influences and prejudices. (6) Engagement: the company as a living organism is a dynamic set of relationships, the value and lifespan of which is related to its ability to contribute to the sustainable development of society (Natura 2020a, b).

Organic India

Organic India, a world leader in the production and distribution of Ayurvedic Tulsi tea blends and herbal supplements, was founded by Bhavani Lev and Bharat Mitra with some of their friends in 1997 in Lucknow, North India. The founders were inspired by the teachings of the Hindu advaita master Hariwansh Lal Poonja (or, as his followers named him, Papaji). The company took the name Organic India in 2006 and strengthened its mission to operate as an ethical, socially, environmentally, and economically sustainable business that promotes regenerative agriculture and provides livelihoods and training to thousands of impoverished farmers in India's disadvantaged rural, tribal, farming communities. It also aims to combine 5000 years of traditional Indian wisdom with world-class technology to produce bio-certified Tulsi teas, herbals, Psyllium, castor oil products, organic foods and spices, and to promote organic production and sustainable agriculture. After twenty years of development, Organic India had annual turnover of 55 million USD in 2017. Based on an annual growth rate of more than 20 per cent in recent years, it expects to have turnover of over 70 million USD by the end of the fiscal year 2020 (The Economic Times 2017; Organic India 2020a).

History: In the 1990s, the founders of Organic India observed the devastation of nature in India as agricultural industrialization based on chemical pesticides, fertilizers, and genetically engineered seeds spread throughout the country. In parallel with this experience, with the help of Ayurvedic and Western physicians, the founders learned about and researched the positive health effects of herbs, recipes, and herbal products, especially in relation to "Holy Basil," also known as Tulsi. Over the following years they established a specific business model based on responsible economic, social, and environmental principles and fair trade partnerships with farmers in order to help reestablish traditional agricultural wisdom and environmentally regenerate thousands of hectares of farmland and forest. By now, Organic India has managed to contribute to the economic and cultural revitalization of rural communities through 3000 farm partnerships, as well as promoting community health care, education, and inclusive social change for women. It has a subsidiary in the United States certified as a B Corporation, and sells its products in more than 40 countries around the world (Organic India 2020a, b).

Core Values: At the heart of the concept of Organic India is love and the intention of expressing consciousness in action. The main goal is to support true well-being and raise consciousness through a holistic, sustainable business model based on respect for all beings and for Mother Nature. Organic India's mission is to be a trustworthy and innovative market leader in the global market, producing genuine organic products and solutions for healthy and conscious living. Its core values are service to all beings, honesty, total commitment to quality, respect and devotion to Mother Nature, and uncompromising integrity (Organic India 2020a).

Patagonia

Deeply committed to environmental and social sustainability in the sales of outdoor clothing and equipment, Patagonia was founded in 1973 by climber and environmental activist Yvon Chouinard. The California-based company employs approximately 2000 people in more than 50 countries on five continents and generated sales of approximately 800 million USD in 2017 and one billion in 2020. The concept of the company, which aims to produce the best outdoor products without doing unnecessary harm, is that the economy and companies can and should be used to alleviate and remediate the present environmental crisis, and encourage others to do the same. Patagonia recognizes that, as a player in the business world, it is part of the problem because it still uses fossil energy, water, and plastics and emits significant amounts of waste and carbon dioxide as by-products. Patagonia's goal is to make its negative effects transparent, and, as a leading "activist company," through a number of initiatives sufficiently reduce and neutralize the former throughout their supply chain. These initiatives include increasing consumer consciousness, enhancing product durability, monitoring their carbon footprint, embracing environmental movements and campaigns, and promoting business transformation by supporting businesses with similar commitments (Patagonia 2020).

History: Even as a child, founder Yvon Chouinard was in love with the beauty of mountains, open nature, and the depth of personal and community experiences they give us. Chouinard was a freedom-loving young man who spent a lot of time in nature and became an excellent climber. From 1957 to 1965 he was involved in the distribution of his own forged climbing equipment through his company Chouinard Equipment. In 1965, in partnership with an innovative fellow climber, Tom Frost, he further developed his products, resulting in a significant increase in demand for them. Returning from a European tour in 1970, encouraged by the great success of sales of shirts with a collar that he bought back from there (since a collar effectively protects the neck from the skin-rubbing effect of a climbing rope), clothing soon became the company's number one product. However, because of an unfortunate climbing accident and consequent lawsuits, Chouinard had to close his former business and give up the sale of climbing equipment. However, in 1973 he was able to establish a new brand and company, Patagonia, from the formerly successful clothing division. The product range was soon extended to other "quiet" outdoor sports that do not require the use of a combustion engine, such as running, hiking, skiing, surfing, fishing, and non-clothing products (such as backpacks and sleeping bags). Due to Chouinard's personal values, derived from a nature-respecting mountaineering culture and Zen Buddhism, environmental and social sustainability has always been important to Patagonia. Accordingly, it has been committed to improving its sustainability performance from the outset. As a result, since 1996 Patagonia has used only organic cotton for all its cotton products and it co-founded the Fair Labor Association to improve the situation of its workers. In 2002, it appointed a corporate social responsibility manager and began working more intensively with its factories. In 2005, a clothing recycling program called Common Threads was started. In 2007, a project called The Footprint Chronicles was launched, which has since transparently tracked the social and environmental impacts of Patagonia products. The company has been rigorously auditing its raw material suppliers since 2011, and in that year an extended version of the previous clothing recycling program called the Common Threads Initiative was started based on the principles of Reduce, Repair, Reuse, Recycle, and Reimagine. In 2013, Patagonia reinforced the clauses in its Code of Conduct that refer to ethical practices in the supply chain with special emphasis on the requirement of providing living wages that support a decent livelihood. Patagonia's products have been manufactured with Fair Trade Certified Sewing certification since 2014, which indicates that the buyer pays a community development premium above market price to suppliers to improve the quality of life in local communities in the long run. In addition, since 2014 Patagonia has only used down feathers for linings that come from 100 per cent traceable sources that exclude the practice of force-feeding and live-plucking of birds. Since 2016, it has managed to implement ethical wool procurement, whereby the fair treatment of animals, and ethical and sustainable land use are ensured throughout the supply chain. In 2017, Patagonia launched a website called Worn Wear through which its customers can return Patagonia products that have been used but that are still in good condition to the company via their stores or the internet or post office. For doing this, customers receive a credit toward their next purchase, and, after cleaning and repair, the products can be repurchased at a significant discount (Patagonia 2020).

Core Values: The ethos of Patagonia grew out of a climbing culture that, in addition to love and respect for nature, is based on a free entrepreneurial spirit, adventurousness, risk-taking, action, independence, self-motivation, and passion. In addition to these principles, for such intentions to be realized a person should be versatile, flexible enough and open to new things so that they can react to any difficulties that may arise in a timely and appropriate manner. Development and adaptability is essential, so that one never stops asking the question how one can do what they are doing better. Striving to improve the environmental and social sustainability of companies may also be compared to a complex climbing activity (similar to Interface's concept of Mount Sustainability), whereby one needs to know the internal characteristics (strengths and weaknesses) and the external circumstances (opportunities and threats), but most of all respect the limits and constraints of nature. A minimalist style, simplicity, and a focus on utility are needed, because all unnecessary burdens endanger the success of a climb, and even the life of the climber. Nevertheless, according to Chouinard, who was inspired by Zen Buddhism, one should not be afraid: just as a samurai is not afraid of death, neither should one be afraid of failure in business. You need to focus on doing your job well, and then you will achieve results; including in financial terms. It is thus the job of a business leader who is conscious of this not to sit in their office all day, but to be among their employees, to talk to everyone in the right tone, to come up with new ideas from outside the company, and to unite efforts to make changes in the right direction. Of course, it is also the great responsibility of a leader—and correspondingly, their company—that if they have the skills, resources, and opportunities to do good things, they should do them. A leader has the greatest responsibility for the origin of all resources that are utilized, and the state of nature. The overarching core values of Patagonia's commitment are a sense of interconnectedness with the natural environment and all beings, the pursuit of harmony, responsibility, cooperation, the intention to foster stakeholders' internal development and self-realization, and spirituality nourished by the latter (Chouinard 2005; Ooley 2013; Patagonia 2020).

Scott Bader

Scott Bader is a global chemical company with turnover of around 200 million GBP that employs almost 700 people and operates in sixteen countries on five continents. It has six manufacturing sites and fourteen offices, and is a market leader in composite, adhesive, and specialty polymer manufacturing. What makes it special is its self-governing structure. Scott Bader Commonwealth Limited is a common trusteeship; a community-owned company in which employees make decisions and manage assets. It is also a registered charity. Scott Bader does not have a corporate social responsibility policy because CSR is not separate element of its business model, but the basis of how it operates. Since the establishment of the current community ownership and corporate governance system in 1951, the core value of the company has been creating value for society. One of the main guidelines for this endeavor is a long-term vision and plan called 2036 Vision, which also functions as a system that prioritizes social and environmental sustainability elements and monitors and measures their development and impact (Scott Bader 2019, 2020).

History: The company was founded in 1921 in London by Swiss-born Ernest Bader and his wife, Dora Scott. They operated it according to the prevailing capitalist corporate governance principles for three decades. After becoming followers of the Quaker religion in the 1940s, the couple became increasingly preoccupied with the idea that acting more ethically to improve the world should also be emphasized as an economic principle. Their idea was that corporate capital should be distributed and operated in such a way that all employees have a real and equal say in the management of the company. Based on basically Quaker principles, a radical decision was made in 1951 to create the Scott Bader Commonwealth from the company (which had by then moved to Northamptonshire in central England). The organization, run by the employee community, was considered a British company until the mid-1960s, and then began to expand internationally. In 1966, in Amiens, France, a new plant was set up in the form of a joint venture in continental Europe to strengthen the position of the organization in the market for technical, commercial, and industrial composites. It launched an Irish subsidiary in Dunboyne, Eastern Ireland, in the mid-1970s, which has since worked closely with suppliers and customers in product innovation and actively participated in the company's charitable activities. In 1992, Scott Bader acquired Swedish Neidert Trading AB, from which the Nordic subsidiary responsible for supplying Northern Europe was formed. A South African unit was established in 1993 after 30 years of manufacturing Scott Bader products in the country under license, meaning that Scott Bader's history now extends back more than half a century in Africa. International expansion continued in the 1990s and 2000s (1992 USA and Czech Republic; 1999 Croatia; 2001 Germany; 2002 Spain and Dubai; 2007 China; 2013 Canada). In recent years, the company has strengthened its presence in markets in which it has been relatively weak so far, such as in Latin America, while in 2020 an Australian subsidiary was created (Jacob 2012; Scott Bader 2020; Simkin 2020).

Core values: Embedded in the creation and operation of the Commonwealth is the socio-economic vision of the founder, Ernest Bader. According to this, a sustainable and socially responsible enterprise cannot exist solely for its own sake, as it is part of the natural environment, society, and the national and international community, so its responsibilities extend far beyond the factory walls. The concept of joint ownership and "trusteeship" can be seen as a third way compared to capitalist and communist economic systems. Management must be based on consensus rather than instruction, and a company must refuse to participate in industry rivalry, international wars, and the armaments industry. The aim is to provide all stakeholders with the opportunity to develop materially and spiritually, for the members of the working community to be mutually responsible, and for work to be based on democratic participation. Scott Bader's core values can be derived from all these elements and the Quaker principles that inspired the company's transformation in 1951. It defines sustainable development in the same way as the Brundtland Commission. Scott Bader seeks to have a positive effect on the life of all beings affected by its activities. The company intends to develop so as to promote the complete evolution of individuals. It maintains equal opportunities for all to enjoy the benefits of the workplace. Everyone is involved, can participate, and has a say in the affairs of the company. Everyone has an opportunity to participate in social and community activities, but should also take individual responsibility. The leaders of Scott Bader lead by example, and conflict resolution is dialogue-based and nonviolent (WCED 1987; Scott Bader 2019, 2020).

TerraCycle

Hungarian-born Tom Szaky founded TerraCycle in 2001 at Princeton University. The company, which has been headquartered in New Jersey ever since, collects and recycles waste that has been declared unsuitable for recycling. It is now present in 21 countries around the world and had more than 200 employees, annual sales of 27 million USD, and profits of over three million USD in 2019. According to the owner-founder, who uses nature as an example for developing his concepts about waste, the whole idea of "waste" should be eliminated, since there is no waste in nature—rather, there is continuous circulation of materials. TerraCycle is the world leader in the management of waste in terms of the complex material flows of the industrial processes that serve the needs of today's consumer societies. TerraCycle considers this waste to be a usable resource, unlike traditional waste processing companies, and has now collected and recycled more than a billion pieces of garbage, supporting the mostly voluntary work of over 202 million people. For every piece of recycled garbage, it donates two cents to schools and charities around the world, and has raised more than 44 million USD so far (TerraCycle 2020).

Tom Szaky was born in Budapest, Hungary in 1982, but grew up in Canada after moving to Toronto with his parents in 1987. He enrolled in the Department of Psychology and Economics at Princeton University in 2001, but due to the increasing success of his work at TerraCycle he stopped his studies to focus entirely on his business. Szaky's background includes being honored for his community work as early as in his teenage years (he also operated three smaller internet businesses). Along with a classmate, Jon Beyer, Szaky founded TerraCycle in 2001 with loans of a few thousand dollars to recycle food waste from the university kitchens. This food waste was processed and, with the help of earthworms, ripe compost was produced, which was then sold to horticultural businesses and individual buyers. In 2003, the business model won Carrot Capital's Business Plan Challenge competition and the accompanying one million USD award. However, Szaky refused to accept the award because the would-be donors asked him to completely overhaul his business model and leave his colleagues. Returning to the original idea, TerraCycle further developed the product and began selling it in liquid form packaged into used soft drink bottles. Thus, the product came to consist exclusively of previously recycled components; i.e., "waste" (TerraCycle 2018, 2020).

In 2004, in a huge step, TerraCycle's plant fertilizer (named Plant Food) entered the Canadian stores of Home Depot and Walmart, and the company began to grow. From the premises TerraCycle was using for free on campus the company moved to its own office building in New Jersey, which was converted from a disused warehouse. During the reconstruction, local and international urban artists participated with TerraCycle, using only recycled materials and recyclable waste. Since then, the walls have been repainted every few weeks to provide space for exhibitions for emerging young artists. In 2005, TerraCycle organized their first volunteer waste collection team called Bottle Brigade, which collects used soft drink bottles for liquid plant manure. In the same year, the company also began selling their products in Walmart and Home Depot stores in the United States generating annual sales of one million USD by 2006. In 2007, the product range was expanded to offer nine different types of nutrient solutions, and a sponsored waste collection program was launched, according to which the producer of the original product that becomes waste (e.g., empty soft drink boxes, yogurt cups) bears the cost of selective collection and recycling. In 2008, market leader brand Capri Sun became the main sponsor of the Drink Pouch Brigade and launched an innovative marketing campaign in Newsweek magazine's environmental special issue, which resulted in 47,000 people returning 800,000 Target-brand plastic promotional bags. These were then used to make carrying bags—the first time this type of mass upcycling event has ever happened (upcycling refers to transforming "waste" into a product with a different function). In 2009, 25 new types of Brigade programs were launched, and TerraCycle began operations in Brazil, Canada, and the United Kingdom. To raise consumer awareness, the company launched a stand-alone TV reality show series called *Garbage Moguls* and opened their own store in Princeton to market their own products. Their first pop-up store opened in New York in 2010. "Hot Spots" have also been set up in Walmart stores (organic product displays) to present original products that can be considered sources of waste (such as Capri Sun soft drinks) and products with novel functions made from waste (such as backpacks and pen holders). By 2010, more than 50 million empty soft drink pouches had been collected and more than one million USD donated to schools and nonprofits. Due to the increase in the number of employees, TerraCycle also expanded its office in 2010 (TerraCycle 2018, 2020).

In 2011, TerraCycle opened offices in Norway, Spain, Germany, Ireland, Switzerland, Denmark, Belgium, and the Netherlands, and the number of employees increased to over 100. To change consumer awareness, they developed their first online game, Trash Tycoon, in which players have to run a waste recycling business. In 2012, the world's first project to recycle cigarette butts was launched. Two-and-a-half billion butts were collected with the participation of 40 million people, and a further six million USD was donated to charity. In 2013, the company's expansion continued both geographically and in terms of supply. With the newly opened Australian and New Zealand branches, TerraCycle was operating in more than 20 countries and running more than 100 types of program. In collaboration with the city of Vancouver, Canada, the first municipal cigarette waste recycling program has been launched. One of the largest German waste management companies, Landbell GmbH, bought a 25 per cent stake in TerraCycle in three German-speaking countries. In 2014, the sale of collection boxes called Zero Waste Boxes for almost all types of waste commenced. This new waste collection format was also made available in Staples, Office Depot, and Home Depot stores. An office was also opened in Japan, and Canada's largest waste management company, Progressive Waste Solutions, bought a 20 per cent stake in the Canadian subsidiary. Another TV series called *Human Resources* was launched on the Pivot network. In 2015, in cooperation with Unilever, the collection of metal boxes for deodorants was organized in 1600 Drogerie Markt stores in Germany, from which bicycles were made and donated to child welfare organizations. In 2016, a pioneering partnership was formed with French water, energy, and waste management company SUEZ, through which SUEZ acquired a 30 per cent stake in TerraCycle's French, British, Swedish, Belgian, Dutch, and Finnish subsidiaries. In the USA, with Henkel, TerraCycle was the first company in the world to develop a program for recycling industrial adhesive packaging and, together with Bausch + Lomb, for contact lenses and their packaging. They also set up a branch in China. In 2017, Procter & Gamble and SUEZ partnered to create the first fully recyclable shampoo bottle made of marine waste. In Australia, together with L'Oréal, the first playground made of recycled beauty waste was opened. A South Korean subsidiary was also launched in 2018. TerraCycle also developed and launched Loop in 2019. This is a circular shopping system that home-delivers and recollects the world's most favorite brand items in durable, refillable packaging in order to reduce the amount of single-use plastics (TerraCycle 2018, 2020).

Core values: as a genuine social and ecological entrepreneur and committed leader, Tom Szaky's most important core values are honesty, transparency, accountability, enthusiasm, passion for hard work, and creativity. He emphasizes these factors during the operation of Terracycle, because only through adhering to these values can he achieve his goal, which is making a significant change to the whole world, so that the economy can better meet the needs of humanity without generating waste, just as nature does. His philosophy is that everything is possible, and that it is the greatest joy when one can see that others enjoy what they are doing. In the collaborative and caring environment created by the founder, there is a strict work ethic, but also openness and empowerment. All mistakes can be forgiven, unless someone is dishonest with themselves. The company's mission, value commitments, and atmosphere inspire many not only within but outside the company, and both TerraCycle's and Szaky's activities and achievements have already received numerous accolades (CNBC 2012; Parvati Magazine 2017; TerraCycle 2020).

Table 5.3 summarizes the main characteristics of the value orientations of the internationally well-known ecologically conscious business organizations under analysis.

Table 5.3 Main characteristics of the value orientations of ecologically conscious businesses in the international sample

Company name	Vision	Values	Means	Outcomes
Green Monday	Global change through constructing an ecosystem of plant-based food to prevent climate change, food insecurity, food-related illness, planetary devastation, and animal suffering	Sustainability, health and well-being, consciousness, simplicity, feasibility, easy-to-implement and easy-to-share solutions, knowledge sharing, Buddhism	Awareness raising and promoting a sustainable lifestyle, grocery stores for plant-based food, sustainability and CSR consulting, ethical capital investment fund, prestigious advocates, and partner organizations	Increasing vegetarian and "once-a-week" plant-based food consumption, local and global community building, shaping food culture and society, feasible implementation of triple-bottom-line approach

Company name	Vision	Values	Means	Outcomes
Houdini Sportsware	Inspiring and enabling mankind to reconnect to nature through leading a healthier and happier lifestyle in partnership with nature, to evolve as individuals and as societies to improve the situation of present and future generations	Responsibility, sustainability, functionality, regeneration and intrinsic value of nature, passion, consideration of future generations, love, holistic approach, circular systems, cooperation, knowledge sharing, transparency, free thinking, setting an example, leading the change, ecosophy, deep ecology	Ethical and sustainable production of functional outdoor clothing, highly innovative product design based on recycled, biodegradable raw materials, local R&D and production, few suppliers and short supply chain, redefining consumption and customer care, dedication to "recycling, reusing, repair, rental," open-source innovation	Sustainability-based business model with nature as the blueprint, on the road to becoming 100 per cent circular: 100 per cent of products circular by 2022, total value chain circular and using only renewable energy by 2030, then moving beyond net zero, creative innovations, high quality, timeless style

(continued)

Table 5.3 (continued)

Company name	Vision	Values	Means	Outcomes
Interface	Doing right for a positive future with moral courage, showing that sustainability is better for business, transforming itself into an agent of restoration, and being a catalyst for the redesign of global industry	Industrial ecology, purpose-driven and restorative economy, sustainability, consciousness, compassion, action, passionate teams, doing well by doing good, well-being, genuineness, generosity, inspiring others, interconnectedness, striving for a better future, pioneering innovations inspired by nature	Globally producing commercial and household modular flooring, own sustainability advisory group using "The Natural Step" sustainability methodology and the concept of "Mount Sustainability," radical product and process innovation, close cooperation and ethical relationship with members of the value chain	Climate Take Back and Mission Zero programs to become carbon negative by 2040, carbon-neutral products, services, recycled materials to eliminate all negative environmental impacts, cyclical, gentle business model with radical redesign of processes and products mimicking nature, improvement of life of all stakeholders

Company name	Vision	Values	Means	Outcomes
Natura	Becoming the best beauty group for the world through nurturing beauty and relationships that foster a better way of living and doing business, the collaboration of four socially and environmentally conscious brands through local and global expression that promote the well-being of people, animals, and the planet	"Well-being well," harmony, empathy, successful, and joyful relationship with nature, people, and the "Whole," pure, transparent relationships, peace, solidarity, striving for continuous development, truth, diversity, human rights and gender equality, circularity, and regeneration	Production and distribution of innovative, natural, ethical, and sustainable beauty care products from four iconic brands (Natura, Aesop, The Body Shop, and Avon), nature-inspired cyclical production system with true value creation throughout entire partner network, fair relationship with suppliers, caring direct sales and consumer awareness raising	High-quality products and services combining traditional and cutting-edge knowledge, 6+ million representatives worldwide, support for local communities, public education and women's causes, carbon neutral in 2019, Vision 2030 to become net zero CO_2 emitters and zero deforestation in Amazon

(continued)

Table 5.3 (continued)

Company name	Vision	Values	Means	Outcomes
Organic India	Being a trustworthy, innovative global leader of consciousness through a holistic and sustainable business model that promotes True Wellness and respect for all Beings and Mother Nature by providing genuine organic products and services that support more conscious and healthy living	Love, respect for and service and dedication to all Beings and Mother Nature, holistic approach, sustainability, real well-being, increasing consciousness, health, inspiring others, reliability, innovation, honesty, accountability, commitment to quality, integrity, Hinduism	Production of organic teas, herbal preparations, spices, fresh and packaged food, fair and lasting relations with farmers, herb collectors, rural development for communities, cooperation with market-leading handicraft product distributor Fabindia	Genuine organic herbal products available worldwide, holistic business model for the benefit of all stakeholders, restorative agriculture for serving and protecting nature, support for farmers, herb collectors, and their communities in rural India

Company name	Vision	Values	Means	Outcomes
Patagonia	Saving the planet through building the best outdoor clothing products and apparel without causing unnecessary harm and using business to lead society and protect and restore the stability, integrity, and beauty of the web of life, and continuously developing new ways to do things	Love and respect for nature, free entrepreneurial spirit, self-motivation, passion, diversity, openness, fearlessness, doing good and well, respect for limits, minimalist style, simplicity, transparency, innovation, humility, interconnectedness, empowerment, courage, meaning, Buddhism	Retailing of ecological outdoor clothing and apparel, leading "activist company" that aims at increasing consumer consciousness, support for environmental movements and campaigns and businesses, and promoting business transformation	Using business to alleviate environmental crisis and encouraging and supporting others to do the same (campaigns, movies, investment fund), monitoring and reducing carbon footprint, material, product and value chain innovations, participation in political activism and regenerative agriculture
Scott Bader	Creating a world in which humanity thrives without compromising the natural systems it depends on through providing essential technologies that address the challenges of a changing society, and being a trustworthy partner that harnesses the power of chemistry as a force for good	Being a part of natural environment, society, national and international community, mutual responsibility, joint ownership and asset management through democratic participation, material and spiritual development of all stakeholders, circular economy, full personal evolution, equal opportunities, participation, leading by example, dialogue, Quakerism	Production, distribution of composite materials, adhesives, special polymers, fireproof-, smoke- and toxin-resistant materials, gel coatings, trusteeship as a unique form of community ownership and corporate governance system, innovation, production, use of "The Natural Step" sustainability methodology	2036 Vision with three pillars: humanity, ecology, business, development without jeopardizing natural systems, use of safe, ethical and transparent chemical industry for public good, knowledge and profit sharing, circular business model, workforce development and cooperation with the wider society Commonwealth Strategy

(continued)

Table 5.3 (continued)

Company name	Vision	Values	Means	Outcomes
TerraCycle	Being a social enterprise that works to eliminate the idea of waste through offering a range of easy-to-use recycling platforms that help everyone to recycle everything and move away from single-use packaging	Honesty, transparency, accountability, credibility, enthusiasm, hard work, strict work ethics, creation, changing the world, everything is possible, cooperative and caring atmosphere, openness, empowerment, community, meaning, circular economy, eco-capitalism ("People, planet, profit" and "Better, greener, cheaper")	Collecting, recycling, reusing waste formerly considered non-recyclable, national-, brand-funded or customer-funded waste collection programs, close cooperation with production companies associated with global and local brands, continuous scientific research to eliminate more waste streams, partnering with millions of individuals, conscious consumers, civil and business communities collecting waste	Implementing multitude of waste collection programs, supporting 200 + million people to collect billions of pieces of garbage, donations to schools and charities, opening subsidiaries worldwide, broadcasting TV series, developing an online game Trash Tycoon, providing value-added consultancy for media, PR, social media, communication, marketing, enhancing brand/consumer loyalty and awareness raising

Source Author's construction

Value Orientations of Ecologically Conscious Business Organizations in the Hungarian Sample

This section first briefly presents the company profiles and value background of the Hungary-based ecologically conscious business organizations that participated in the sample. During the examination of their value orientations, an exhaustive exploration of the value profile of the individual enterprises was not the primary focus. Through aggregation of the interviews with fourteen businesses, the general value characteristics of the Hungarian sample were analyzed to identify similar motives and patterns.

Skanska Hungary

Sweden-based Skanska is one of the world's leading project development and construction groups, with expertise in construction, residential, and commercial property development. Skanska Property Hungary (https://www.skanska.hu/) is its Hungarian subsidiary, with several decades of experience. Its main goal is building for a better society and creating shareholder value alongside social responsibility, and creating innovative and sustainable solutions for a sustainable future for all stakeholders (employees, customers, and communities). Further core values include commitment to security, ethical and transparent operations, green and community investments, diversity, inclusion, protection of life, cooperation, joint development, and commitment to partners.

Nekedterem Hungary

Nekedterem (https://nekedterem.hu/) was founded to provide consumers with a web shop and home delivery service for high-quality fresh vegetables, fruit, and food products from local small-scale producers in Budapest and its surroundings. Its main goal is buying and selling local, artisanal Hungarian products that also meet special customer dietary needs (organic, sugar-free, gluten-free, GMO-free, lactose-free, paleo, vegan, etc.), minimizing the length of supply chain, using recyclable, biologically degradable packaging materials, and selective waste collection. Core values include offering a personal, reliable, friendly service, fostering direct relationships between producers and consumers, saving time for customers, community building.

Réthy Fashion

Réthy Fashion (http://rethy-fashion.com/) is a small family business founded by fashion designer Éva Réti with the aim of rethinking the relation between fashion and environmental protection through recycling and reusing jeans-based clothing and materials. Its main goal is to create high quality, new, innovative jeans products, combined with environmental awareness raising, the promotion of selective waste collection, social value creation, and the employment of disadvantaged people. Réthy Fashion is engaged in climate protection by fighting against global warming and striving for a circular economy.

Bio-Drog Berta

Bio-Drog Berta Ltd. (https://www.bioberta.hu/english/pages/about_us/) was founded to produce organic vegetables, herbs, and fruits. It integrates the work of 50 families who produce 30 species of plants on 70 hectares of irrigable land. Its core values cover value creation for the community, use of their own talent and skills in a novel way, producing as many innovative products as possible, utilizing the largest proportion of processed plants as possible from an excellent agricultural area, building an international reputation, and supplying products that promote the health of consumers, especially Hungarian ones.

Ecoizm/Zöldbol*t*

Ecoizm/Zöldbolt (https://www.ecoizm.com/) launched its service to provide consumers with eco-friendly products in one place (on its webshop and in two bricks-and-mortar shops). Its goal is to offer real, eco-friendly alternatives in almost all areas of everyday life that represent small ways of helping to protect the environment. Ecoizm strives for quality, not quantity, and strictly selects the items it trades. Core values include using everyday products that have some significant environmental benefits over substitute products, the continuous monitoring of innovation and the promotion of environmental awareness, use of natural ingredients, minimal use of synthetic chemicals, durability and ease of repair, pollutant- and hazardous-waste-free, recycled, recyclable, and reusable materials, minimal or natural packaging materials, locally available products, fair trade, handmade, and organic products.

ALTEO Energy

ALTEO Plc. (https://alteo.hu/?lang=en) is an energy service and trading company engaged in renewable and natural gas energy production, energy trading and bespoke energy services, and development for small and large companies. It strives to help meet climate protection goals while maintaining an appropriate cost level and security of supply. ALTEO promotes the principles of democratized energetics, customized service, and sustainable business benefits for customers. Its core values are adaptability, innovation, leading by example, efficiency, flexibility, long-term economic, environmental and social value creation, responsible corporate governance, operating ethically, protection of human life and security, equal treatment, right to a healthy environment, environmental responsibility throughout the supply chain, building lasting and mutually beneficial partnerships, and transparency.

Hajtás Pajtás

Hajtás Pajtás (https://hajtaspajtas.hu/) was the first Hungarian bicycle courier enterprise and is still the market leader. It is also engaged in civil activism to promote bicycling, a more livable environment, and a more sustainable urban lifestyle. Its core values include service based on trust, reliability, transparent and law-abiding business operations, sustainability, environmentally conscious activity, the avoidance of unnecessary pollution, and social responsibility.

Pannonhalmi Abbey Winery

Pannonhalmi Abbey Winery (https://apatsagipinceszet.hu/?lang=en) is an enterprise based on a thousand years of tradition and the Benedictine monks' values (a balance between spiritual life and physical activity, love of work, self-sustainability, education, and the dissemination of culture based on the Regula of Saint Benedict) that is attempting to revive viticulture and wine-making traditions. Its goal is also to make the nonprofit activities of the abbey (operating social, educational, and cultural institutions) economically sustainable, and to produce its own altar wine. Core values include a community based on the values of the gospel that functions well in terms of everyday life and has a positive spirit. Monastic and secular participants are organically united as regards shared values including responsibility, sustainability, preservation, and preserving resources for future generations.

NES Shoes

Designer Andrea Szilágyi graduated in Paris and founded her brand, NES Shoes (https://nesshoes.com/home/) to promote environmentally friendly shoes. Focusing on individual and customized orders and driven by sustainable practices intrinsic to the design and message, NES products are created exclusively from natural, biodegradable, vegan, recycled, and/or recyclable raw materials in an increasingly ecological way. Production is now based in Eastern Hungary at a biomass-heated manufacturing plant that also uses solar electricity from panels and strives to source local raw materials. Core values include supporting the self-expression of self-aware women and men through the provision of comfortable and sophisticated yet affordable shoes, ecological consciousness, social and individual responsibility, aesthetics and joy, and forward-looking, ever-evolving ethical manufacturing and design.

Béres Pharmaceuticals

Béres (https://www.beres-international.com/?en/) is one of the most well-known brand names in Hungary. The family-owned and managed Béres Pharmaceuticals was named after the legendary inventor, Dr. József Béres Sr. His invention, Béres Drops, a unique trace element supplement, was created in 1972 to maintain health by improving the functioning of the immune system. Core values of the company, based on the founder family's deeply felt Christian values, include the prevention of disease using natural products, human-centeredness, supporting people in need, education, culture, science, righteousness, reliability, predictability, social, national, and environmental responsibility, high quality products, perseverance, diligence, compassion, commitment, successful organization, team spirit, a transparent and efficient organization, and an attractive working environment. Béres is also engaged in eco-friendly wine production through a subsidiary.

Kör Architect Studio

Kör Architect Studio is a micro enterprise based on the personal engagement and enthusiasm of the architectural designer Attila Ertsey (http://www.ertseyattila.eoldal.hu/). The company designs ecological, sustainable buildings, and is also involved in educational activities within Hungarian higher education. It strives for an ecological approach based on Rudolf Steiner's anthroposophy and commitment to the idea of a self-governing society. It represents a complete social alternative to the prevailing social system by focusing on the freedom of spiritual life, direct democracy, and the solidarity economy. Core values also include healthier economic operations on the basis of alternative economics (not building on the principle of profit or the exploitation of natural and human resources), cooperation, a focus on the human scale, and harmony between human and environment.

Pipacs Bakery

Pipacs Artisan Bakery (https://pipacspekseg.com/) is an organic bakery that supplies healthy, additive-and-preservative-free bread. Core values of the founder-owners Ádám Fülöp and Márton Tóth and their company are human-centeredness, the material and moral appreciation of employees, avoiding the night shifts that are common to the industry, the importance of ecological values, connection to nature, respect for all the elements and community of the value chain, protection of life and health, and promoting human relationships with partners based on trust and mutual responsibility.

Pendits Vineyards and Winery

Pendits (https://www.pendits.com/) is a small family business, founded by Márta Wille-Baumkauff and her husband in Eastern Hungary, that follows the principles and values of organic, biodynamic farming, and crafts wines as a philosophy of life. Its spiritual approach based on anthroposophy means that the owners seek harmony with nature and the organic oneness of man, plants, animals, and habitat, timing work in the vineyard to natural cycles. The economy is seen as an organism that should have self-sustaining ability and autonomy. Core values also include building on regional values, products, and relationships, creating a clean, healthy product of the finest quality, social responsibility, conservation of terroir, sustainable development, and strengthening and utilizing environmental, cultural, and local community values, innovative research, and supporting family farms.

MagNet Bank

MagNet Bank (https://www.netbank.hu/en) is the largest financial institution in 100 per cent Hungarian private ownership, and has operated profitably for over two decades in Hungary. It is a commercial bank that started as a savings cooperative but became a triple-bottom-line focused values-based community bank that strives to promote sustainability (i.e., to be an ethical, sustainable, and impact-based bank), as well as environmental and social responsibility, human relationships based on respect and trust, consciousness, innovation, transparency, and human-centeredness. MagNet Bank is a member of the Global Alliance for Banking on Values and is committed to advancing positive change in the financial sector through sustainable economic, social, and environmental development, with a focus on helping individuals fulfil their potential and building stronger communities.

Radar charts of the enterprises' value profiles were drawn up (Appendix 2) based on the interviewees' responses (on a seven-item Likert scale) to the following question: how important to the operation of their business do they consider each of the thirteen ecological values identified from the literature? The figures show the differences between the businesses.

Figures 5.1 and 5.2, show more clearly what the radar charts indicate. The opinion of the fourteen Hungarian businesses is that the most important ecological values are responsibility, trust, openness to mystery, respect for ecosystems, love, temperance, and reciprocity. Respondents consider humility, a holistic approach, the intrinsic value of natural beings, natural embeddedness, and biodiversity to be important values, but less decisive. The value of non-possession appears to be unimportant to them.

Figure 5.2 shows more accurately the direction and intensity of deviations from the mean value (which takes a value of four, as indicated by the vertical line in the middle of the diagram) than other types of figures (Robbins and Heiberger 2011). In the illustration, the color red indicates a value of 1 ("least important"), while dark green represents 7 ("most important"), and dark gray indicates a lack of response, or the

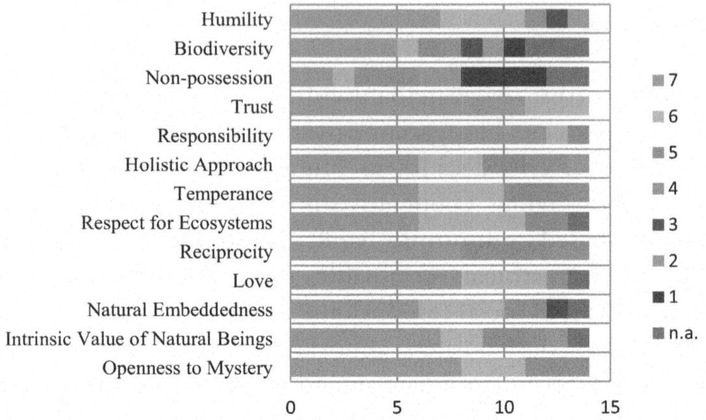

Fig. 5.1 Stacked bar chart of the importance of ecological values for selected Hungarian businesses (*Source* Author's construction)

response "not relevant." In the middle of each colored field, the number of interviewees who chose that particular value is listed.

The importance of the thirteen ecological values was also examined through content analysis of the whole texts of the interviews in order to reveal the presence of these values in the responses of the interviewees. Table 5.4 summarizes the frequency of occurrence of the ecological values identified during the content analysis. The most frequently identifiable values were responsibility, a holistic approach, and temperance. In addition, typical values included respect for ecosystems, trust, and reciprocity. The values of natural embeddedness, biodiversity, openness to mystery, humility, love and the intrinsic value of natural beings occurred rather less often. The value of non-possession was not identifiable using this method either.

The value orientations of the Hungarian businesses were also mapped using an inductive approach, in addition to the deductive method described above. During the content analysis of the transcripts of the interviews, patterns were explored that could characterize the value background, motivation, culture, and way of thinking of the given enterprise through coding and categorizing the meaningful content that could be identified in each paragraph. During the analysis and interpretation of the meaning of 36 patterns that were identified, consolidated sets were

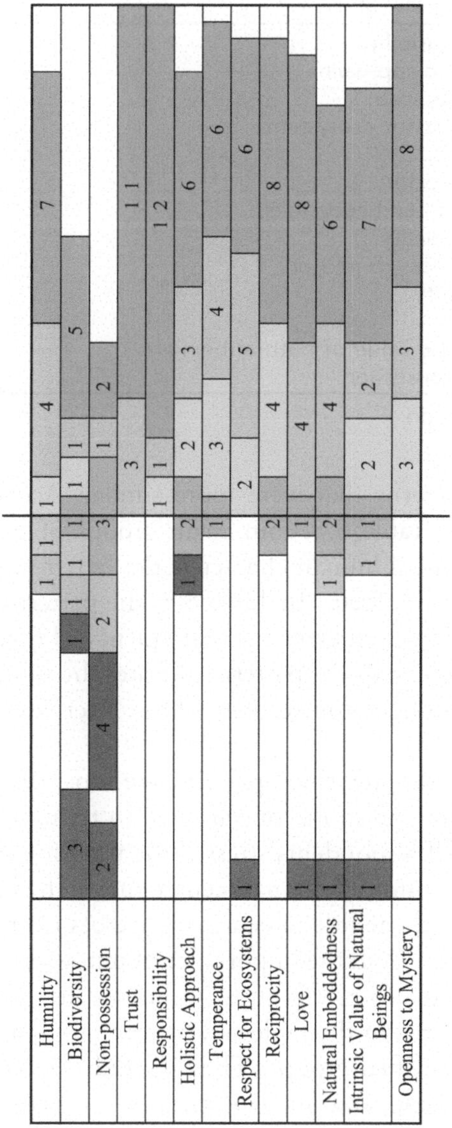

Fig. 5.2 Diverging stacked bar chart of the importance of ecological values for selected Hungarian businesses (*Source* Author's construction)

Table 5.4 Frequency of occurrence of ecological values in the interviews with selected Hungarian businesses

	Ecological value	Frequency
1	Responsibility	57
2	Holistic approach	49
3	Temperance	46
4	Respect for ecosystems	25
5	Trust	22
6	Reciprocity	20
7	Natural embeddedness	13
8	Biodiversity	11
8	Openness to mystery	11
10	Humility	10
11	Love	9
12	Intrinsic value of natural beings	8
13	Non-possession	0

Source Author's construction

formed from those patterns that were more similar. According to the clustering presented in Table 5.5, four main groups of patterns could be defined: namely, general human characteristics, environmental focus, social focus, and economic focus. In Table 5.5, the patterns are listed in order (from top to bottom) pursuant to the frequency of their occurrence (the number after the name of the pattern indicates the number of interviewees out of the sample of fourteen in whose interviews the pattern could be identified).

Based on Table 5.5, the identified patterns are most diverse in terms of human characteristics and most concentrated in terms of an environmental focus. Almost all respondents stressed the need for value creation for social and local communities, human-centeredness, the importance of human relationships, and the role of economic factors (difficulties, challenges, and success factors) and the importance of innovation and quality. Besides the creation of the former groups, an interesting phenomenon is that the lower five patterns in the table can be recognized as overarching the four previously identified groups. These include (1) consciousness, search for meaning, (2) cooperation, avoidance of competition, (3) environmental, social, and economic sustainability, (4) self-sustainability, self-management, autonomy, adaptability, resilience, and (5) organicity.

Table 5.5 Clustering of patterns identified in the interview transcripts in selected Hungarian businesses

Sample of Hungarian ecologically conscious businesses			
Human characteristics	Environmental focus	Societal focus	Economic focus
Commitment 11	Environmental consciousness 13	Social utility, local communities 13	Economic factors, need for entrepreneurial, business knowledge 14
Non-harming, non-violence 11	Education, environmental education 9	Humaneness, human relationships, human-centeredness, human scale 12	Innovation 13
Optimism, hope, gratitude 11	Recycling 5	Health, protection of life 7	Quality 10
Life philosophy, worldview 10		Culture, aesthetics 6	Value-based, ethical operation, transparency 7
Setting an example 10		Mission 6	Certification 5
Authenticity 6		Lack of social demand 6	Labor shortage 4
Dedication, perseverance 5		Tradition 2	Lack of comparative advantage 1
Negative expectation, disappointment, hopelessness 5			
Harmony with nature, connection with nature, interconnectedness 5			
Struggle, fight 4			
Self-confidence 3			
Self-realization, joy 3			

(continued)

Table 5.5 (continued)

Sample of Hungarian ecologically conscious businesses			
Human characteristics	Environmental focus	Societal focus	Economic focus
Respect 3			
Common sense, practicality 2			
Patterns overarching the four groups			
Consciousness, search for meaning 10			
Cooperation, avoidance of competition 9			
Sustainability, triple bottom line 6			
Self-sustainability, self-management, autonomy, adaptability, resilience 5			
Organicity 5			

Source Author's construction

These umbrella patterns may be seen as factors that help synthesize the operations of the businesses.

Summary

For the ecologically conscious business organizations in the international sample, the most important values are circularity, well-being and health, respect for nature and future generations, cooperation and knowledge sharing, passion, sustainability, transparency, responsibility, genuineness, honesty, credibility, accountability, setting an example, regeneration, simplicity, consciousness, and action. Values such as innovations inspired by nature, feasibility, ecology and ecosophy, a holistic approach, doing well by doing good, inspiring others, interconnectedness, diversity, empowerment, free thinking, fostering the material and spiritual development of all stakeholders, love, openness, and meaning are also important to them. Respondents also consider compassion, generosity, humility, respect for limits, solidarity, integrity, harmony, peace, equal opportunities, fearlessness, self-motivation and quality to be relevant, but these values were less emphasized, as identified during the case analyses.

For Hungary-based ecologically conscious business organizations, the following values are the most important: responsibility, holistic approach, trust, openness to mystery, respect for ecosystems, love, temperance, reciprocity, consciousness, cooperation, human-centeredness, commitment, non-harming, optimism, education, knowledge, innovation, and quality. Values such as humility, the intrinsic value of natural beings, natural embeddedness, biodiversity, authenticity, transparency, and aesthetics are important but not decisive for them. Non-possession is a value that they do not consider relevant to them at all.

In brief conclusion, the operation of the ecologically conscious business organizations in the sample under study is overwhelmingly based on similar values, and concerning their value orientations no sharp distinction can be drawn between international and Hungarian cases.

The raison d'être of the international and Hungarian business organizations in the sample is the pursuit of multidimensional (social, ecological, and economic) sustainability and the exercise of authenticity. Their basic goals often include the protection of health, the integrity of people in general, and of nature, preserving the quality of life, and supporting domestic culture, society, economy, and local communities. The businesses strive to produce high quality products and services, and do not pursue growth at all costs but rather organic development, as well as self-realization, and the expression of the personal values of the owners and managers.

Both the international and the Hungarian ecologically conscious businesses interpret success in a multidimensional way. Financial profit is not the only objective, but a means of ensuring the long-term survival of the enterprises. Real success means simultaneously harmonizing, nurturing, preserving, and restoring social and ecological values. An important element of their definitions of success is how well the businesses take into consideration the well-being of the whole stakeholder network, as defined in a wide sense.

Appendices

Appendix 1 Interview Guide for Research on the "Value Orientation of Ecologically Conscious Businesses" in Hungary

1. Characteristics of the business

    1.1. Basic characteristics of the enterprise: foundation, activities, number of employees, annual sales, economic situation.

    1.2. Does the enterprise have a written mission statement, and are there any written documents regarding its value commitment?

    1.3. How do the former relate to the personal value commitment of the founder/manager?

2. The interpretation and value orientation of ecological consciousness

    2.1 What do you understand by the term ecological consciousness?

    2.2 Are you committed to a worldview (religion, spirituality, community, …)? How do the values of this worldview relate to ecological consciousness?

    2.3 As an entrepreneur, do you have any value commitments that are not related to ecology? What is the relation between these values and ecological values?

    2.4. Please rate how important the following ecological values are in your entrepreneurial life!

Humility	0	1	2	3	4	5	6	7
Biodiversity	0	1	2	3	4	5	6	7
Non-possession	0	1	2	3	4	5	6	7
Trust	0	1	2	3	4	5	6	7
Responsibility	0	1	2	3	4	5	6	7
Holistic approach	0	1	2	3	4	5	6	7
Temperance	0	1	2	3	4	5	6	7
Respect for ecosystems	0	1	2	3	4	5	6	7
Reciprocity	0	1	2	3	4	5	6	7
Love	0	1	2	3	4	5	6	7
Natural embeddedness	0	1	2	3	4	5	6	7
Intrinsic value of natural beings	0	1	2	3	4	5	6	7
Openness to mystery	0	1	2	3	4	5	6	7

Other value(s)

0	1	2	3	4	5	6	7
0	1	2	3	4	5	6	7
0	1	2	3	4	5	6	7

3. Ecological aspects of the operation of business
   3.1. What does ecology mean in terms of the operation of your enterprise? In what areas does a "green" approach prevail, and how? (for instance, product development, new investments, production, office activities, transportation, etc.)
   3.2 In which areas is your ecological performance best, and where do you think further development and progress is needed?
   3.3 Do you have certified (environmentally friendly, organic, etc.) products? If so, why was it important to become certified?
   3.4 Does the enterprise have an environmental management system, and does it use an environmental management standard (for example, ISO 14000)? If so, what are your experiences with this? If not, do you consider it important to obtain one? If not, why is it not important to you?
   3.5 What was the main motivation for using progressive ecological practices? Where did the incentive come from? (for instance, from a manager, owner commitment, external benefits, etc.)
   3.6 How important are state regulations or subsidies in stimulating and promoting ecological and environmental activities, and what do you think of these instruments?
   3.7 How important are civil organizations, NGOs, and social support in stimulating and promoting ecological and environmental protection activities, and what do you think of these organizations/types of activity? Do you have a relationship with any NGOs? If so, what is their nature (what do they do)?
4. Competition and ecology
   4.1. How would you rate the strength of competition in your business sector?

0	1	2	3	4	5
Do not know	Very weak	Weak	Moderate	Strong	Very strong

4.2 How would you evaluate your competitors' ecological consciousness in your business sector?

0	1	2	3	4	5
Do not know	Very weak	Weak	Moderate	Strong	Very strong

4.2 In general, is ecological consciousness an advantage or disadvantage in this business sector?

0	1	2	3	4	5
Do not know	Significant disadvantage	Disadvantage	Indifferent	Advantage	Significant advantage

5. Does the ecological consciousness of a business represent an advantage?

   5.1. Does having a business with an ecological consciousness bring advantages to owners and managers?

0	1	2	3	4	5
Do not know	Definitely not	Not	Partly yes, partly no	Yes	Definitely yes

5.2 Does the ecological consciousness of a business influence the performance and motivation of employees?

0	1	2	3	4	5
Do not know	Definitely not	Not	Partly yes, partly no	Yes	Definitely yes

5.3 Do future managers/employees find businesses attractive because of their ecological consciousness?

0 Do not know	1 Definitely not	2 Not	3 Partly yes, partly no	4 Yes	5 Definitely yes

5.4 Does the ecological consciousness of a business contribute to the loyalty of customers?

0 Do not know	1 Definitely not	2 Not	3 Partly yes, partly no	4 Yes	5 Definitely yes

5.5 Does the ecological consciousness of a business have an impact on relationships with suppliers and partners?

0 Do not know	1 Definitely not	2 Not	3 Partly yes, partly not	4 Yes	5 Definitely yes

5.6 On the whole, does the ecological consciousness of a business pay off in the context of the present Hungarian economy?

0 Do not know	1 Definitely not	2 Not	3 Partly yes, partly no	4 Yes	5 Definitely yes

6. Prospects for an ecological consciousness in the Hungarian economy
    6.1. How do you rate the chances of an ecological consciousness developing in today's Hungarian economy?
    6.2. How can the economy and businesses be made more ecology-oriented?
    6.3. What kind of changes do you expect in the next 5-10-25 years with regard to the ecological consciousness of business?
7. Which other ecologically conscious businesses do you know? Who would you recommend that we include in the research?
8. Do you have any other comments or questions about the topics we have discussed?

Appendix 2 The Importance of Ecological Values for Ecologically Conscious Business Organizations in the Hungarian Sample

Radar charts of the value profiles of each business compared to the arithmetic mean and the median of the importance of values.

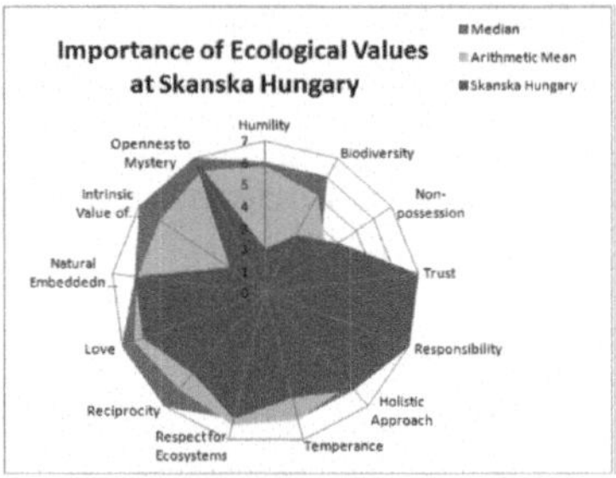

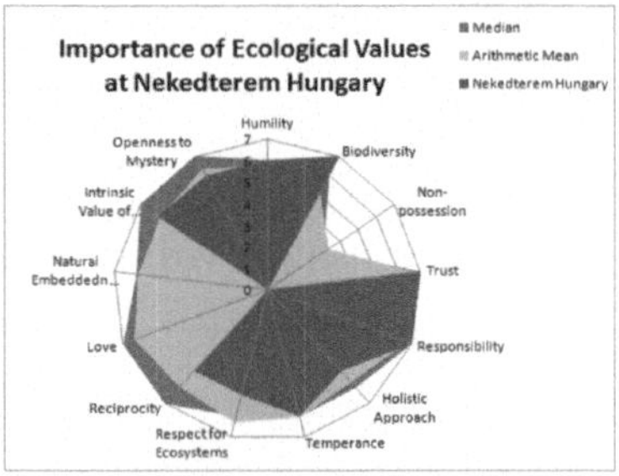

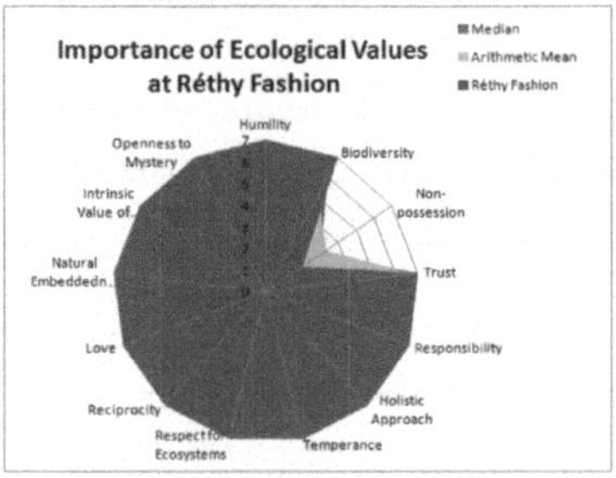

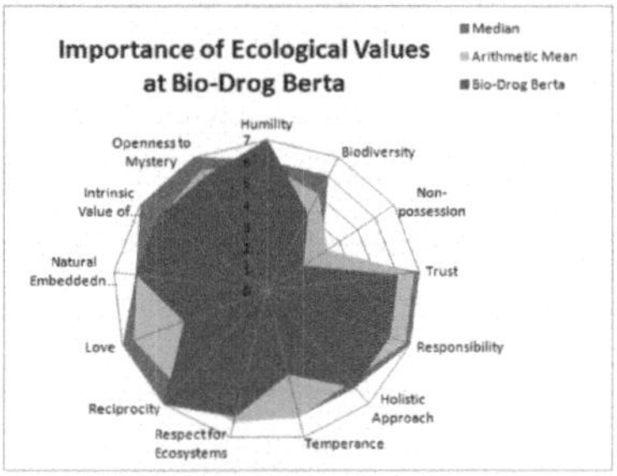

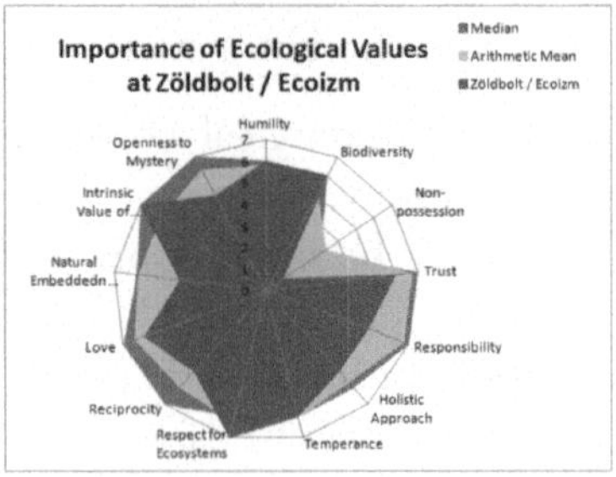

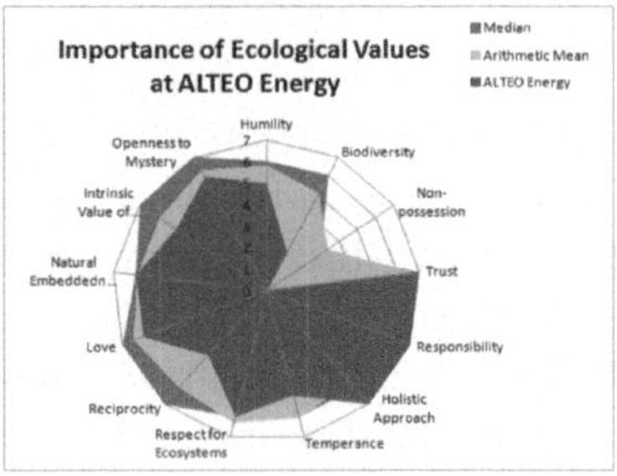

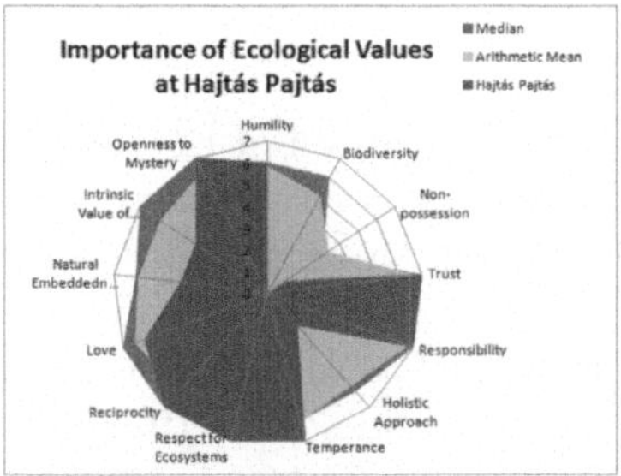
Importance of Ecological Values at Hajtás Pajtás
Median
Arithmetic Mean
Hajtás Pajtás
Humility
Biodiversity
Non-possession
Trust
Responsibility
Holistic Approach
Temperance
Respect for Ecosystems
Reciprocity
Love
Natural Embeddedn...
Intrinsic Value of...
Openness to Mystery

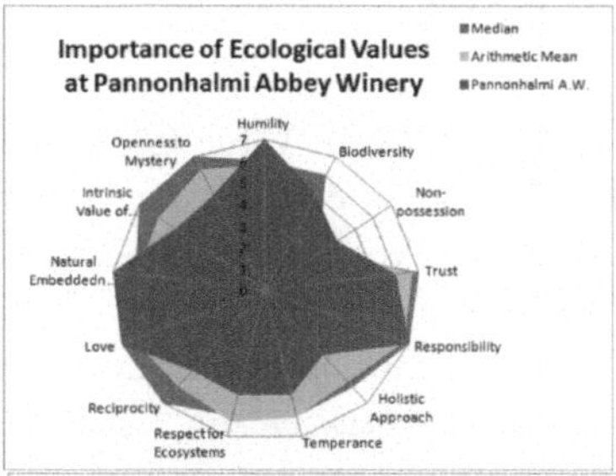
Importance of Ecological Values at Pannonhalmi Abbey Winery
Median
Arithmetic Mean
Pannonhalmi A.W.
Humility
Biodiversity
Non-possession
Trust
Responsibility
Holistic Approach
Temperance
Respect for Ecosystems
Reciprocity
Love
Natural Embeddedn...
Intrinsic Value of...
Openness to Mystery

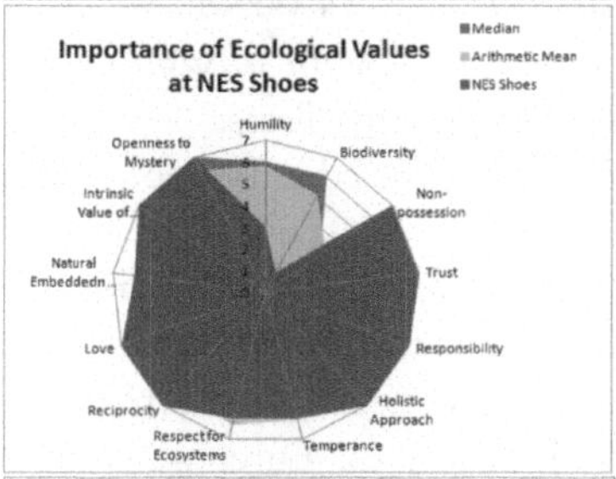
Importance of Ecological Values at NES Shoes
Median
Arithmetic Mean
NES Shoes
Humility
Biodiversity
Non-possession
Trust
Responsibility
Holistic Approach
Temperance
Respect for Ecosystems
Reciprocity
Love
Natural Embeddedn...
Intrinsic Value of...
Openness to Mystery

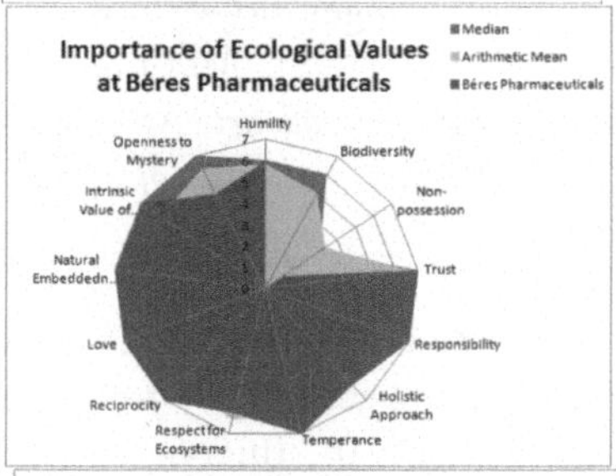
Importance of Ecological Values at Béres Pharmaceuticals
Median
Arithmetic Mean
Béres Pharmaceuticals
Humility
Biodiversity
Non-possession
Trust
Responsibility
Holistic Approach
Temperance
Respect for Ecosystems
Reciprocity
Love
Natural Embeddedn...
Intrinsic Value of...
Openness to Mystery

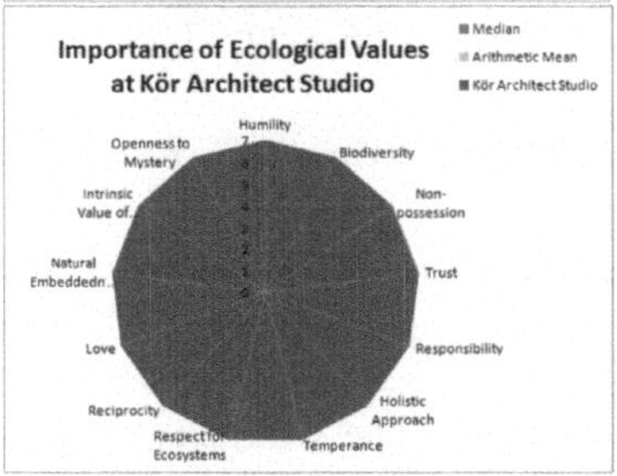
Importance of Ecological Values at Kör Architect Studio
Median
Arithmetic Mean
Kör Architect Studio
Humility
Biodiversity
Non-possession
Trust
Responsibility
Holistic Approach
Temperance
Respect for Ecosystems
Reciprocity
Love
Natural Embeddedn...
Intrinsic Value of...
Openness to Mystery

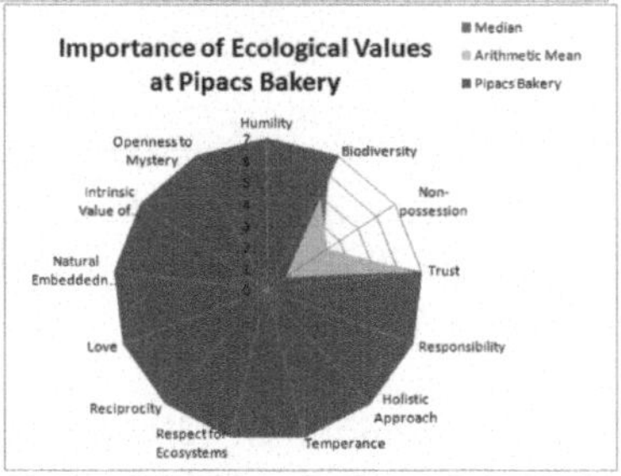
Importance of Ecological Values at Pipacs Bakery
Median
Arithmetic Mean
Pipacs Bakery
Humility
Biodiversity
Non-possession
Trust
Responsibility
Holistic Approach
Temperance
Respect for Ecosystems
Reciprocity
Love
Natural Embeddedn...
Intrinsic Value of...
Openness to Mystery

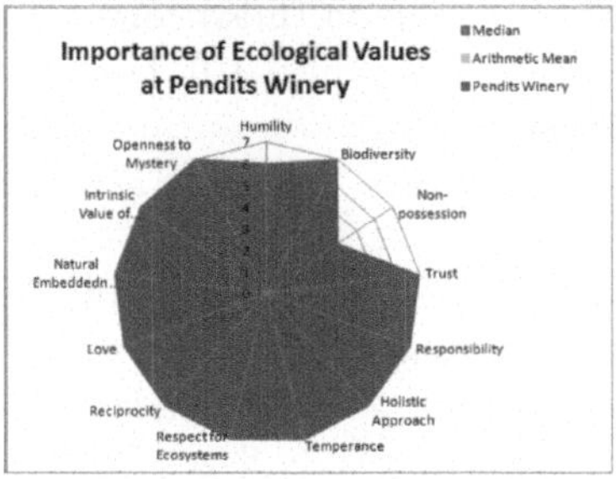
Importance of Ecological Values at Pendits Winery
Median
Arithmetic Mean
Pendits Winery
Humility
Biodiversity
Non-possession
Trust
Responsibility
Holistic Approach
Temperance
Respect for Ecosystems
Reciprocity
Love
Natural Embeddedn...
Intrinsic Value of...
Openness to Mystery

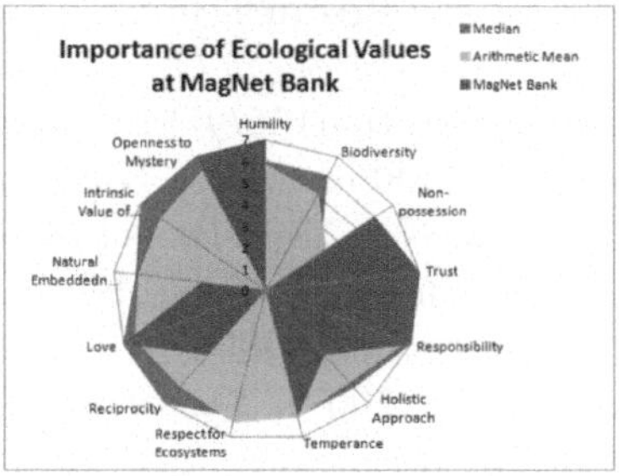
Importance of Ecological Values at MagNet Bank
Median
Arithmetic Mean
MagNet Bank
Humility
Biodiversity
Non-possession
Trust
Responsibility
Holistic Approach
Temperance
Respect for Ecosystems
Reciprocity
Love
Natural Embeddedn...
Intrinsic Value of...
Openness to Mystery

References

Allinson, R. E. (2009). Value Creation as the Foundation of Economics. In L. Zsolnai, Z. Boda, & L. Fekete (Eds.), *Ethical Prospects: Economy, Society and Environment* (Vol. 1, pp. 63–87). Dordrecht: Springer. https://doi.org/10.1007/978-1-4020-9821-5_4.

Allinson, R. E. (2011). The Ethical Producer. In L. Zsolnai (Ed.), *Spirituality and Ethics in Management*. Issues in Business Ethics (Vol. 19, pp. 53–73). Dordrecht: Springer. https://doi.org/10.1007/978-94-007-1153-2_4.

Anderson, R. C. (1998). *Mid-Course Correction: Toward a Sustainable Enterprise: The Interface Model*. Atlanta: The Peregrinzilla Press.

Babbie, E. (2008). *The Basics of Social Research* (4th ed.). Belmont: Thomson Wadsworth.

Balch, O. (2013, March 18). Natura Commits to Sourcing Sustainably from Amazon. *The Guardian*. https://www.theguardian.com/sustainable-business/natura-sourcing-sustainably-from-amazon. Accessed 8 June 2020.

Barlow, C. A. (2010). Interviews. In A. J. Mills, G. Eurepos, & E. Wiebe (Eds.), *Encyclopedia of Case Study Research* (pp. 495–499). Thousand Oaks: Sage. https://doi.org/10.4135/9781412957397.

Boyatzis, R. E. (1998). *Transforming Qualitative Information: Thematic Analysis and Code Development*. London: Sage.

Bowen, G. A. (2009). Document Analysis as a Qualitative Research Method. *Qualitative Research Journal, 9*(2), 27–40. https://doi.org/10.3316/qrj0902027.

Cassell, C., & Symon, G. (2004). Introduction: The Context of Qualitative Organizational Research. In C. Cassell & G. Symon (Eds.), *Essential Guide to Qualitative Methods in Organizational Research* (pp. 1–10). London: Sage. https://doi.org/10.4135/9781446280119.

Chouinard, Y. (2005). *Let My People Go Surfing: The Education of a Reluctant Businessman*. New York: Penguin Group.

CNBC. (2012, June 24). *I Am American Business: Tom Szaky*. CNBC. https://www.cnbc.com/id/100000748. Accessed 10 June 2020.

Creswell, J. W. (2007). *Qualitative Inquiry and Research Design. Choosing Among Five Approaches* (2nd ed.). Thousand Oaks: Sage. https://charlesbickenheuserdotcom.files.wordpress.com/.../creswell_2007_qualitative_inquiry_and_research_design__choosing_among_five_approaches__2nd_edition.pdf. Accessed 4 March 2018.

FAO—Food and Agriculture Organization of the United Nations. (2006). *Livestock a Major Threat to Environment—Remedies Urgently Needed*. http://www.fao.org/newsroom/en/news/2006/1000448/index.html. Accessed 7 June 2020.

Fereday, J., & Muir-Cochrane, E. (2006). Demonstrating Rigor Using Thematic Analysis: A Hybrid Approach of Inductive and Deductive Coding and Theme Development. *International Journal of Qualitative Methods., 5*(1), 80–92. https://doi.org/10.1177/160940690600500107.

GlobeScan. (2019). *The 2019 GlobeScan/SustainAbility Leaders Survey* (Report). https://globescan.com/wp-content/uploads/2019/07/GlobeScan-SustainAbility-Leaders-Survey-2019-Report.pdf. Accessed 7 June 2020.

Green Monday. (2020). https://greenmonday.org/en/. Accessed 6 June 2020.

Hawken, P. (1993). *The Ecology of Commerce: A Declaration of Sustainability*. New York: HarperBusiness.

Houdini. (2018). *Planetary Boundaries Assessment 2018: This Is Houdini*. https://api.houdinisportswear.com/storage/2A69199BFCBA925CC9260D61F41301EA566C760FB9A727B5DABB2C330C13D1BC/08df8496f36f49f0bb821fdeafdd775e/pdf/media/e5eec5e201b242e9a2aa14aba9c3b696/Houdini_Planetary_Boundaries_Assessment_2018.pdf. Accessed 6 June 2020.

Houdini. (2020). https://www.houdinisportswear.com/en/. Accessed 6 June 2020.

Hsieh, H.-F., & Shannon, S. E. (2005). Three Approaches to Qualitative Content Analysis. *Qualitative Health Research, 15*(9), 1277–1288. https://doi.org/10.1177/1049732305276687.

Hunyadi, L., Mundruczó, G., & Vita, L. (1997). *Statisztika [Statistics]*. Budapest: Aula Kiadó [in Hungarian].

Interface. (2019). *Annual Report 2019*. https://s22.q4cdn.com/139673446/files/doc_financials/2019/ar/tile20191229_10k_web.pdf. Accessed 7 June 2020.

Interface. (2020). https://www.interface.com/US/en-US/homepage. Accessed 8 June 2020.

Jacob, A. (2012, August 28). Scott Bader—A Long Term Commitment to Composites. *Reinforced Plastics Magazine*. https://www.materialstoday.com/composite-industry/features/scott-bader-a-long-term-commitment-to-composites/. Accessed 9 June 2020.

Jamieson, S. (2004). Likert Scales: How to (Ab)Use Them. *Medical Education, 38*(12), 1217–1218. https://doi.org/10.1111/j.1365-2929.2004.02012.x.

King, N. (2004). Using Interviews in Qualitative Research. In C. Cassell & G. Symon (Eds.), *Essential Guide to Qualitative Methods in Organizational Research* (pp. 11–22). London: Sage. https://doi.org/10.4135/9781446280119.n2.

Krippendorff, K. (2004). *Content Analysis: An Introduction to Its Methodology* (2nd ed.). Thousand Oaks: Sage.

Kvale, S. (1994). Ten Standard Objections to Qualitative Research Interviews. *Journal of Phenomenological Psychology, 25*(2), 147–173. https://doi.org/10.1163/156916294x00016.

Kvale, S. (1996). *Interviews: An Introduction to Qualitative Research Interviewing*. Thousand Oaks: Sage. https://books.google.hu/books/about/InterViews.html?id=lU_QRm-OEDIC&redir_esc=y. Accessed 12 April 2020.

Kvale, S. (2006). Dominance Through Interviews and Dialogues. *Qualitative Inquiry, 12*(3), 480–500. https://doi.org/10.1177/1077800406286235.

Lapadat, J. C. (2010). Thematic Analysis. In A. J. Mills, G. Eurepos, & E. Wiebe (Eds.), *Encyclopedia of Case Study Research* (pp. 925–927). Thousand Oaks: Sage. https://doi.org/10.4135/9781412957397.

Largest Companies. (2020). http://www.largestcompanies.com/company/Houdini-Sportswear-AB-227636. Accessed 7 June 2020.

Lázár, I. (2011). Spirituality and Human Ecosystems. In L. Zsolnai (Ed.), *Spirituality and Ethics in Management*. Issues in Business Ethics (Vol. 19, pp. 95–105). Springer. https://doi.org/10.1007/978-94-007-1153-2_6.

Magnuson, J. C. (2007, August). Pathways to a Mindful Economy. *Society and Economy,* 29(2), 253–284. Sustainability and Sufficiency: Economic Development in a Buddhist Perspective. https://doi.org/10.1556/SocEc.29.2007.2.8.

Maréchal, G. (2010). Constructivism. In A. J. Mills, G. Eurepos, & E. Wiebe (Eds.), *Encyclopedia of Case Study Research* (pp. 220–225). Thousand Oaks: Sage. https://doi.org/10.4135/9781412957397.

Mason, J. (2002). *Qualitative Researching* (2nd ed.). London: Sage. www.sxf.uevora.pt/wp-content/uploads/2013/03/Mason_2002.pdf. Accessed 12 April 2020.

Maxwell, J. A. (2013). *Qualitative Research Design: An Interactive Approach* (3rd ed.). London: Sage.

McLeod, S. A. (2008). *Likert Scale.* https://www.simplypsychology.org/likert-scale.html. Accessed 12 April 2020.

Miles, M. B., Huberman, A. M., & Saldana, J. (2014). *Qualitative Data Analysis: A Methods Sourcebook* (3rd ed.). Thousand Oaks: Sage.

Mills, A. J., Eurepos, G., & Wiebe, E. (Eds.). (2010). *Encyclopaedia of Case Study Research*. Thousand Oaks: Sage. https://doi.org/10.4135/9781412957397.

Natura. (2020a). https://www.naturabrasil.fr/en-us/. Accessed 8 June 2020.

Natura. (2020b). https://www.naturabrasil.com/. Accessed 8 June 2020.

Natura & Co. (2020). *Creating the Best Beauty Group FOR the World* (2019 Report). https://naturaeco.com/report_2019_en.pdf. Accessed 8 June 2020.

Ooley, A. (2013, March 11). *15 Quotes to Inspire Small Business Owners from Yvon Chouinard*. LogoMaker. https://www.logomaker.com/blog/2013/03/11/15-quotes-to-inspire-small-business-owners-from-yvon-chouinard/. Accessed 9 June 2020.

Organic India. (2020a). https://www.organicindia.com/. Accessed 8 June 2020.

Organic India. (2020b). https://organicindiausa.com/. Accessed 8 June 2020.

Parvati Magazine. (2017, April 17). Community: TerraCycle, with Tom Szaky. *Parvati Magazine*. http://parvatimagazine.com/2017/04/community-terracycle-tom-szaky/. Accessed 10 June 2020.

Patagonia. (2020). http://eu.patagonia.com/hu/en/home/. Accessed 9 June 2020.

Pataki, G., & Takács-Sánta, A. (Eds.). (2005). *Természet és gazdaság. Ökológiai közgazdaságtan szöveggyűjtemény [Nature and Economy. Key Texts of Ecological Economics]*. Budapest: Typotex Kiadó [in Hungarian].

Patton, M. Q. (2002). *Qualitative Research and Evaluation Methods* (3rd ed.). Thousand Oaks: Sage.

Robbins, N. B., & Heiberger, R. M. (2011). Plotting Likert and Other Rating Scales. In *JSM Proceedings, Section on Survey Research Methods* (pp. 1058–1066). Alexandria: American Statistical Association. www.montana.edu/msse/Data_analysis/Likert%20Survey%20Graphs.pdf. Accessed 12 April 2020.

Scott Bader. (2019). *Annual Report 2018*. https://www.scottbader.com/wp-content/uploads/Annual-Report-2018.pdf. Accessed 9 June 2020.

Scott Bader. (2020). https://www.scottbader.com/. Accessed 9 June 2020.

Simkiñ, J. (2020). *Ernest Bader*. http://spartacus-educational.com/JbaderE.htm. Accessed 9 June 2020.

Stan, L. (2010). Content Analysis. In A. J. Mills, G. Eurepos, & E. Wiebe (Eds.), *Encyclopedia of Case Study Research* (pp. 225–230). Thousand Oaks: Sage. https://doi.org/10.4135/9781412957397.

TerraCycle. (2018). https://www.terracycle.com/en-US/. Accessed 5 July 2018.

TerraCycle. (2020). https://www.terracycle.com/en-US/. Accessed 10 June 2020.

The Economic Times. (2017). *Organi India Eyes Rs 500 Crore Turnover by FY20 End*. https://economictimes.indiatimes.com/industry/cons-products/fmcg/organic-india-eyes-rs-500-crore-turnover-by-fy20-end/articleshow/62240529.cms. Accessed 8 June 2020.

WCED—World Commission on Environment and Development. (1987). *Our Common Future*. Oxford, NY: Oxford University Press.

Zimberoff, L. (2017, June 12). *This Guy Is Trying to Break Hong Kong's Meat Addiction*. Bloomberg. https://www.bloomberg.com/news/articles/2017-06-12/this-guy-is-trying-to-cure-hong-kong-s-meat-addiction. Accessed 7 June 2020.

Zsolnai, L. (2001). Ökológia, gazdaság, etika [*Ecology, Economy, Ethics*]. Budapest: Helikon Kiadó [in Hungarian].

6

Comparative Analysis of Ecologically Conscious Business Models

This chapter analyzes the business models of ecologically conscious business organizations in the international and the Hungarian sample. The elements and characteristics of the business models are presented in six main dimensions, as defined by Chesbrough and Rosenbloom (2002). These dimensions include value propositions, market segment, cost structure and profit potential, structure of the value chain, position within the value network, and competitive strategy. This approach makes it possible to compare the results of the case analyses of the international and the Hungarian enterprises.

Ecologically Conscious Business Models in the International Sample

In this section, the business models of ecologically conscious enterprises in the international sample are presented in a uniform way.

A. Ócsai, *Ecologically Conscious Organizations*, Palgrave Studies in Sustainable Business In Association with Future Earth,
https://doi.org/10.1007/978-3-030-60918-4_6

Green Monday

Value propositions: Green Monday's activities are aimed at helping combine the seemingly small but easy-to-implement steps of individuals who are looking to change their lifestyles to create global-level change. The method it promotes supports and indicates reductions in the carbon footprint, while leaving individuals free to decide when and how to reduce their meat consumption. For instance, people can stop eating meat for a full day once a week, or every lunchtime. They can also reduce the amount of meat they consume during meals, or omit red meat, which has a high environmental impact, from their diet. An important element of Green Monday's value proposition is that consuming less meat has a significant impact on the planet as well as on humans. The production of plant-based food may have a carbon footprint that is only about 3 per cent of meat production, and use a tenth of the water. It can help reduce global hunger, because using one unit of land for crop production can provide more than ten times as many people with proper nutrients than if that same unit is used to produce meat. A plant-based diet can have the following beneficial effects on human health: it can reduce the risk of lung and kidney problems, breast cancer, strokes, heart attack, cardiovascular disease, infertility, osteoporosis, type-two diabetes, and obesity. Additionally, it increases the intake of antioxidants, flavonoids, fiber, polyphenols and micronutrients, and the number of healthy life years due to the beneficial effects of the former (Green Monday 2020). Founder David Yeung also considers business sustainability to be important and is therefore a proponent of the triple-bottom-line concept. He wants to make his mission-based business economically successful while making favorable environmental and social impacts (Zimberoff 2017).

Market segment: Green Monday is a platform that has both a social and a business segment. The social branch, led by the Green Monday Foundation, engages in awareness-raising, dissemination, and knowledge promotion campaigns about climate change, Earth Day activities, restaurant network development, and food aid campaigns to promote sustainable lifestyles. The business side consists of three main areas. (i) As an active market player, Green Monday intends to expand its sustainable food retail supply through an initiative called Green

Common. Its network of stores sells plant-based food products and sustainable household items, and provides advice on how to prepare plant-based food at home. (ii) Green Monday Solutions offers sustainability and social responsibility consulting (involving the themes of sustainable development, CSR, employee loyalty, marketing and business development, and the introduction of Green Monday products and services) to domestic and international companies (restaurants, event organizers, food producers, supermarkets, and marketing companies). (iii) Green Monday Ventures is a private equity fund for impact investing that supports innovative and ethical business ideas whose business models, operations, products and services address global climate change, food safety, health, or animal welfare issues (AVPN 2016; Green Monday 2020).

Cost structure and profit potential: The business side of Green Monday has become successful and the company has been recognized with a number of business awards since its inception (Green Monday 2020). Partner companies have also benefited from the successful operation of Green Monday and the successful dissemination of a sustainable lifestyle. For example, England-based PizzaExpress, which has 20 stores in Hong Kong, has seen double-digit growth in vegetarian menu sales on Mondays. As a side effect, the company has also boosted its total daily turnover on Mondays. The vegetarian community has also evolved significantly, as proven by the increase in the number of vegetarian restaurants in Hong Kong from 130 to 250 from 2013 to 2017. Success is also reflected in company finances. Green Monday's total retail and reseller sales approached 12 million USD in 2017, and have since increased significantly. The sales and profit outlook is favorable, as the global market for alternative protein rose to about 2.2 billion USD in 2019, compared to a global meat market of 1.7 trillion USD. Market forecasts estimate that the alternative meat market could be worth between 90 billion USD and 470 billion USD by 2040. Green Monday is now present in five countries in Southeast Asia, in the United Kingdom, and in the United States. Its products are available in ten countries and will be in ten more within the year (Zimberoff 2017; Green Monday 2020; Yusof 2020).

Structure of the value chain: according to the concept of Green Monday, it is not enough to shed light on things that should be changed; feasible alternatives must also be provided in order for real change to take place in people's behavior and lifestyles. Important elements of the value chain are therefore research and development and knowledge sharing, implemented in part through the Green It Yourself community program that provides sustainability advice regarding housekeeping and food preparation and organizes community programs (with a focus on recipe databases, cooking tips, cooking competitions, and blogger meetings) (AVPN 2016; Green Monday 2020). The Green Knowledge & Research Center aims to raise awareness about sustainability and share best practices, mainly in the Hong Kong region. Its research interests range from environmental and behavioral change associated with climate change, cultural phenomena, sustainable consumption, innovation, and environmental policy to regional development. It shares its latest results and news with its stakeholders through international events and a monthly newsletter (Green Monday 2020). Its research and development activities also include the development of new plant-based foods and meals. As part of its Right Treat initiative, the type of food innovations are studied that will bring long-term benefits to the planet, humanity, and animals alike, and will not impose additional liabilities and suffering on other beings and future generations. The first major achievement of this program was the development of a mushroom-, rice-, and pea-based pork substitute called Omnipork that took place over a year and a half with Canadian researchers. However, Green Monday does not only innovate by itself. Among others, it financially supports research by the California-based company Beyond Meat, which makes plant-based burgers. Green Monday also supports Perfect Day, a cell-based farming enterprise that produces dairy products from cell cultures, and a food-design-based technology company called Lighter (AVPN 2016; Zimberoff 2017; Mannion 2018; Green Monday 2020).

Food and other products sold in Green Common stores are sourced from strictly sustainable and ethical suppliers. The main sourcing principles are meat-free, healthy, and fair trade. Green Monday prefers local products from Hong Kong's organic producers, social enterprises, small-, and medium-sized enterprises and fair trade organizations (AVPN 2016; Green Monday 2020).

Green Monday Ventures can be seen as a seed investment fund that invests in companies that serve social or environmental causes (reducing the ecological footprint, increasing health and well-being, and supporting individuals and businesses to become sustainable), which are also capable of generating a profit. In addition to financial investments, in many cases Green Monday has also supported companies through appropriate forms of synergy. For California-based Beyond Meat, for example, providing access to Asian commercial channels has represented significant help for their development (AVPN 2016).

Green Monday's mission is actively supported by many renowned and popular personalities, from domestic and international artists and government officials to opinion leaders. Its clients include a number of major financial institutions, including the Bank of China and HSBC, public utility companies like Hong Kong International Airport, real estate management businesses, food companies such as Beyond Meat and Del Monte, retail businesses like Quiksilver and Procter & Gamble, and service companies such as eBay and Google. It also serves more than 1000 restaurants mainly from the region, but also others in the USA, Peru, the UK, Italy, Australia, and Japan, and over 2000 schools in 33 countries. Around 600 domestic universities such as the University of Hong Kong, Chinese University of Hong Kong, Hong Kong Baptist University, and Tsinghua University, and numerous foreign universities like Columbia University, Washington University in St. Louis, University of California Los Angeles, and Wharton School are among its partners. Green Monday also supplies governmental organizations such as the Hong Kong Office of Health, the United States Consulate in Hong Kong and Macao, and the Canadian and Italian Chamber of Commerce (Green Monday 2020).

Green Monday's value chain also includes the Green LUCK Banquet program, which works with event management companies, food aid, and shark rescue organizations to make events healthy, sustainable, and free from food waste. By developing event management culture, the program aims to reduce the carbon footprint of events through providing vegetarian food, eliminating food waste, serving the community (offering leftover food to Hong Kongese families in need), and not harming the world (by reducing waste and protecting sharks by avoiding traditional dishes made from shark fins) (Green Monday 2020).

Position within the value network: Green Monday's social and business branches work together across a wide range of areas. According to its own surveys conducted in cooperation with market researcher Ipsos Hong Kong, the reputation of Green Monday and its mission rose between 2014 and 2016 from 22 to 45 per cent among 15–24-year-olds, and 22 to 33 per cent of the total female population (percentages indicate the proportion of respondents who recognized the company name). In 2020, an independent survey showed that more than 45 per cent of people in Hong Kong know about the company's activities (Green Monday 2020; Yusof 2020). Another significant impact is that, due to Green Monday's activities, by 2016, 1.6 million people, (22 per cent of Hong Kong's total population—where per capita meat consumption is among the highest in the world—had become "flexitarians," meaning people who mostly eat a vegetarian diet but sometimes consume meat (AVPN 2016; Hackett 2019). Figures from 2008 showed that only 5 per cent of people in Hong Kong were flexitarians. By 2020, the proportion of vegans and flexitarians in Hong Kong had risen to 34 per cent. More than three million people worldwide have joined the Green Monday movement through taking a "Pledge to go Green Monday." All these steps and changes have reduced CO_2 emissions by 900,000 tons a year, which would have required 40 million trees to absorb. In addition, the lives of 300 million animals (cattle, pigs, and poultry) have been saved along with 375 billion liters of water—enough to supply more than 500 million people (Green Monday 2020; Yusof 2020).

Green Monday's activities were recognized with significant awards as early as in the year after its foundation. These included the "Best Idea of the Year 2013" award and the East Week "Outstanding Corporate Strategy Award." In 2014, founder David Yeung received an award for being one of the "100 Most Creative People in China" from *Fast Company* magazine, and Green Monday received the magazine's "Top 100 Most Innovative Companies in 2014 China" award. In 2015, Green Monday also won Fast Company's "Top 50 Most Innovative Companies in China" award, the title of one of the "Asian 100 Pioneers" from Purpose Economy, Conscious Company Magazine's "17 Rising Social Entrepreneurs" award, and the "Ten Outstanding Young Persons in Hong Kong" award. In 2018, the chief executive officer was named "Social Entrepreneur of the Year" by the World Economic Forum and Schwab Foundation. Green Monday was awarded "Company of the Year" by the animal rights organization People for the Ethical Treatment of Animals in 2019 (Green Monday 2020; Yusof 2020).

Competitive strategy: When Green Monday was established, there were only a few vegetarian restaurants in Hong Kong. Since its inception, it has not only expanded the supply with its own business portfolio, but also inspired others to launch vegetarian restaurants and food services by taking advantage of growing awareness about sustainable lifestyles and diets. However, Green Monday did not primarily see this as an increase in the strength of the competition, but as the spread of its concept and values, which they see as a positive development, meaning they are able to work with an increasing number of partners. Opportunities for cooperation have been consciously sought from the outset. One of these involved joining the global Meatfree Monday movement, which has made significant strides in reducing meat consumption in countries including the United States and Great Britain through more than 20 worldwide campaigns. Through its corporate partners, Green Monday is involved in many sectors, and has the primary target of connecting different stakeholders throughout the entire value chain and ecosystem of the sustainable food industry (from producers and traders to consumers) and developing mutually beneficial forms of collaboration (AVPN 2016; Green Monday 2020).

Houdini Sportsware

Value propositions: The most important element of the value propositions of Houdini is sustainability, which does not influence the company's operations as a separate functional area, but is an integral part of all its activities. For Houdini, sustainability is not the opposite of good business, but rather a precondition for it. Nature has intrinsic value and provides the blueprint for transforming the current business system into a circular one. Nature is the most important source that makes it possible to earn a living, so Houdini intends to do everything to protect it and improve its current state (Houdini 2020).

Market segment: Houdini is a men's, women's and children's clothing retailer. It specializes in the production and distribution of functional clothing in an ethical and sustainable manner. It offers its products primarily to ecologically conscious customers to whom sustainability is important. In addition to ecological and social principles, it wants to reach all consumers who like outdoor sports through offering high quality and timeless product design (Houdini 2020; Largest Companies 2020).

Cost structure and profit potential: In the financial year ending April 2019, annual sales increased by 11 per cent to 16.8 million EUR, indicating a doubling in the growth rate compared to the previous year. The average growth rate of revenue was around 20 per cent in previous years. Profit had been stable at around 2 per cent before 2017. It then dropped to a loss of 6.6 per cent in 2017, which was likely due to the increase in expenses associated with growing sales, a significant increase in assets (by 33 per cent to 9.5 million EUR), the number of employees (from 37 to 42), and rising current liabilities. Earnings before taxes were less than 1 per cent in 2018 and minus 1 per cent in 2019. The amount of current liabilities has fluctuated, but as turnover has grown steadily, it is now at a healthy ratio. Due to stable demand, brand popularity, industry recognition, and the company's continuous innovation activity, financial indicators can be expected to remain acceptable and turnover and asset expansion can continue on a path of organic development (Largest Companies 2020).

Structure of the value chain: Based on a holistic approach, Houdini seeks to roll out the principle of sustainability along its entire value chain. This effort is manifested in its business model innovations, mainly within the field of the collaborative economy, the goal of which is to decouple growth from the use of resources. Houdini has introduced several services for extending product lifetime, such as "Care," "Repair," "Reuse," and "Rental." In its brick-and-mortar retail stores and an e-commerce channel, through the application of green building design the company inspires, educates, assists, and guides its community of consumers to engage in better product care, provides a repair service, and creates a marketplace for the reuse of second-hand yet fully functional Houdini products. Houdini considers sharing and product-as-service solutions to be alternatives to conventional ways of consuming. Through its rental initiative, Houdini provides access to otherwise expensive products as an alternative to ownership while eliminating unnecessary resource demand for fabrics that may be used less frequently (Krarup et al. 2015; Houdini 2018, 2020).

The principle of sustainability is strictly applied from the product design phase onwards. For each product idea, and in several phases during product development, Houdini utilizes a Designer's Checklist, involving asking the questions: Does this product deserve to exist and is it versatile and durable enough? Is nothing added that is not needed? Will the product last long enough, age with beauty, and be easy to repair? And is there an "end-of-life" solution for the product? Houdini also adheres to strict principles (weather resistance, safety, visibility, and timelessness) when choosing from its own self-developed color set, so that its customers can use their comfortable, functional, and eye-catching products for as long as possible (Houdini 2018, 2020).

The environmental footprint of clothing products largely depends on the raw materials that are used. Since the fall of 2019, Houdini's new products have been made of fabrics that are 100 per cent recycled, recyclable, renewable, biodegradable, or sustainable Bluesign® certified. Sixty-three per cent of that collection was produced in a completely circular way, and Houdini's goal is to be 100 per cent circular by 2022 (Houdini 2020). Polyester-based fabrics are widely used due to their durability, fast drying, moisture repellency, reusability, easy handling, and favorable properties due to the lower energy and water requirements of production. In collaboration with a Japanese company called Teijin, Houdini has been using polyester fibers from a fully closed-loop recycling system (Eco Circle®) for its products since 2007 (Krarup et al. 2015). In the case of natural fabrics, merino wool, which has the most favorable properties in terms of retaining heat and repelling moisture and bacteria of nearly all natural materials, has been used since 2011. For Houdini's wool products, full traceability of wool origin was achieved in 2016, which is an important milestone in its sourcing policy that is associated with strict animal welfare standards. In order to preserve biodegradability and reusability, natural fiber fabrics are blended during manufacture solely with natural fibers (e.g., silk), not synthetic fibers (Houdini 2020). A project called the Houdini Menu was initiated in 2016 to prove that the properties of the company's materials are also favorable in terms of sustainability, during which second-hand Houdini clothes made of 100 per cent renewable organic materials were composted. Using this compost, vegetables and spices were grown that were then served as part of a menu at the world's first vegetarian reception of its kind in April 2017 (Di Ciancia 2017). In the fall of 2018, Houdini also opened a composter for worn-out sportswear in Rosendals Garden, Stockholm, to test on an ongoing basis how its natural clothes can be transformed into healthy soil (Houdini 2020). In the design of materials, Houdini strives to use the simplest and fewest possible ingredients to improve their recyclability. In order to utilize the residue generated during cutting, a project called Scrap Me Up was launched in 2010. During this event, a series of a limited number of pieces was made from materials previously classified as waste (Krarup et al. 2015). Of the various fabric treatment materials (used for improving water repellency, and with antibacterial effects), after eight years of research and experimentation, highly harmful fluorinated substances (PFOA, PFOS) were entirely replaced (by 2018). During these activities, Houdini worked closely and continuously with raw material suppliers. The company co-creates, when necessary, new materials that are not protected by patents. Such open-source innovation thus helps the use of ecological materials to gain ground (Houdini 2018, 2020).

True to its strict environmental principles, Houdini exercises great care in selecting its manufacturing partners and manufacturing processes. The company has consciously decided to form partnerships with a minimal number of suppliers and manufacturers so that environmental- and human-rights-related conditions can be managed (monitored two to five times a year) through long-term, close, and stable forms of cooperation. Almost all Houdini products are now made in Europe (in the Baltics, Poland, and Portugal), with only 3.5 per cent being produced in China. Since 2019, all materials have been recycled, renewable, recyclable, biodegradable, or closed life cycle materials. Fabrics are sourced mainly from Japan, Italy, USA, Lithuania, Taiwan, and Sweden. Houdini's suppliers are not Fairtrade-certified, but, according to the company, its own internal standards are stricter than Fairtrade standards, so Houdini does not plan to join the Fairtrade certification scheme (Krarup et al. 2015; Houdini 2018, 2020).

Attitudes toward customers are also in line with Houdini's set of principles. The company tries to redefine the concept of consumption by reducing overconsumption as much as possible. Since 2012, Houdini has allowed its consumers to try out outerwear products (jackets and trousers) by renting them on a short-term basis. Conscious customers can consider whether it is necessary to buy and possess those products, or if it is sufficient to just rent them for a while. With this approach, fewer products are enough for more customers, while the value of use and enjoyment is not reduced. For a similar reason, Houdini has also launched a second-hand clothing sales service in its stores, which it occasionally links to charitable offerings. Customer appreciation is also increased by providing a lifetime warranty for all Houdini products. If a product is damaged through the customer's own fault, it is replaced at a lower price than a new one. However, after a while products wear out from regular use, and if they can no longer be repaired, they can be dropped off at Houdini stores and partner stores to be included in Houdini's own recycling system (Houdini 2020).

Position within the value network: Houdini is a leading representative and supporter of sustainability principles across its entire value network. It has continuously worked to transform consumption patterns, and its products are increasingly being rented, reused, and repaired. Besides these efforts, based on the Stockholm Resilience Center's concept of Planetary Boundaries, Houdini has been working with the organizations Albaeco and Mistra Future Fashion to develop an open-source, holistic environmental assessment system that will allow any business to measure its performance in line with the above-described concept and the UN Sustainable Development Goals (SDGs). The goal is to eliminate all negative effects in the shortest possible time, which can be achieved through knowledge sharing and innovation involving interdisciplinary collaboration. In line with these aspirations, in 2018 the first ever corporate Planetary Boundaries analysis was created. This kind of assessment makes visible factors that are often omitted. Adding social boundaries to the nine planetary boundaries highlights not only the ecological areas that it is important to consider, but also the conditions that influence the well-being of people working within the value chain. To further increase the transparency of its environmental performance, Houdini publishes a Planetary Boundaries Assessment report every three years, and details about its seasonal sustainability status twice a year. These statistics show the current status of all Houdini products regarding what proportion have been made from recycled, recyclable, biodegradable and renewable, Bluesign®-certified and circular fabrics (Houdini 2018, 2020).

Houdini's achievements have been recognized. In 2010, CNBC named Houdini one of the 25 most creative companies in Europe for its work on sustainability. Svenskt Sportforum awarded the title "Woman of the Year in the Sports Industry" to Houdini's CEO Eva Karlsson in 2011. In 2012, Houdini won the Swedbank Sustainability Prize for their commitment to sustainability and profitable growth. In recent years, several of its products and raw materials have won sustainability awards (the ISPO Eco Achievement 2014, Scandinavian Outdoor Award Sustainability Gold 2015, ISPO Award Gold 2015 and 2020). In 2017, Houdini received one of the most prestigious awards in the fashion industry, the "H&M & Elle Conscious Award," for its commitment to sustainability and its role in renewing the industry. In 2017, Eva Karlsson was winner of the "Pontus Schultz Award for a humane economy" for uniting function and sustainability and adapting research on Planetary Boundaries to make it relevant to Houdini, while also making a profit and inspiring others. In 2018, Karlsson was deemed the winner of the "NMC Award for Sustainable Leadership" for her wholehearted commitment to sustainability and striving to work within Planetary Boundaries (Houdini 2020).

Competition strategy: Houdini has repeatedly confirmed and demonstrated through its operations that its sustainability-related work occurs in close cooperation with other industry players. For example, in a multi-annual research project, the company worked together with raw material suppliers, industry partners (including Bergans, Norrona, and OrganoClick) and a higher education institution (the University of Borås) to develop a revolutionary and innovative material to replace fluorinated carbon-based fabric treatments that are extremely harmful to the environment. It is part of Houdini's strategy to make its discoveries as widely available as possible, so, for example, patents are not used to protect the materials the company has developed in order to make them freely available and usable. Building a sustainable future is possible only through knowledge sharing and innovation via interdisciplinary cooperation. Houdini emphasized this at a sustainable fashion seminar held in the Swedish parliament, for example. Eva Karlsson talked about Houdini's experience with environmental issues and her expectations in relation to decision-makers, including a number of fashion industry players, researchers, and politicians. In the otherwise highly competitive outdoor clothing industry, at the international level (which includes the companies Columbia, Patagonia, and Timberland) and in Sweden (Boomerang, Filippa K), several players are focusing their business models on sustainability and inspiring each other, too (Krarup et al. 2015; Di Ciancia 2017; Houdini 2020).

Interface

Value propositions: The main goal of Interface is to become the most valuable company in the world that offers modular carpets and related services, while leading a world-changing sustainability movement in parallel with eliminating its negative environmental impacts and developing activities that regenerate nature. Even when Interface was founded, there was a focus on making a change, as Ray Anderson began manufacturing modular carpets, which were at that time unknown. In 1994, inspired by Paul Hawken's book *The Ecology of Commerce* (Hawken 1993), he also started on a major transformation of the conventional industrial business model ("take-make-waste") into a renewable, cyclical, more gentle one. Anderson questioned the principles on which petroleum-based carpet manufacturing were based by acknowledging that the traditional business model exploits the Earth and destroys symbiotic ecosystems. He decided that Interface had to become an environmentally sustainable and ultimately nature-regenerating company. The new focus has been on the radical redesign of processes and products and the introduction of new technologies and systems that reduce or even eliminate waste and emissions while increasing the use of renewable materials and energy. Interface's Mission Zero defines the target of eliminating all negative environmental impacts by 2020. Anderson described the process of creating a completely sustainable company as being like climbing a mountain ("Mount Sustainability") that has seven faces, all of which must be scaled. The seven key areas on which Interface focuses its development-related efforts and monitors its performance are the following: (i) eliminating all types of waste related to all activities; (ii) eliminating the use of toxic substances in all products, vehicles, and facilities; (iii) operating its buildings with 100 per cent renewable energy; (iv) redesigning processes and products to close the technological cycle through recovering materials and using bio-based materials; (v) transporting people and products in a more efficient way so that waste and emissions can be eliminated; (vi) creating a culture based on the principles of sustainability to improve the lives of all stakeholders (employees, partners, suppliers, customers, investors, and communities); and (vii) developing a new business model that demonstrates and nurtures the value of sustainability-based business (Gingerich 2016; Interface 2020a).

Market segment: Interface is a global flooring company that specializes in the design, production, and sales of carpet tile and resilient flooring, including luxury vinyl tile and rubber flooring. It is a global leader in the commercial carpet tile industry, accounting for around a third of the approximately 39 billion USD global commercial flooring market. Interface has recently entered into the residential and luxury vinyl flooring segment, and, through acquisition of nora Holding GmbH in 2018 (which also operates in the market segment of rubber flooring for customers mainly in healthcare, life sciences, and education), has more than doubled its customer base in a few years (Interface 2019, 2020b; Grand View Research 2020).

Cost structure and profit potential: The market segments served by Interface are associated with the largest margins for any type of flooring, and the company's products represent a premium category in terms of design, sustainability, and innovation, with the potential for more profit than the industry average. So far, most of the clients of Interface have been architects, designers, and end users, which earns more money for Interface than if it primarily traded with distributors. Since 2017, Interface has been executing a market diversification strategy to increase its presence and market penetration for modular carpet in non-corporate office market segments such as government, education, healthcare, hospitality, and retail space. As a result, in 2019 its net sales increased by almost 14 per cent to over 1.3 billion USD, net income grew by more than 57 per cent to 79 million USD, and earnings per share also significantly increased by nearly 7 per cent. Radical innovations that have steadily and substantially reduced the company's negative environmental impact over the years have also helped cut material and energy costs. The example of Interface indicates that a sustainable business model that supports a livable future has the potential to be financially sustainable (Interface 2019, 2020b; Grand View Research 2020).

Structure of the value chain: During the radical sustainability turn in 1994, Interface did not have the opportunity to rely on past experience, so the company used external knowledge. It set up an expert group of researchers, environmental activists, and entrepreneurs called the Eco Dream Team. These individuals helped Interface to create a business-friendly sustainability framework and keep this under review. The Swedish The Natural Step methodology, developed by Dr. Karl-Henrik Robert to preserve the quality of terrestrial living systems, was also used to create a new business model. According to this concept, in a sustainable society, in order to preserve nature, the concentration of substances derived from the Earth's crust (carbon dioxide, heavy metals, and minerals), substances produced by society (such as antibiotics and endocrine-disrupting chemicals), and the extent of physical destruction (deforestation and ground-water depletion) must not be increased. Additionally, nothing should place limits on human health, potential for impact, knowledge, impartiality, and meaning (The Natural Step 2014, 2020; Interface 2020a).

One of the essential elements of Interface's value chain is radical innovation driven by the principle of sustainability in the field of product and process design and development. Its research and development department is recognized by industry peers, and generated 17.8 million USD in 2019, an increase of more than 27 per cent on 2017. Interface actively collaborates with developers of fabric, yarn, and carpet backing suppliers. Many of its new products and technological innovations were the first in the world to solve industry problems or improve a technological step by making it cleaner, faster, or more environmentally friendly. For example, the environmental footprint of the company's TacTiles glue-free installation system is more than 90 per cent less than that of traditional carpet adhesives. The company's "i2" products, inspired by nature (biomimicry), vary in terms of patterning and coloring so that the tiles can be installed in any order and orientation. In this way, their harmonious appearance is maintained during wear and module replacement over time, and they can be installed faster, repaired more easily, and recycled. Accordingly, they generate approximately 90 per cent less waste than traditional broadloom carpets. As a result of the circularity of the production processes, the carbon footprint of Interface's products has been reduced by more than 50 per cent since 1994, and in 2017 they created the world's first carbon-negative carpet prototype. To offset the remaining carbon footprint and greenhouse gas emissions, the company works throughout the total product life cycle with raw materials that are carbon neutral, as verified by an independent certifier. It also supports emission reduction and offsetting projects worldwide, such as reforestation efforts, anti-deforestation campaigns, wind farms, and domestic heating modernization. Expanding into new market segments, Interface insists on adhering to strict principles. In 2017, the company entered the market for modular resilient flooring (customers can combine fully integrated hard floor and soft carpet coverings on demand). Using this combined system, the materials used for each module can be produced in a controllable way and completely reused at the end of their life through Interface's recycling program, called ReEntry. The company holds numerous United States and foreign patents and multiple trademarks for its products and production processes (Lampikoski 2012; Interface 2019, 2020a).

Interface has eight manufacturing locations in seven countries on four continents (USA, Netherlands, UK, Thailand, China, Australia, and Germany), so it can provide local solutions to its customers in all markets. The raw materials needed for production are also sourced from regional and global external sources to increase security of supply, and recycled fabrics are used for the bottom layer of carpets. An ISO 14001 environmental management system is in place. Four of its product groups have the GreenCircle Certified Environmental Facts label, and 99 per cent of products have an Environmental Product Declaration certified by an independent certifier that authentically describes the related ingredients and environmental impacts, supported by comprehensive life cycle analysis. All Interface products are certified by the United States Green Building Council according to the Leadership in Energy and Environmental Design (LEED) assessment system that transparently demonstrates and certifies the environmental impact of buildings and construction activities. Since 2011, Interface has been actively involved in the development of a new product certification (a "Health Product Declaration") which provides full transparency through disclosing the ingredients in products, and encourages their further development. As a result, the use of halogen- and heavy-metal-based flame retardants, fluorinated stain-repellent coatings, aqueous yarn paints, and liquid carpet adhesives has been eliminated in standard products manufactured in the United States (Lampikoski 2012; Interface 2019, 2020a).

At the end of 2019, Interface was employing more than 4100 employees worldwide, 59 per cent of whom were engaged in manufacturing, with the help of 225 temporary staff. There are also trade unions in several countries, and management maintains a good, active relationship with them. In addition to environmental sustainability, Interface takes the principles of ethical business seriously, with a special focus on respect for human rights and labor standards. Its code of ethics includes anti-corruption and anti-bribery measures, as well as supplier clauses. A hotline and online interface for reporting fraud and ethical misconduct anonymously and confidentially are also available to employees (Interface 2019, 2020a).

The majority of Interface customers (51 per cent of them at the end of 2019) are office building investors or tenants. The company also supplies educational institutions, the hospitality sector, healthcare institutions, retail and financial enterprises, governmental customers, and individual households. The principal geographical markets are the Americas, Europe, and Asia Pacific. In 2019, these areas accounted for approximately 57, 29, and 14 per cent of total net sales, respectively (Interface 2019, 2020b).

Position within the value network: Interface is one of the most innovative companies in the world, with a sincere commitment to sustainability and design. Important recognition of this is the fact that Interface has been the only company to be mentioned, for over 20 years, as being among the best companies for sustainability performance in The GlobeScan-SustainAbility Leaders Survey. Ray Anderson's work and Interface's environmental performance and purpose-driven culture have been recognized many times. From these awards, just a few are highlighted here: in 1996 Ernst & Young's Entrepreneur of the Year award; in 2007 *Time* magazine's Heroes of the Environment award; in 2010 the American Society of Interior Designers' Design for Humanity Award; and in 2016 Ethical Corporation, Responsible Business Awards: Best Company (GlobeScan 2019; Interface 2020a).

Interface sets an example to other market players through its activities and performance in order to help create a viable future. The company demonstrates that it is possible to operate a business model that is carbon neutral or even carbon negative. The results of Interface's Mission Zero so far speak for themselves. Since 1996, the company has reduced its greenhouse gas emissions by 96 per cent, the amount of waste-to-landfill by 92 per cent, water intake by 89 per cent, and the carbon footprint of its products by 69 per cent. Eighty-nine per cent of its energy comes from renewable sources, and 54 per cent of all raw materials used are organic or made of recycled materials. Its sustainability mission, called Climate Take Back, has defined goals that even more ambitious. In addition to having zero negative environmental impacts, Interface wants to change the prejudice against carbon dioxide so it is no longer considered an "enemy" but a resource. The company also strives for revolutionary industrial transformation that can create a better future for humanity, and regenerate the climate control capacity of the biosphere (Interface 2020a, b).

Competitive strategy: Interface operates in a highly competitive global market that includes a large number of players, even after significant consolidation in recent years. The company is a global leader of commercial flooring solutions, but several of its competitors (including Milliken,

Mohawk, Tarkett Tandus Centiva, Shaw, and Bentley) are working in more market segments and may have greater financial capacity. However, Interface is serving an increasing number of segments with hard and soft surface flooring, which generate the largest margins. Its market value has expanded from four to nine billion USD in a couple of years, and it can now successfully compete in terms of design, sustainability, and innovation. The principal competitive factors in Interface's markets are brand recognition, quality, design, service, broad product lines, product performance, marketing strategy, pricing and sustainability. In most of these, Interface has a competitive advantage, so premium prices and industry-leading margins appear to have been secured for the company for the coming years. In addition, Interface's deep commitment and decades-long effort and successful practice of ecological sustainability clearly differentiate and highlight the company, enhance the brand, and represent a strategic advantage (Interface 2019, 2020b).

Natura

Value propositions: Brazil-based Natura's vision is to become a group of global brands with a local and global presence through its responsible operations, caring relationships, and high-quality ethical products and services. The members of this group, as a community committed to building a better world, have better relationships with themselves, others, nature, and with everything as a whole. Natura's mission is to contribute to improving the state of the world by building on its commitment to transparency, sustainability, and well-being. Based on its core values—a close relationship with nature, science and technology—, Natura works to expand and mobilize its network. In addition, the company strives to develop creative solutions for a life inspired by beauty, happiness, and sustainability. Natura recognizes that the source of life is nature, and this provides inspiration and creativity for all the activities of the company. Natura, therefore, turns to nature with great love. The company studies and utilizes both traditional and state-of-the-art knowledge because the products of the best scientific and technological research are essential for making high-quality products. Natura nurtures relationships so that all stakeholders who share similar values can join its mission. The company's basic goal is to have the greatest possible positive impact during its operation and the smallest possible negative one (Natura 2020a, b, c).

Natura established the Natura & Co. global cosmetics group in 2017. At that time the former was a collaboration of three similarly committed brands (Brazilian Natura, Australia-based Aesop, and The Body Shop, headquartered in the United Kingdom) dedicated to creating a positive economic, social, and environmental impact, and co-creating value in all of its businesses, brands, and geographical regions around the world. In line with the spirit of its motto, "Nourish through intelligent interactions," Aesop pays special attention to details, and keeps the importance of maintaining a diversity of needs and sensory pleasure in mind. It strives to display this care in all its products through intellectual commitment, and respect for environmental conditions and the wholeness of life. The Body Shop seeks to fight for a fairer and more beautiful world by offering high quality, naturally inspired products that are produced ethically and sustainably. According to the principles of the founder, Anita Roddick, the company wants to use commerce to change the world and make business a force for good. The Body Shop has been engaged in championing equality, helping women achieve financial independence, sourcing natural ingredients, cooperating with farmers and suppliers in a fair manner, and helping local communities develop. The company has been campaigning against animal testing for cosmetics for more than three decades. In 2019, Natura announced its acquisition of the US-based Avon, which concluded in January 2020. The acquisition expanded the group with an iconic beauty brand that is recognized world over for its strong purpose, business model based on female entrepreneurship and empowerment, powerful relationship-based selling model, and heritage in relation to bringing break-through innovation to the mass market (Natura 2020a, b; Natura & Co. 2020).

Market segment: Natura is present in three major market segments: fragrances, cosmetics (beauty and body care), and gifts. Natura's main market is Brazil but through its group of global brands—Natura & Co.—the company has global reach, and is considered to be the world's fourth-largest multi-channel, direct-selling global beauty giant. The global market value of beauty products increased to more than 150 billion USD in 2019, and its steady rise is expected to continue during the coming years. The biggest global beauty companies include L'Oréal, Unilever, The Estée Lauder Companies, Procter&Gamble, Shiseido, Coty, Louis Vitton Moët Hennessy, Beiersdorf, and Johnson&Johnson. Natura's special market segments are natural and organic cosmetics and premium cosmetics, both of which make up around a quarter of the whole market, with above-average growth expectations of about five to 6 per cent. Geographically, North America and Asia Pacific are the dominant markets, accounting for about 60 per cent of the total market, in which areas Natura has been an increasingly important player in combination with its partner brands. Brazil is the home market for the company, where it has maintained its market-leading position (with market share of 16 per cent in 2019). Natura is followed by the Boticário Group, Unilever, Procter&Gamble and L'Oréal (Melo 2018; Alves 2020; Natura 2020c; Natura & Co. 2020; Shahbandeh 2020, Technavio 2020).

Cost structure and profit potential: Following challenging collaboration among its businesses in diverse regions, in 2019 Natura & Co.'s consolidated net revenue increased by almost 8 per cent to 3.6 billion USD, while EBITDA improved by 7.5 per cent to nearly 500 million USD. As a result, the parent company Natura Cosméticos S.A., headquartered in Brazil, took in more than 2.2 billion USD, thereby growing by almost 7 per cent. The annual sales of subsidiaries also grew significantly (The Body Shop by more than 6 per cent to more than one billion USD, and Aesop by over 22 per cent to 325 million USD, with an improvement of 30–40 per cent in their EBITDA ratios). In Natura's fiftieth anniversary year, collaboration between the three major cosmetics brands thus continued on favorable financial terms.

Nonetheless, the consolidation of the organizations, the revitalization of the business model, and the strengthening of growth potential still required further efforts, so Natura refreshed its strategic pillars. The goals are now to strengthen the power of the brand, pursue greater differentiation and innovation in its product categories, integrate online and offline direct selling, and accelerate digital transformation and entry into international markets to promote scalable growth. With the acquisition of Avon, such synergies permit the group of brands as a whole to invest in the expansion of each brand, particularly in areas such as research and development, digitalization and marketing. Natura & Co. also has greater influence in terms of advocacy of its main causes, including women's empowerment, climate action, the banning of animal testing in cosmetics, and local community development.

As innovation and marketing are key success factors in the beauty cosmetics market, research, and development, and advertising expenses play an important role in driving growth and profitability. In order to keep up with these trends, Natura has continuously been increasing its investment in innovation, which grew from 2.2 to 2.4 per cent of net revenue to over 200 million USD in 2019. The company also initiated an omnichannel strategy to simultaneously implement e-commerce, relationship selling, and traditional retail. In addition, in January 2020 Natura & Co. began trading on the New York Stock Exchange to further improve its financial conditions. Based on these factors and favorable global and domestic market forecasts, Natura's expansion and profit potential seem to be feasible (Alves 2020; Natura 2020c; Natura & Co. 2020; Technavio 2020).

Structure of the value chain: Natura's aim is to create a cyclical production system inspired by nature that is able to reproduce and regenerate itself. Natura wants to become a company that creates a positive impact that not only neutralizes the negative effects of its operations, but also creates value throughout its entire network of relationships. The following results have been achieved in product design, product development, and operations through Natura's "Standing Forest," "More Beauty, Less Waste," and "Every Person Matters" initiatives: Natura has been carbon neutral since 2007, and emission offsetting includes the impact created throughout the value chain until 2018. The company invested over 450 million USD in the Amazon region between 2010 and 2019, thereby helping support the livelihood of more than 5100 supplier families and local communities, non-governmental organizations, and public authorities and conserve rainforests. These efforts have contributed to the conservation of 1.8 million hectares of forest land, which area is equivalent to half the size of Holland. Natura has banned animal testing related to all products and its exclusive raw materials since 2006, and 80 per cent of its portfolio is vegan. In 1984, as the first such initiative in the world, Natura introduced refillable packaging. In Brazil, the company's product packaging now contains 50 per cent recyclable materials, almost 9 per cent post-consumer recycled material, and the half of the volume of waste generated from packaging is recycled in a reverse logistics process. The number of women in management positions grew from 30 per cent in 2017 to over 40 per cent in 2019, and the plan is to reach 50 per cent in 2020. The company allocated more than eight million USD to supplier communities for purchasing inputs and benefit sharing and training, and 7 per cent of its Brazilian work force is disabled. Natura has constantly been improving the income of its consultants and has organized an educational platform for them. The company also aims to increase consumer awareness through its brands, so product information shows the environmental and social impact of products bought via e-commerce (Natura 2020a, c).

Natura only had direct sales until 2012. It then acquired a more balanced sales system, complemented by Aesop and The Body Shop brands and their stores, franchise and wholesale partners, and online platforms. The expansion of the company into a global brand group also had an impact on the geographical area they supply. Natura, which was present in only seven countries in 2012, by 2020 was selling the group's products in more than 100 countries. Among the sales channels, the brick-and-mortar store network has developed dynamically due to the presence of subsidiaries. Starting from a few dozen fully owned Natura shops at the beginning of the decade, by 2019 Natura had 490 stores in ten countries (including franchise stores), while Aesop was operating 240 stores in 23 countries, and The Body Shop about 3000 retail locations in more than 70 countries. In 2019, Natura alone was responsible for 6800 "co-workers," of whom 5000 were working in Brazil, along with 1.8 million personal and online consultants in relationship selling. In the same year, the Natura & Co. group had more than 40,000 employees and associates, and more than 6.3 million consultants and representatives in over 100 countries worldwide. E-commerce is of great importance for the future of the cosmetics industry, and the number of Natura consultants connected to the company's digital platform reached 1.6 million, 680,000 virtual stores having been opened. This increase in the share of e-commerce will be supported by the experience and success of Aesop and The Body Shop in this field and the focus on digitizing Avon's business, as planned by the group (Natura 2020c; Natura & Co. 2020).

Natura & Co.'s corporate governance structure underwent significant changes in 2019 following the Avon acquisition. It led to the creation of the Natura & Co. Holding Company, which took over full control of both Avon and Natura Cosméticos S.A., which in turn controls Aesop and The Body Shop as subsidiaries. The Board of Directors also was complemented with Avon representatives. Via this international group of brands, it should be possible to exploit significant synergies while maintaining the autonomy of the four brands. Accordingly, the four brands will continue to have their own leadership, while the "Group Operating Committee," comprising the chief executive officers of the respective business units, will be responsible for the maintenance of group synergies (Natura & Co. 2020).

Position within the value network: Natura's efforts to operate in an environmentally and socially responsible manner have been recognized in many ways, of which only a few can be mentioned here. Reductions in the company's greenhouse gas emissions and combating climate change are due to the Natura Carbon Neutral Programme that started in 2007 and were recognized by the United Nations Global Climate Action Award in 2019. From the 670 projects that were submitted, Natura was the only Brazilian company featured on the list of 15 winners. The company has been featured on the Canadian media and research company Corporate Knights' Global 100 ranking of the most sustainable companies for 11 years. This list assesses around 7500 companies in 21 countries, and is announced annually during the World Economic Forum at Davos. Since 2004, Natura has been listed on the São Paulo stock exchange Corporate Sustainability Index. The index was developed with the support of the World Bank, the Brazilian Ministry of the Environment, and a number of environmental organizations to demonstrate the sustainability of its member companies based on economic efficiency, environmental sustainability, social justice, and corporate governance. Natura, the only company in the market segment for personal products, has been listed on the Dow Jones Sustainability Index for emerging markets for seven years. Only one-tenth of the 800 largest companies in the Standard & Poor's Global Broad Market Index can be included in the index based on their advanced economic, environmental, and social sustainability practices (S&P Global 2020; Natura 2020c; Natura & Co. 2020).

Natura has been a "B Corp" since 2014, which certifies its commitment to promoting positive economic, social, and environmental impacts. The company was awarded Best for Environment three times, and Best for Changemaker in 2019. Natura was listed in fifth place in the GlobeScan-SustainAbility Leaders Survey, among the best sustainability companies (including Unilever, Patagonia, IKEA, Interface, Danone, Nestlé, Marks & Spencer, Tesla, and BASF). Natura is the most well recognized regional sustainability leader in Latin America, and the only emerging market company to appear in the top ten. For seven years, the Ethisphere Institute, a global organization committed to enhancing business practices, has deemed Natura to be one of the most ethical companies in the world. Chief executive officer João Paulo Ferreira of Natura & Co. Latin America was listed among the ten business leaders with the best reputation in Brazil. Natura does not conduct animal tests, and is thereby certified with the Leaping Bunny certification from the organization Cruelty Free International. The Union for Ethical BioTrade has also attested to the sustainability of the natural ingredient supply chain for the Ekos product line (GlobeScan 2019; B Lab 2020a; Natura 2020c).

Since 2000, Natura has been reporting in accordance with the Global Reporting Initiative standard, the first Latin American company to do so. The company presents, in a transparent manner, the year's results and progress in line with the United Nations' Sustainable Development Goals objectives and its own long-term sustainability plan 2050 Sustainability Vision. Since 2016, Natura has disclosed its negative environmental impacts according to Environmental Profit and Loss methodology. In 2019, its externalities represented 6.8 per cent of its net revenue, a slight decline compared to 2018. Since the first calculation, which was based on 2013 data, the accumulated gain in efficiency in EP&L/Net revenue has been 1.8 percentage points. The valuation of the company's social impacts in the form of Social Profit and Loss started in 2019 among its consultants and supplier communities. Following these achievements, Natura intends to develop its Integrated Profit and Loss assessment to express its environmental, social, and human externalities in an integrated way to support strategic decisions (Natura 2020b, c).

Natura's mission involves serving society and leveraging positive socio-economic impact in its network through promoting education, women's rights, and healthcare. One way of doing this has been investing all the profit from the sale of the Crer Para Ver non-cosmetic product line, launched in 1995, into supporting children's education. This work has been promoted by Instituto Natura (set up in 2010) to further improve the results of earlier initiatives. This includes supporting school projects, education, the training and development of teachers, civil servants, and consultants. In 2019, in Brazil and the Latin American region, almost 100,000 consultants, nearly 10,000 schools, more than 46,000 teachers and coordinators, and over 1.5 million students benefited from this program (Natura 2020c).

Within the group Natura & Co., each brand is committed to social and environmental responsibility. To highlight a few of the recent related achievements, the following may be mentioned: Adding up the brands' contributions so far, over one billion USD has been donated to the most important women's causes, such as women's empowerment, entrepreneurship, and well-being. Since the inception of the Aesop Foundation in 2016, it has donated over three million USD to 30 charitable projects in Australia aimed at promoting literacy and storytelling. Aesop has also transitioned over 70 per cent of its plastic product packaging range into recycled plastic. In 2019, The Body Shop launched a Community Fair Trade Programme in partnership with plastic waste pickers in India, especially women, to incorporate more than 250 tons of recycled plastic into packaging, which amount is expected to reach 900 tons within two years. Last year, The Body Shop joined Natura as a B Corp, and Aesop was also in the process of being certified. To help employees prepare for environmental, social, and business challenges, the brands provide their associates and leaders with sustainability, purpose-driven leadership, and customer care training. They also strive to pay a fair income and living wage to the members of their networks (B Lab 2020d; Natura & Co. 2020).

Competition strategy: In the 1970s and 1980s, the Brazilian cosmetics market was relatively closed to imports. The competitors of Natura were local multinational companies such as Unilever that were not deterred by the country's political instability and hyperinflationary economy. This situation until the early 1990s favored Brazilian companies, which provided local customers with high-quality products. Due to the consolidation of the economy and globalization, consumer markets changed rapidly; new consumer groups with greater purchasing power appeared, and the number of companies that wanted to serve them increased within a short time. In times of intensifying competition, economies of scale, globalized operations, a high level of product development and marketing expenditure were the criteria for success. Natura's main competitor in the direct sales segment was Avon, which is now part of the group. In the retail segment the Boticário Group, Unilever, Johnson & Johnson, Procter & Gamble; and in terms of selective sales channels, L'Oréal, Nivea, Louis Vuitton and Chanel, have been the most important market players. Today, the competition perceived by Natura has intensified in both domestic and international markets, as its competitors sell products with similar functionality. Products of competitors may also appear within Natura's direct sales channels because consultants can sell products from the brands of different companies. Nevertheless, Natura has been the market leader in its largest market in Brazil based on its commitment to environmental and social sustainability and continuous innovation, and respect for and protection of Brazil's values and strong brands. A differentiated strategy of maintaining close relationships via the omnichannel shopping experience of customers and innovative technologies also supports the company's competitive advantage. Becoming a global group of similarly strong and environmentally and socially responsible beauty brands has further increased Natura's potential to be successful both locally and globally (Jones and de Pinho 2006; Melo 2018; Alves 2020; Natura 2020c; Natura & Co. 2020; Shahbandeh 2020, Technavio 2020).

Organic India

Value propositions: Organic India aims at achieving social, environmental and economic sustainability and is committed to the production of genuine organic food and products. It has a unique business model that strives to create benefits for all stakeholders through close-to-nature, sustainable organic farming practices that serve and conserve nature and support the livelihoods and well-being of farmers and tribal "wild-crafters" in rural India. Organic India works with thousands of small family farmers who are engaged in sustainable organic farming on more than 20,000 hectares in seven states of Central and Northern India. Organic India is among the most geographically extensive organizations in the country. Its products symbolize the chain of interconnectedness between Nature, producers, and consumers, which the organization completes by supporting environmental and social sustainability and offering training and a dignified life for farmers, and contributing to the health, happiness, and well-being of consumers (Organic India 2017, 2020a, b).

One important commitment of Organic India is supporting and promoting regenerative agriculture. The goal of the company is not only to produce high-quality organic crops, but also to reverse the degradation of the natural environment. It seeks to improve the condition of land by enriching biodiversity and restoring soil fertility. To this end, Organic India continuously trains its partners, farmers, and tribal wild-crafters about the principles and practices of organic, renewable, biodynamic, and traditional Indian (*vriksha ayurveda*) agriculture, which treats each piece of land as a unique living organism. No synthetic chemicals, genetically modified plants, or radiation are used in its farming activities. However, the following gentle technologies are applied: comprehensive soil fertility management, seed collection, maintaining the diversity of species, composting, water treatment, crop protection and crop rotation, and consideration of lunar and other natural cycles during planting and harvesting. These techniques renew local ecosystems through carbon sequestration and improving water and soil conditions, thus also positively affecting the global ecosystem. By using these methods, more than 4000 hectares of chemically heavily contaminated land had been made fertile again by 2017 (Organic India 2017, 2020a, b).

Market segment: All of the products of Organic India are organically certified. Originally, the company used to make teas and herbal preparations, although its product range now includes a number of other products such as spices, ginger, seeds, beans and cereals, and fresh vegetables. Its main product segments are tulsi teas and tea blends, herbal preparations, and other packaged foods (including ghee, coconut oil, honey, stevia, and apple cider vinegar). The products are sold in 25 of its own shops and 15,000 India-wide partner stores, and online. Organic India also exports to more than 40 countries, accounting for 60 per cent of its annual turnover. Its largest foreign markets are the United States (where a subsidiary has been operating with B Corp certification since 2015), Canada, Europe, the Middle East, and Australia (ASSOCHAM – Ernst & Young 2018; B Lab 2020b; Organic India 2020a, b).

Cost structure and profit potential: From the 1990s onwards, the global market for organic products (food, beverages, textiles, health maintenance, and beauty products) has been growing almost 60 per cent faster than the market for conventional products. This can be mainly attributed to a rise in living standards, growing consumer awareness, and government subsidies. In addition to the countries most engaged in organic production (Australia, Argentina, and China) and consumption (USA, Germany, and France), India is among the world leaders in terms of the number of organic farmers (India is first, with more than 830,000 farmers) and size of area used for growing herbs (after Finland and Zambia, India is third with 4.2 million hectares). The size of the Indian organic market was about 570 million USD in 2018, which may triple by 2020, mainly due to a significant increase in exports, as domestic consumption is still low (1 per cent of total consumption). In addition to this favorable growth potential, the margin on organic products is also above average—ranging from 10 to 40 per cent more than conventional products. Key to Organic India's success, in addition to operating faithfully in line with its core values, is the growing health consciousness of consumers. The company expects further growth in this consciousness and an increase in domestic demand, so annual turnover may rise from 55 million USD in 2017 to 70 million USD by 2020. The successful development of Organic India may also be supported by the planned expansion of the product range, and opening up to new segments (organic skin and body care products) (*The Economic Times* 2017; ASSOCHAM – Ernst & Young 2018; Organic India 2020a, b).

Structure of the value chain: The value chain of Organic India is based on the philosophy of the "whole herb," which is potent and full of life. Herbs are complex, synergistic mixtures of hundreds of compounds (nutrients, minerals, and vitamins) that contain complex "information," as well as natural mechanisms that mitigate harm to health. When plants are used in their entirety, they have a beneficial balancing effect on the human body, unlike when their ingredients are utilized after artificial decomposition into individual ingredients. Four decades of scientific research have proven this fact, which was already known from the ancient Vedic wisdom. Organic India therefore uses whole plants in their purest form for its products. All its ingredients are organic, hand-picked, and locally processed. Owing to advanced processing methods and drying technology, the content of herbs may be efficiently preserved, so that they can be used in the creation of products of the best quality, efficiency, and purity on the market (Organic India 2017, 2020a).

Tulsi tea blends are at the heart of the product offerings. Tulsi, or basil, is one of India's sacred plants and is often referred to as the "queen of herbs" because of its regenerating and healing effects. It is also a key element in Ayurveda, the traditional holistic healing system in use throughout India. Tulsi is considered by science to be an adaptogenic plant that, by exerting complex effects, balances the vital functions of the body, and enhances resilience to environmental, physical, and emotional stress (Organic India 2020a).

Organic India is particularly committed to applying the principles of its holistic quality assurance system (honesty, accountability, and responsibility) throughout the whole production process (seed production, sowing, cultivation, harvesting, processing, marketing, and sales). The quality of its products has been proved through auditing and certification by independent third-party organizations. Accordingly, Organic India is one of the few herbal companies in India to be certified according to the schemes of Good Manufacturing Practices, Hazard Analysis & Critical Control Points, ISO 9001: 2015, and Orthodox Union's kosher quality certification. It also meets the standards of The Indian National Program for Organic Production, the Organic Certification of United States Department of Agriculture, Control Union Certifications World Group, the European Union's Organic Certification, the British Soil Association, GMO Free and Non-GMO Project Verification, and Fairtrade America. Organic India has recently been awarded Cosmos certification by ECOCERT for its core principles of respect for biodiversity, use of clean manufacturing processes, green chemistry, and transparency to consumers (Organic India 2020a).

Organic India values its partners, who include the farming families and tribal wild-crafters that provide the high-quality raw materials, many of whom are women, widows, disadvantaged, elderly, or illiterate people. In addition to organic, biodynamic, regenerative, and traditional Indian agricultural education and practices, it also provides them with training in self-sufficiency and self-development, which also improves the opportunities of future generations. Such relationships are based on mutual respect, dignity, and interconnectedness. The company is committed to improving the lives of its partners in production, which it strives to do on several levels. Organic India buys crops from them on terms more favorable than the normal market ones. It also pays the cost of obtaining the necessary organic certification. Farmers can grow their own crops on their land in rotation, alongside crops for selling to Organic India, giving families a more stable income and source of healthy food. The company provides them with health care, gender equality programs, and improves their infrastructural conditions. As a result of these investments, and through the success of individual families, villages can also start to develop, and the quality of life of local communities can be significantly improved, laying the foundation for more successful, healthier, happier lives for future generations (Organic India 2017, 2020a).

An important element of the value chain is Organic India's close collaboration with Fabindia, India's largest private retail platform for craft-based products. Fabindia acquired a 40 per cent stake in Organic India in 2013 and then increased its stake to 51 per cent in 2015. Fabindia buys home furnishing and decorative items, clothing, and organic food products from rural artisans across the country and exports them around the world (Organic India 2020a).

Position within the value network: For more than 20 years, Organic India has been committed to achieving social and environmental sustainability through a holistic business model. Its successful operation proves that a sustainable and ethical business model can create value not only for the company but also for its entire value network. The quantifiable results of this in 2017 were as follows. Over two decades, more than 2000 marginalized family farmers across India, and hundreds of tribal wild-crafters have been supported. More than 8000 people have been provided with free health care in Organic India's own health center, and almost as many have participated in its health maintenance programs. More than 200 people are employed in the raw material processing plants of the company, 95 per cent of whom are women. Through its restorative agricultural technologies and production partners, the fertility of more than 4000 hectares of chemically ravaged soil has been restored. Organic India's product range includes more than 100 types of herbal teas, dietary supplements, and organic food items, and it sells more than 240 million cups of organic Tulsi tea per year across the world (Organic India 2017, 2020a).

Organic India's products meet a number of quality and organic certification standards, but the company has made further improvements to increase its sustainability performance. The boxes of its flagship product, Tulsi tea, are made from 100 per cent recycled paperboard, at least a third of which is post-consumer content. Additionally, Tulsi tea bags are made entirely of unbleached, chemical-free, biodegradable, and therefore safely compostable paper, and will soon be produced without metal clips. In the near future, Organic India will open a new factory on the outskirts of Lucknow, housed in a building that will be certified in line with the world's strictest environmental certification scheme, LEED (Leadership in Energy and Environment Design). In order to preserve natural ecosystems, tribal wild-crafters will be supported through training about environmentally sustainable, regenerative, and hygienic methods of procuring herbs and fruits on more than 1.4 million hectares of certified organic forests, and will then be supervised and certified (Organic India 2017, 2020a, b).

Organic India is also seeking to add value to its entire value network by establishing the "Earth Seer" standard, which certifies ethical, trustworthy, holistic, socially, environmentally, and economically responsible sustainable business behavior that is committed to promoting well-being and respect for all beings and Mother Nature. The certification also encourages its holders to go beyond expected requirements by improving their business processes and supports the emergence of conscious consumption through collaboration with all stakeholders (Organic India 2017, 2020a).

To support its stakeholders, the company created the Organic India Dharti Mitr Award, which is given to organic farmers whose work significantly contributes to improving the agricultural, ecological, and social conditions of India. In addition to moral recognition, the award, which also includes a cash prize, also serves as a platform for strengthening relationships and sharing knowledge between committed actors in the field (IFOAM 2017).

In recognition of its accomplishments in relation to the common good, social and environmental sustainability, local communities, and ethical behavior, Organic India's US subsidiary received the "Best for Changemakers" award in 2018 and the "Best for the World Overall" award in 2018 and 2019. With this result, Organic India is now recognized as being among the best ten per cent of 2500 B Corporation certified companies in 150 industries in 50 countries around the world (B Lab 2020b).

Competitive strategy: The production and consumption of organic products has been increasing more than that of conventional products, mainly due to rising living standards, the spread of health-conscious lifestyles, the expansion of the urban population, and government subsidies (for example, in 2016, the entire agricultural area of the Indian state of Sikkim was converted to organic production). In India, a number of successful organic enterprises share a market that is growing 50 per cent faster than the world average. In addition to the market leader Organic India (with 25 per cent market share), the largest companies are Sresta Natural Bioproducts (14 per cent), Morarka Down to Earth (9 per cent), Conscious Foods (8.5 per cent), and Ecofarm (6 per cent). As a world market leader, Organic India is also very popular among consumers, the loyalty of its regular customers is strong, and brand recognition is significant. However, organic products are still considered a luxury in India, so Organic India intends to change this to "reintroduce" natural, healthy, and sustainable organic products to the market and make them available to all members of society. The company seeks to make producers, consumers, and decision-makers realize that organic production is the only long-term sustainable solution. Thus, Organic India encourages a growing range of stakeholders to raise their awareness and change their lifestyles. It uses digital and print media marketing tools based on the potential of the positive impact of experts and opinion leaders, influencers, and community building to increase brand awareness. Organic India is further developing its unique product offerings and is strengthening its presence in different geographical regions (for example, in China) and is also targeting new market segments (skin and body care products). The goal is to make its holistic health-conscious conception available in most product segments related to consumer welfare (ASSOCHAM – Ernst & Young 2018; Srivastav 2018; Organic India 2020a, b).

Patagonia

Value propositions: Patagonia's mission is to produce the best products without causing unnecessary harm, and to contribute to resolving the environmental crisis through the company's activities and continuously developing new ways to do things. These goals are rooted in a love of nature and a feeling of close connection with it, which constantly encourage Patagonia to act in order to preserve nature, improve its condition, and protect and restore the stability, integrity and beauty of the web of life. The culture and practice of mountaineering based on simplicity and utility can also be seen in Patagonia's value provisions, and is most evident in their product design and process organization (Patagonia 2020).

Market segment: Patagonia manufactures and distributes sustainable, ecological outdoor women's, men's and children's clothing, accessories (caps, scarves, and gloves), and apparel (sleeping bags, backpacks, blankets, and mugs) worldwide in its own stores as well as via resellers and the internet. According to industry analyses, the global outdoor clothing market accounted for almost 13 billion USD and is expected to reach more than 19 billion USD by 2026. The total value of the global outdoor apparel market was about 43 billion USD in 2016 and has been forecast to increase steadily by around 5 per cent per year until 2024. North America is one of the leading regions, with continuous demand for innovative products, but the Asia Pacific market is expected to expand significantly in the coming years owing to emerging demand by fitness inclined young generations. So far, offline stores have been dominant in sales, but the convenience of buying and online discounts could drive the e-commerce segment (Gaille 2018; GlobeNewswire 2019; Statista 2019; Business Wire 2020; Patagonia 2020).

Cost structure and profit potential: Committed to environmental and social responsibility, Patagonia's production costs are higher than the market average. For example, the company pays higher wages than its competitors in order to respect fair trade principles and to support the livelihood of local communities. However, Patagonia's brand, which is well known for its genuine commitment to sustainability, is strong, and, thanks to customer loyalty, the company has sufficient stable profit for its long-term success. This is true despite the fact that the company's advertising is minimal, and Patagonia sometimes uses anti-consumption campaigns such as its famous New York Times advertisement "Don't Buy This Jacket" in response to a Black Friday campaign in November 2011. The latter drew attention to the catastrophically harmful environmental effects of overconsumption and ways of mitigating these. Patagonia has since encouraged its consumers to consciously change their shopping habits. Despite these unusual methods, Patagonia's profits are enough to finance its functioning and long-term value commitments. For instance, as co-founders of the One Percent for the Planet initiative, the company donates the equivalent of 1 per cent of its annual gross sales in the form of a combination of monetary, in-kind, and promotional support directly to local environmental nonprofit organizations that are working to protect air, land, and water around the globe (since 1985, over 89 million USD has been donated to support environmental protection). Market expectations are favorable for Patagonia, as they expect further expansion by more than 5 per cent in the outdoor clothing and apparel segment during the coming years. North American and Asia Pacific markets may well develop significantly due to increasing consciousness among people about fitness and healthy lifestyles. After having stagnated in the middle of the decade, the European outdoor market has recovered and is expected to grow at a moderate speed. Most of the market segments for Patagonia products (clothing, backpacks, hiking, and climbing apparel) have also strengthened due to an increase in marketing activity aimed at encouraging women and families to engage in more outdoor activity. The Latin American outdoor clothing and apparel market may also grow moderately over the next five to six years, but because of the low per capita income in the region, interest in Patagonia's products may be subdued (Jans 2017; Chen 2018; GlobeNewswire 2019; Statista 2019; Business Wire 2020; Patagonia 2020).

Structure of the value chain: Patagonia strives to promote environmental and social sustainability throughout its entire value chain. Its fundamental goal is to mitigate and neutralize the negative effects of climate change, and to develop and apply practices that can improve the state of nature. In this endeavor, product design based on simplicity, usability, durability, and repairability is the starting point. In addition, Patagonia focuses on the following goals: (i) mitigating the environmental impact of its supply chain through monitoring its carbon footprint, and increasingly using renewable energy, brownfield investment, and green offices. Patagonia supports "car-free to work" initiatives. Its high-quality raw materials come from traceable sources. (ii) The company helps local grassroots environmental movements worldwide by making donations funded by a self-imposed "Earth tax" that is equivalent to 1 per cent of its total annual revenue. Patagonia also provides employees with an extra 320 hours for voluntary work, in lieu of working hours. (iii) Patagonia promotes systemic change by leveraging the company's popularity and brand strength. This includes embracing various environmental campaigns and environmental issues. (iv) The company provides consumers with high-quality, repairable products and also ensures the reuse of second-hand products via its Worn Wear project. (v) Patagonia is engaged in regenerative organic agriculture, and operates its own business called Patagonia Provisions to trade in sustainable and organic food. (vi) The company has been helping develop new ways of doing business. In 2013, a venture capital fund (Tin Shed Ventures) was launched with share capital of 20 million USD to fund start-up companies that address environmental issues, including the development of renewable energy infrastructure and regenerative organic agriculture, protecting water resources, neutralizing waste, and developing sustainable materials (Patagonia 2020; Patagonia Provisions 2020; Tin Shed Ventures 2020).

Patagonia has been operating as a certified B Corp oration since 2012. In line with this certification (by nonprofit organization B Lab), in 2019 Patagonia achieved over 151 points out of a maximum of 200 points, maintaining the level of a year earlier. This independent external evaluation appraises company performance in terms of impact on the environment, employees, customers, community, and transparency. Patagonia prepared an Annual Benefit Corporation Report in 2018, which was organized around its six main commitments. In relation to these, the following primary results were achieved in terms of increasing environmental and social sustainability.

One per cent for the planet: between 1985 and 2017, 89 million USD was donated to environmental organizations. In 2017, nearly half a million dollars was donated to 1000 organizations. Five hundred Patagonia employees participated in the distribution of grants.

Best product without no unnecessary harm: in 2017, according to the company's internal product evaluation system related to sustainability impact, Patagonia products achieved an average of 8.77 out of a maximum of 10 points. Almost a third of the materials they used were recycled, while a fifth were renewable, and the proportion of newly produced polyester and nylon-based materials was reduced from 58 to 51 per cent in two years. More than 70,000 of Patagonia products were repaired at 54 repair centers worldwide. Due to Patagonia's Fair Trade program, 26,000 of its workers received higher-than-market wages in 2017. The number of workers supported by the program has recently grown to 66,000. Patagonia now uses 100 per cent traceable down for its products, 72 per cent of its product line is made from recycled materials, 76 per cent is Fair Trade Certified sewn, and more than 150 farmers are taking part in its Regenerative Organic Cotton Pilot Program.

Operations causing no unnecessary harm: an environmental impact assessment focusing on the topics of energy, water, and waste was conducted in 32 Patagonia stores. The company reduced car commuting by almost 900,000 km under its "Drive-Less Program" (a decrease of 6 per cent). Although in Europe and South America Patagonia managed to reduce both electricity use and pollutant emissions (by 13 and 31 per cent, respectively) in 2017, both indicators increased worldwide by about 10 per cent due to growth in the largest markets (United States, 6–7 per cent, and Japan 24–37 per cent). Since then, Patagonia has met 100 per cent of its electricity needs in the United States with renewable electricity, and 76 per cent of its global needs. The company's goal is to switch to 100 per cent renewable electricity and become a zero-waste-to-landfill company by 2020, and to become carbon neutral by 2025.

Sharing best practices with other companies: five factories held chemical treatment training for 130 workers that they shared at meetings of the Outdoor Industry Association. Patagonia made over 400 public appearances at industrial and public forums, and organized more than 2000 free community events in its North American stores. Over 30 Patagonia employees held management or consulting positions in more than 40 industry, academic, and environmental organizations.

Transparency: Patagonia has published a list of its factories for 14 years, placing the company at the forefront of the industry. More than 30 studies and posts have been published about various sustainability topics. In 2017, the Fair Labor Association, an independent third party, accredited Patagonia's social responsibility program with regard to improving the position of employees.

Supportive work environment: all employees are provided with health insurance premiums free of charge. Half of Patagonia's employees are women. Almost half of the company's executives are women, while the US average is around one third (Rose Marcario was formerly Patagonia's CEO, while fewer than 5 per cent of US companies are led by a woman). Nearly every other weekend included a three-day break for Patagonia workers. Around 80 employees took part in internships at environmental organizations using fully paid leave of up to two months. Eighty workers received non-violent civil disobedience training about how to participate in civil movements in a dignified manner. There were also on-site childcare and development programs for 130 children of mothers employed by Patagonia (Patagonia 2018, 2020; B Lab 2020c).

Position within the value network: For almost five decades, Patagonia has been a committed advocate of sustainability and fair trade, and is playing a pioneering role in solving environmental and social problems and supporting the social movements involved in those efforts. As an "activist company," Patagonia has embraced a number of initiatives and used its brand and the organization's resources to serve the common good. In 2018, the company launched an activism platform ("Action Works") to connect committed individuals to organizations working on environmental issues in the same community. Via this initiative, it has supported initiatives for improving and regenerating agricultural soil, the health of terrestrial and marine ecosystems, climate and atmosphere, species diversity, and fostering environmental justice, civic democracy, sustainable communities, and indigenous people. Patagonia's recent environmental campaigns include attempts to protect Tasmania's rainforests, dismantle offshore oil rigs, prevent the construction of river hydropower plants in the Balkans and the expansion of the Keystone oil pipeline in North America, and the extraction of oil and gas in protected areas in Alaska. To increase consumer consciousness, Patagonia has actively participated in the creation, publishing, and distribution of several books and films on relevant topics, including *Unbroken Ground,* and *DamNation.*

Over the years, Patagonia has increasingly engaged in political activism in order to live up its values and foster the specific goals related to these. An example of Patagonia's peremptory attitude is the several cases in which it has stood up for its value commitments against the US government. In 2017, for example, Patagonia organized a boycott against a prestigious outdoor fair in Utah in protest of the state's intention to reverse a previous presidential decision to establish the Bears Ears National Monument National Park. Also in 2017, in line with several environmental and local community organizations, Patagonia sued the US government and president in relation to a decision to significantly reduce the area of two national parks. In 2018, the company urged over 400 companies to provide employees with a day off to vote on election day, as Patagonia itself did, also becoming the first brand to endorse specific political candidates (Friedman 2017; Gelles 2018; Fast Company 2020; Patagonia 2020).

The performance of Patagonia has continuously been recognized. Just a few of the most recent awards are highlighted here: in 2018, *Fast Company* magazine ranked Patagonia the sixth best among "The World's 50 Most Innovative Companies" for leading the way in promoting long-term solutions to environmental problems and growing its business in line with amplifying its social mission. The list included more than 350 companies, including Apple, Netflix, and Amazon. In addition, in the category of "Social Good" Patagonia was first that year. In the GlobeScan-SustainAbility Leaders Survey, Patagonia has been mentioned among those companies with the best sustainability performance since 2013. The company was ranked second behind Unilever, followed by companies such as IKEA, Interface, Natura, Danone, Nestlé, Marks & Spencer, and Tesla. Patagonia has been certified as a B Corporation since 2012. It has been awarded the "Best for the World" prize in the categories of Environment, Community, Changemaker, and Overall since 2017. With these results, Patagonia has continuously been among the best 10 per cent of the 2500 B Corporation certified companies in 150 industries in 50 countries around the world for years (Fast Company 2018, 2020; GlobeScan 2019; B Lab 2020c; Patagonia 2020).

Competitive strategy: Trends in the North American outdoor clothing and apparel market are dominant factors in the industry. Although the market is fragmented and several brands are responsible for the majority of the market, the most significant US-based players (such as Nike, VF Corporation, Hanesbrands, Under Armour, Canada Goose, North Face, Columbia Sportswear, G-III Apparel Group, Newell Brands, and Outdoor Research) also have global influence. Other major non-US brands include Adidas, Puma, Hugo Boss, ASICS, and the Mizuno Corporation. However, due to some new market trends, even smaller or recently established players have been able to rapidly gain significant market share and brand awareness. One notable phenomenon is that traditional sports retail chains have been losing ground against direct-to-consumer selling manufacturers. Direct sales, associated with transparent pricing, have been gaining popularity among consumers and allow manufacturers to benefit from higher margins by omitting interaction with merchants. The other trend is the proliferation of lifestyle marketing, which, along with direct sales, can result in deeper and more credible customer relationships. Younger generations increasingly prefer wellness and outdoor lifestyle and lifestyle brands. The owners and managers of these brands, partly through their own approaches to life, are sincerely committed to representing brand values. In addition to Patagonia, Fjällräven, HippyTree, Kühl, and Blackyak are also popular and increasingly successful emerging brands. It seems that the values faithfully represented by Patagonia for almost half a century are becoming more favorably received in the market owing to the increase in consumer consciousness and emphasis on genuine value commitment. Patagonia can thus continue to rely on its genuine core values, work closely with its stakeholders, and focus on customers committed to sustainability and a minimalist style. It can also maintain its success in financial terms, creating a sufficient financial base on which to advocate and support the sustainability issues it considers important (Chen 2018; GlobeNewswire 2019; Statista 2019; Business Wire 2020; Patagonia 2020).

Scott Bader

Value propositions: As set out in its long-term plan, "2036 Vision," based on the three pillars of Business, Ecology, and Humanity, Scott Bader seeks to become a sustainable chemical company that operates in line with the company's ethos and the founder's vision. Scott Bader imagines a world in which humanity develops without endangering the natural systems that support its living conditions. Scott Bader promotes this development by responding to the challenges of a changing society by using the chemical industry to promote the common good. The company defines its values in terms of seven strategic goals. (i) Through leading the way in the creation of a circular economy, Scott Bader works with its partners to create a closed-loop value chain free of waste and negative impacts. (ii) Acting beyond compliance: As a reliable, proactive market leader of a safe, transparent, and ethical chemical industry, it produces products and processes that protect people and the planet while setting an example to others. (iii) Scott Bader promotes sustainability by sharing its vision, knowledge and profit and supplying products and services that create real value for society. (iv) While striving for excellence, as a purpose-driven company Scott Bader continually improves all of its processes and products to deliver world-class business performance and meet all the expectations of its customers. (v) Through initiatives and innovations at all levels of the organization, the diversity and creativity of empowered and motivated employees gives the company its strength. (vi) In order to encourage working together for success, Scott Bader is an integral part of a global network of mutually beneficial supplier, consumer, and alliance-based partnerships that share its vision and mission. (vii) Through the ethical use of natural resources and as a proponent of clean energy, freshwater conservation, and zero emissions, Scott Bader is a strong advocate of environmental protection and a shift toward sustainability (Scott Bader 2019, 2020).

Market segment: Scott Bader's main activities are the production of adhesives and composites such as resins and gelcoats and specialty polymers in the geographical markets of Europe, North America, South Africa, the Middle East, the Far East, and Australia. Its products and services are mainly used in the automotive-, construction-, chemical-, transportation-, marine-, and wind energy industries, and, to a lesser extent, in households and the sector of graphic arts in more than 100 countries worldwide. In 2018, 58 per cent of total annual sales came from Europe (131 million GBP), about a third of which came from the UK, where Brexit has not yet had any tangible effects, but the uncertainty of potential scenarios has been a constant subject of discussion and the company has taken various measures to prepare for all possible outcomes. European sales of composites increased by 1.3 per cent due to strong demand for specialty products, resulting in an increase of over 5 per cent on the margin per ton. The adhesives sector continued to grow significantly (by 13 per cent) in all product types and geographic regions, but the margin per ton declined by 3 per cent because price increases could not be passed on to customers. Sales volumes and margins of the specialty polymer business remained at the levels of the prior year, although the polidene business was divested as it no longer fit with strategic plans (Scott Bader 2019, 2020).

Cost structure and profit potential: Due to the uncertainty of Brexit scenarios, threats of further consolidation of the industry, and a continuously tightening regulatory framework, market conditions were fairly difficult for Scott Bader in 2018. However, the company was able to grow in terms of volume, sales, turnover, and profit, and considered the year to be a successful one, with progress on several fronts. Sales increased by almost 12 per cent to 226 million GBP, while profit before tax and exceptional items grew by 7 per cent to six million GBP. Net cash at year end amounted to more than 13 million GBP, including profit on the sale of the polidene business. Mainly due to the impact of the product mix, which was due to significant growth in resin sales, margin per ton decreased compared to 2017. Operating costs increased, while trading cost per ton declined by about 5 per cent. In the Middle East, 2018 was an outstanding year with record sales that increased by 54 per cent based on strong local sales and exports. However, major construction projects have been hit by the regional geopolitical situation. South Africa has yet been suffering from recession. Challenges in relation to ensuring safe access to key raw materials continued, as in previous years, along with a significant number of force majeure incidents along the supply chain, and the adverse effects of climate change (for instance, the low level of the Rhine River) notably impacted raw material supply. Scott Bader expects this trend to continue and is preparing to mitigate such effects. As a part of efforts to spread the risk and enter potential markets, in 2018 Scott Bader established a Japanese subsidiary to better serve the growing demand in the region, and planned to upgrade its Indian production facility during 2019. In June 2020, after ten years of cooperation, the company also acquired the assets of Summit Composites Pty, thereby establishing an Australian subsidiary to distribute resins, gelcoats, and adhesives, all built on Summit's reputation for product quality, performance, and reliability (Scott Bader 2019, 2020).

Structure of the value chain: A special feature of Scott Bader's value chain is the corporate governance structure derived from community ownership and leadership. The company has no external shareholders, so it can take into account different, longer-term aspects in its operation compared to the average company. The three main governing bodies are the Group Board, the Commonwealth Board, and the Members'

Assembly. The nine-member Group Board acts as a board of directors and is responsible for business affairs (finance, legal, and strategy), but also ensures that the business is run in accordance with defined principles and helps promote charitable objectives. An Audit Subcommittee also assists its work. The Group Chief Executive Officer reports to the Group Board on a monthly basis. The nine-member Commonwealth Board operates as a holding company and is the company's registered charity. It is responsible for discussing strategic matters, acquisitions, profit distribution, decisions determining long-term development, and monitoring compliance with community principles and legislation related to charity law. The Members' Assembly is the group's democratic forum to which the Group Board is accountable. The Assembly monitors adherence to the principles defined by The Commonwealth. The five largest sites (UK, South Africa, Dubai, Croatia, and France) each have Local Councils that represent members when discussing local issues (Scott Bader 2019, 2020).

Scott Bader puts meeting special customer needs at the heart of its strategy, so innovation is the soul of the value chain. Every year, the company comes up with new solutions and new products so that it can maintain its technological leadership in the markets for its key products. Scott Bader does not intend to compete on price and volume, but on the highest possible technological and service solutions that will enable the enterprise to firmly differentiate itself from its competitors (Jacob 2012; Scott Bader 2020).

Based on its core values and its deep commitment to sustainability, Scott Bader embarked on a long-term strategic sustainability project across the whole group in 2017. In collaboration with advisory groups The Natural Step Germany, and Sustainable Growth Associates, it redefined its vision and strategic goals and the steps required to achieve these. The three main pillars of the plan "Vision 2036" are Business, Ecology, and Humanity (Sustainable Growth Associates 2018, Scott Bader 2020; The Natural Step 2020).

Within the pillar "Ecology," the reduction of the company's environmental impact is captured in the following achievements from 2018. The first 100 tons of bio-based resin were sold, serving as a cost-effective, "greener" solution for the market. All but one site made significant energy savings through process optimization and a higher rate of asset utilization. Over the last two years, energy consumption per ton has been reduced by almost 14 per cent. A third of all production sites now run on 100 per cent renewable electrical energy. The Croatian site has signed the "Responsible Care" global charter, showing Scott Bader's commitment to dealing with chemicals safely over the total life cycle. Also in Croatia, 50 per cent of the factory's cooling water consumption came from rainwater. Scott Bader played a very active role in an industry initiative led by its UK subsidiary involving defining what a circular composite economy could look like, which project also continued during 2019 (Scott Bader 2019).

In the pillar "Humanity," Scott Bader focused on the strategic goal of "Striving for Excellence." Project management, sustainability, and coaching training were provided to more than 200 employees across the group. A "Company Employee Ownership Day" was organized at all manufacturing sites to improve teamwork and strengthen community spirit. Scott Bader's largest site in the UK won the "Investors in People Gold Award" for its outstanding performance at effectively managing and supporting the development of its people. The company's "Values in Action" program was extended globally for a second year to recognize the teams or individuals who exemplify commitment to organizational values, fairness, teamwork, and responsibility through their activities. In 2017, the general manager of the Amiens site was given new management responsibilities at a group level, and his position was reorganized into a collegial management structure, thereby strengthening Scott Bader's progress toward increasing self-management. In the same year, a major project was launched to review the reward and appraisal system to make Scott Bader more competitive at finding and retaining talented and skilled people, and also to create the right human resource background for underpinning the company's progress toward sustainability (Scott Bader 2018, 2019).

In 2018, progress was made in the field of occupational health and safety performance, but more work is needed to improve this as planned. "Lost Time Accidents" related to chemical processes and engineering declined from three to one, but the "Lost Time Incident Frequency Ratio" (the number of accidents at work that resulted in an injury, per one million working hours) disappointingly rose above the industry benchmark. In 2018, the first global Health and Safety survey was conducted, while local improvement action plans have been implemented at all sites during 2019, and this area has remained a key focus, with behavioral safety and change management targeted for improvement (Scott Bader 2019).

Position within the value network: As a leader in innovation and technology, Scott Bader prioritizes getting its internal processes and products audited and certified by third-party organizations in all markets and geographical regions. The company has been certified according to ISO 9001:2015, ISO 14001:2015, ISO 45001:2018, and BS OHSAS 18001:2007. In addition to these qualifications, Scott Bader's commitment to social and environmental sustainability has already been recognized by several awards. In 2017, the UK site received the "Gold Investors In People Award" (IIP); an important form of recognition for organizations that effectively ensure the development and leadership of their employees. This represented a major step forwards after Scott Bader joined the IIP evaluation scheme in 1997, and took home the IIP Silver Award for several years. A significant milestone in the company's environmental sustainability development was the acquisition of a Silver EcoVadis rating for its sustainable procurement practices in 2018. EcoVadis evaluates the global supply chain of more than 40,000 companies according to four main themes (Environment, Ethics, Labour/Social, Supply Chain) in line with 21 indicators based on several sustainability schemes (such as the UN Global Compact, and ISO 26000). Through an online platform, EcoVadis provides ratings, based on which Scott Bader was in the top 17 per cent of companies in its industry in 2019. This represents a slight decline compared to 2018 but reassessment has been under way, with several performance indicators now addressed in Scott Bader's "2036 Vision" (Scott Bader 2020).

Scott Bader plays an exemplary role through its active charitable activities. It donates to charities with similar goals at local, national, and international levels. Each year, grants go to beneficiaries through the "Global Charity Fund," which is financed by a specified percentage of the company's yearly income. In 2018, donations worth 222,100 GBP were distributed to more than 200 charities in 23 countries in relation to initiatives involving education, training (41 per cent), health and disabilities (23 per cent), community (22 per cent), and sustainable livelihoods (14 per cent). Through the Central Fund, four large African projects were also supported with 25,000 GBP each, based on the votes of Commonwealth Members at the annual general meeting. In addition, group companies paid 30,000 GBP of donations directly to numerous charities. Scott Bader also helps charities by giving employees an extra day off each year to contribute to the work of an NGO of their choice through volunteering. In 2018, there was record uptake in the number of volunteering hours, which reached almost 1000 hours (Scott Bader 2019).

Competitive strategy: The market segments targeted by Scott Bader are characterized by high volatility and an extremely strong competitive situation involving numerous players of different sizes. The key success criteria are low production costs and sales prices, and increasingly personalized customer service through adequate innovation and customer care. Scott Bader is strong mainly in terms of innovation capability and meeting specific customer needs, as well as in some niche markets. There is also strong emphasis on working closely with partners because, being true to its core values, Scott Bader does not want to engage in fierce industry struggles (involving cost and price competition). Accordingly, it is also a member of 12 trade associations on four continents. By concentrating on these strengths, Scott Bader can hold its own against its competitors, which are usually larger. In addition, the special ownership and management structure can give the company a competitive advantage because short-term market effects have less influence on its operations. Scott Bader can be successful based on its long-term strategic approach and committed, mutually beneficial partnerships. During 2017–2018, the company had to cope with significant challenges due to several factors (rising raw material prices, issues with security of supply, economic and geopolitical uncertainty in certain geographical regions, and tightening of the regulatory environment). It is generally expected that competition in its key markets, cost, and price pressure will remain significant, raw material supplies will be uncertain, regulation of the chemical industry in line with safety and environmental standards will increase, and the impacts of Brexit will be unpredictable for the time being. As a strategic response, Scott Bader plans to continue to focus on its core values and leverage its strengths in product development and technical service to intensify its presence in niche markets where it can maintain its long-term success through serving specific customer needs. In addition, expansion and quality improvement have been planned in geographical regions (e.g., Brazil, India) that have not received much emphasis so far (Jacob 2012; Scott Bader 2019).

TerraCycle

Value propositions: The essence of TerraCycle's business model is that, based on the triple principle of "People, Planet, Profit," the company creates profitable business solutions for the selective collection, recycling, and reuse of waste traditionally classified as non-recyclable for its individual, corporate, institutional, and civil partners. Such waste includes, for example, cigarette butts, empty coffee capsules, drink pouches, yoghurt cups, confectionery packaging, worn-out baby seats that usually end up in landfills or incinerators, and even plastic ocean waste. For wastes that are difficult to recycle, TerraCycle develops national selective collection platforms (such as voluntary waste collection teams, and Zero Waste Boxes) whose operation is financed by the producers of the related brands, retailers, municipalities, small businesses, NGOs, or individual consumers. Waste that is collected can be used in its original form (reuse), with a changed, even upgraded function (upcycled), or as processed raw material for use in the manufacture of new products (recycled). When possible, TerraCycle seeks to create new products with the least possible additional energy input, thus moving closer to the implementation of the circular economy concept (by which the by-products or end products of material flows serve as inputs for another process cycle at the end of their lives). Costly selective collection can be still profitable for TerraCycle's partners because, in addition to generating measurable benefits in financial terms (working in an ecologically conscious way can generate more sales, greater market share or margins, and lead to more donations), the company can provide its partners with numerous additional services (e.g., media, PR consulting, social media, communication and marketing services) and added value. Such value may include the auditing and innovative redesign of products and production processes, creating more sustainable operations, higher customer turnover, brand enhancement, stronger consumer loyalty, and cleaner city streets. From this point of view, therefore, waste is positively evaluated rather than negatively. With the help of innovative solutions, the amount of waste and raw materials that need to be extracted can also be reduced. Another important value proposition of TerraCycle is that by focusing on the principles of "better, greener, cheaper" of eco-capitalism, it can promote solutions that are environmentally, socially, and economically sustainable in the long term (Vaccaro 2009; Eliances 2017; TerraCycle 2020a).

Market segment: TerraCycle is a global market leader in the collection and recycling of waste. It deals with all kinds of waste, in addition to the traditionally selectively collected paper, glass, metal, and rigid plastic waste. The company has four principal business divisions: (i) National recycling operations, whose shipping, storage, and recycling costs are sponsored by the manufacturers and traders of over 80 consumer brands. Major brand partners include Procter & Gamble, Garnier, Bausch & Lomb, Santa Fe Natural Tobacco, Colgate, Tom's of Maine, and Kiehl's. (ii) Zero Waste Boxes, which can be used to collect a specific waste stream (such as coffee capsules) or a defined category of waste (such as non-compostable kitchen waste). Including pre-paid shipment, these boxes are paid for by waste-collecting customers, and, once filled, can be delivered by UPS to a TerraCycle recycling facility. (iii) The sale of raw materials refers to the sale of pellets made from recycled plastics to plastic product manufacturers such as Green Mantra, Nexus Fuels, Akshar Plastics, and Ultra Poly Corporation. (iv) Regulated waste recycling helps businesses to manage regulated, universal and hazardous waste such as fluorescent lamps, bulbs, batteries, e-waste, organic waste, medical waste, and other types of waste potentially harmful to the environment (TerraCycle 2020a, b).

TerraCycle US Inc., the largest subsidiary of TerraCycle that accounts for the majority of the company's total annual sales, generated annual sales of more than seven million USD in 2018 from about 80 brand-sponsored national recycling programs. The subsidiary generated revenue of 3.6 million USD from more than 100 categories of (available-to-the-public) Zero Waste Boxes, 2.3 million USD from material sales, and over seven million USD in the regulated waste division. Within the material sales division, since 2017 TerraCycle has developed a "storied plastic" segment to sell recycled materials at premium prices. The name refers to the fact that the origin of these materials is known (for example, beach/ocean plastic), so new products (such as cosmetics packaging or shoes) made from these plastics can be associated with special meaning and unique marketing-related value. Main partners in this segment are Procter & Gamble, REN Skincare, AXE, Microsoft, and a network of organizations that is cleaning up beaches in more than ten countries. This initiative is now one of the world's largest beach/ocean plastic collection programs (TerraCycle 2020a, b).

Cost structure and profit potential: TerraCycle's business model is based on zero or negative cost waste, because producers, retailers, and consumers sponsor their waste collection and recycling programs. The company can thus potentially operate at below-market cost and generate greater profits even while providing additional services to differentiate itself from its competitors. The company's financial results, based on 2018 and 2019 data available for the US subsidiary, were as follows. In 2019, in the United States, TerraCycle saw a significant increase in total annual sales in the largest market by 35 per cent to 27 million USD. The reason for this was primarily the significant growth of the two largest business units, as new Sponsored Waste programs were launched and the Zero Waste Boxes segment was expanded to individual and corporate customers. In addition, large new deals in the Material Sales business were concluded. Costs were mainly due to logistics expenses, the redemption of charity points, the cost of employees engaged in delivery services, sales-related expenses, and general and administrative expenses. Total expenses increased, but by less than net sales, so net income grew by more than 160 per cent to a record 3.2 million USD. With regard to general market trends, TerraCycle expects that the awareness-raising impact of the World Economic Forum and Ellen MacArthur Foundation will strengthen global efforts to achieve a circular economy, and more and more companies will incorporate a sustainability element into their operations. In the United States, the government's denial of climate change may also stimulate individual initiatives to reduce personal environmental impacts; as a result, demand for TerraCycle products and services will continue to increase in its market segments. Based on its strong and positive reputation, TerraCycle plans to launch new business platforms and improve its product mix to increase premium-priced offerings that will allow the company to expand and grow profitably (PR Newswire 2020; TerraCycle 2020b).

Structure of the value chain: the core elements of TerraCycle's value chain are innovation and applied scientific research, through which the composition of different types of waste and the conditions of their generation are studied. Through such analyses, TerraCycle explores the recyclability of these wastes and investigates how to reduce the content of waste streams. Innovation activity also includes the development of new business models and marketing and communication plans, with which the collection, processing, and sale of specific types of waste can be made profitable in a strictly financial sense. Most waste management companies only deal with the collection and shipment of waste to landfills, so TerraCycle's concept of innovation and research and development activity is among the few exceptions (TerraCycle 2020a, b).

Important actors in the value chain include waste collectors and civil, corporate, and official communities. Over 202 million people have participated in related waste collection programs since the founding of TerraCycle. These people represent all areas of society regardless of age, gender, religion, financial status, and political sympathy. The role of employees is also an important human factor in the value chain. At TerraCycle, a strong work ethic prevails, and the atmosphere is cheerful and informal. Office furnishings are made from waste, and walls are covered in graffiti and are repainted every few weeks. Dress style is relaxed, but expectations about employee and managerial conduct are very high. However, TerraCycle's mission, value background, and meaningful jobs are very attractive to committed people, so dozens of students spend their internships with them in the summer, for example, and the most experienced employees have been working at TerraCycle for almost two decades (Bhasin 2011; *Parvati Magazine* 2017; TerraCycle 2020a, b).

TerraCycle does not have its own processing capacity because of capital requirements and technological inflexibility, as the processing of each type of waste can require different equipment, requiring new investment and financing. On the other hand, TerraCycle's processing partners are happy to cooperate with the company because TerraCycle now has two decades of experience and much know-how in market segments ignored by other market players, offering promising opportunities for expansion for those who work with them. The company also relies on third-party services for the shipment of collected waste (principally UPS in the United States), and warehouses for storage (TerraCycle 2020a, b).

Significant contributors to the performance of the value chain are the companies that produce and distribute the global brands that are cooperating with TerraCycle within the framework of national recycling programs and the brand-sponsored waste collection programs that have been developed for each type of waste. Some of the more than 100 corporate partners and brands include 3 M, AstraZeneca, Barilla, Bausch & Lomb, Coca-Cola, Colgate, ESPN, Garnier, GlaxoSmithKline, Gillette, Hasbro, Home Depot, L'Oréal, Nespresso, Nestlé, PepsiCo, Procter & Gamble, Royal Canin, Rubbermaid, Schwarzkopf, Subaru, Tom's of Maine, and Walmart (TerraCycle 2018, 2020a, b).

An important goal of TerraCycle is to increase consumer awareness, so activities directly related to consumers have been awarded priority in the value chain. To support these, in addition to major trading partners, TerraCycle opened its own retail outlets in Princeton in 2009. In 2010, the company set up so-called "Hot Spots" eco-displays in Walmart stores, which pair original products such as Capri Sun soft drinks pouches with upcycled products made from waste (e.g., bags, caps, balls, and penholders). Individual consumers were targeted by the 2009 reality show series *Garbage Moguls* on The National Geographic Channel, in 2014 in the multi-season TV series *Human Resources*, and by *Trash Tycoon*, the first online game about repurposing waste. Recently, TerraCycle has launched Loop, a circular shopping system for delivering popular brands to households and recollecting them in durable, refillable packaging to eliminate single-use plastics (TerraCycle 2018, 2020a).

Position within the value network: TerraCycle is a global market leader at recycling "unrecyclable" waste, and a committed and tireless advocate of waste elimination initiatives, the promotion of the circular economy, and eco-capitalism. The founder, CEO Tom Szaky, is the author of three books on the topic, and a frequent author and interviewee on professional online platforms, websites about social and public life, and notable newspapers such as Inc., Entrepreneur, Chief Executive, and Smart CEO. Szaky and his company have been recognized more than 200 times as leading sustainable social and environmental actors for their pioneering work. A few of these awards include *Inc.* magazine awarding Szaky the "# 1 CEO in America under 30" award in 2006, and the United States Environmental Protection Agency recognizing the company's business model as consistent with the agency's solid waste strategy. In 2011, the founder was included in *Forbes* magazine's "Impact 30" list. In 2012, Szaky was awarded the United Nations' "Leader of Social Change Award" and TerraCycle was awarded the *Entrepreneur* magazine's "Brilliant 100 Companies" award. In 2013, Szaky won the Schwab Foundation's "Social Entrepreneur of the Year" award. In 2017, TerraCycle was awarded the United Nations' "Momentum for Change Lighthouse Activity" award for the first fully recyclable shampoo bottle made from ocean plastic waste, developed in collaboration with Procter & Gamble and the French water, energy and waste management company SUEZ. In 2018, TerraCycle received the "BIG Innovation Award" and Szaky was awarded the Ernst & Young "Entrepreneur of the Year Regional Winner." In 2019, the company was number ten on *Fortune* magazine's "List of 52 Companies Changing the World," as well as on "Inc's 5000 List," and Tom Szaky was named one of the "Top Most Influential Doers and Shakers in Purposeful Retail" (TerraCycle 2020a, b).

TerraCycle's significant impact within its value chain is clearly illustrated by the fact that it is working on solving a global social and economic problem that no other company has taken on so far. Coping with more than 23,000 billion pieces of consumer waste (including five million tons of plastic waste per year) is an extreme challenge for the planet and for human health. The recycling rate of waste is very low, and environmental education and awareness raising have not been awarded high priority so far. TerraCycle's mission is to change people's perceptions of waste, mobilize individuals to engage in selective waste collection, encourage companies to support recycling programs, and support educational, community, religious, and charitable NGOs from its income. The company also takes responsibility for its local environment. It has chosen economically disadvantaged New Jersey as its headquarters to create jobs for locals through its operations, and to provide education and training for young people who can participate in service of a good cause. TerraCycle also provides urban artists with a creative, exhibition space (TerraCycle 2018, 2020a).

TerraCycle's Sponsored Waste Programs involve offering individuals and organizations that collect waste a reward in the form of "TerraCycle charity points," which can be converted into donations to charities. Points are awarded based on the net weight of waste items that are collected, and can usually be converted into a 0.02 USD payment per waste item to a charity or school selected by the collector. So far, almost eight billion waste units have been collected and more than 44 million USD has been donated.

In 2018, TerraCycle formed TerraCycle Global Foundation to address the complex challenges of collecting and recycling waste in emerging countries such as Thailand, China, Indonesia, Vietnam, Sri Lanka, and the Philippines. Through this organization, the company engages with local governments, communities, and nonprofit and corporate partners to offer waste collection and recycling platforms, with special emphasis on preventing plastic pollution from entering aquatic systems. It creates charitable organizations that cooperate with social, environmental, and educational organizations to enhance recycling efforts and improve the conditions of the waste pickers who work to clean up waterways and are engaged in land-based plastic collection (TerraCycle 2020a).

Competition strategy: No other company is collecting and recycling most of the waste categories treated by TerraCycle, so there is no direct competition. In its main market segments, the following factors characterize the development of competition. National recycling programs and Zero Waste Boxes are unique in the market. Working closely with its partners, TerraCycle helps them with not only sustainability, logistics, marketing, and PR services, but also with innovative research and development activities to become more sustainable and operate more effectively. There is significant competition in the regulated waste recycling segment, with larger, stronger companies than TerraCycle dominating the market. Nevertheless, the company can successfully differentiate itself from traditional players and gain market share in the medium term by building on the company's brand, reputation, special services, and competencies that contribute to improving the awareness and popularity of partners' brands. In the material sales business, TerraCycle does not deal with conventionally collected and recycled HDPE and PET-type plastics, but with categories not treated by others. In this special segment, the company has a market-leading position, which gives TerraCycle significant room to determine supply and pricing. Competition has been growing in the "Storied Plastic" segment, as other companies are increasingly inclined to deal with ocean plastics due to their increasing market value. However, TerraCycle's competitive advantage as a market leader may last over the coming years. An important phenomenon in terms of competition is that, in addition to working closely with its stakeholders in more than 20 countries, TerraCycle has also partnered with the largest conventional waste management companies (Progressive Waste Solutions in Canada, Landbell GmbH. in Germany, and SUEZ in France) since 2013. The latter companies are becoming closer partners and now own 20–30 per cent of all shares in TerraCycle's subsidiaries in Canada and nine European countries. Thus, in addition to the strategy of focusing on special market segments, innovation, and differentiation, the current direction of development also involves more industry collaboration (TerraCycle 2020a, b).

The main characteristics of the ecologically conscious business models in the international sample are presented in Table 6.1.

Table 6.1 Main characteristics of ecologically conscious business models in the international sample

	Value propositions	Market segment	Cost structure and profit potential	Structure of the value chain	Position within the value network	Competitive strategy
Green Monday	Construction and operation of a plant-based food ecosystem to counter planetary devastation, food insecurity, food-related illness, and animal suffering, and promoting local and global community building, implementing triple-bottom-line approach	Social: awareness-raising campaigns for promoting a sustainable lifestyle; Business: grocery stores for plant-based food, sustainability, CSR consulting, impact investing	Rapid turnover growth since foundation, stable profitability, good prospects, geographical expansion because of successful business based on increasing consumer consciousness and lifestyle changes	R&D, sustainable, ethical suppliers, knowledge sharing, community platform, own store network, program for sustainable event management, seed investment fund for sustainable start-ups, prestigious advocates and partner organizations	Good reputation, popularity, real impact on the culture of consumption and people's lifestyle in Hong Kong and the region, numerous entrepreneurial awards immediately after its foundation, market leader with intention to further develop the whole market segment and promote feasible lifestyle change around the world	Shaping consumer consciousness, inspiring other businesses, increasing network of partners involving knowledge sharing and value transfer, strengthening sustainable food industry cooperation

	Value propositions	Market segment	Cost structure and profit potential	Structure of the value chain	Position within the value network	Competitive strategy
Houdini Sportsware	Nature is of intrinsic value and is blueprint for creating circular systems through creativity, high quality, timeless style, sustainability-based business model for highly innovative, ethical and sustainable functional clothing	Ethical and sustainable production and retail sale of functional outdoor clothing for ecologically conscious consumers living an active lifestyle who prefer timeless minimalist style	Steady organic development of revenue with fluctuating profitability due to significant increase in assets and number of staff, continuous innovation, stable demand due to popular brand	Highly innovative product design based on sustainability, recycled, biodegradable raw materials, open-source innovation, local R&D, production in Europe, few suppliers, short supply chain, redefining consumption and consumer care	Leader in sustainability, transforming consumption patterns, first ever Planetary Boundaries Assessment, social boundaries added to measure well-being of value chain, interdisciplinary collaboration, transparency, prestigious business and industry awards	Striving for sustainability in close cooperation with other industry players, even competitors to inspire each other, joint research projects, making company-developed materials freely available

(continued)

Table 6.1 (continued)

	Value propositions	Market segment	Cost structure and profit potential	Structure of the value chain	Position within the value network	Competitive strategy
Interface	Production of modular carpets and services, elimination of negative environmental impacts, restoration of nature, renewable, cyclical, gentle business model, radical redesign of processes, products, improvement of life of all stakeholders	Manufacture and sales of mainly commercial modular carpets for office and retail sector, expanding to household and luxury vinyl floors and rubber flooring mainly for healthcare and education sectors	Largest margin segment, premium products, profit potential greater than industry average, radical innovation to lessen environmental impacts and reduce cost, increase turnover and profitability	Company culture based on sustainability, own sustainability advisory group, "The Natural Step" methodology, radical product and process innovation, close cooperation with value chain, fair and ethical relationship with stakeholders	Pioneering innovator committed to sustainability, design that mimics nature, recognized among the best performers, numerous entrepreneurial awards, role-model for others approaching zero negative impact, striving for revolutionary transformation of industry	Highly competitive global market, global leader in its segment, successfully competes on sustainability and innovation, excellent brand due to ecological commitment and performance

	Value propositions	Market segment	Cost structure and profit potential	Structure of the value chain	Position within the value network	Competitive strategy
Natura	Production and sales of natural, ethical, sustainable, innovative beauty care products through four iconic brands, nature-inspired cyclical system to protect nature, fair, caring relationships and value creation throughout entire partner network	Fragrances, beauty and body care cosmetics, gifts mostly positioned in the natural, organic and premium market segment, originally in Brazil, now worldwide through its group of brands Natura & Co.	Significantly increasing group size, revenue, profitability, synergistic cooperation of global brands Natura, Aesop, The Body Shop, Avon, plans to harmonize and strengthen brands, R&D, digital transformation, innovation	Striving for cyclical production system neutralizing negative impact on nature and creating value for stakeholders in rainforests and partner network, product development, fair relationships, multi-channel sales, consumer awareness raising	Exemplary transparency, continuous monitoring, reporting of sustainability performance, improving environmental and social impacts, widespread recognition of leading practices, support for local communities, reforestation, public education, social justice, women's empowerment and well-being, B Corp	Strong global competition, significant product development, marketing expenditure is key, Brazilian market leader, globally fourth based on environmental, social performance, innovation, strong brands, reputation

(continued)

Table 6.1 (continued)

	Value propositions	Market segment	Cost structure and profit potential	Structure of the value chain	Position within the value network	Competitive strategy
Organic India	Production of genuine organic teas, herbal products and food, holistic business model for the benefit of all stakeholders, promoting restorative agriculture that serves and protects Nature, support for farmers, wild-crafters in rural India	Production and sales of organic teas, herbal preparations, spices, ginger, seeds, fresh vegetables and packaged foods (ghee, coconut oil, and honey), main product Tulsi (basil), certified organic, organic, GMO free	Growth rate of global and Indian organic product market, margins significantly higher than for conventional products, increasing consumer health consciousness and product range can further improve profit potential	Based on "whole herb," traditional holistic healing system Ayurveda, cutting-edge technology, holistic quality assurance system and certification, fair trade, development of farmer communities, regenerative agriculture, close cooperation with market-leading distributor	Business model restores health of soil and plants, continually adds value to marginalized rural farmers, tribal wild-crafter families, quality and organic certification, initiatives to improve environmental, social sustainability performance, recognized by awards, created own ethical standard, award for organic farmers, B Corp	Global market leader in a growing market segment, popular brand, strong customer loyalty, expansion of product range and geographic reach, wants to make organic products available to all

	Value propositions	Market segment	Cost structure and profit potential	Structure of the value chain	Position within the value network	Competitive strategy
Patagonia	Provision of the best quality, simple, useful outdoor products without causing unnecessary harm, using business to solve the environmental crisis via leading society to protect and restore nature, supporting activism and regenerative agriculture	Manufacture and retail of sustainable, ecological outdoor clothing, accessories, apparel designed for utility in simple, minimalist style via own and partner stores worldwide and internet	Higher costs than market average due to application of natural, innovative materials, fair trade in the supply chain, steady growth, sufficient profit expected based on strong brand, customer loyalty, increasing awareness	Design of durable, repairable, reusable products using recycled, renewable, fair trade materials, transparency of factories, footprint of operation monitored and reported, supportive working environment, women's empowerment, regenerative agriculture	Pioneer in industry, promoting environmental, social, political activism, raising consumer consciousness, publishing books, films, 1% of annual sales to grassroots environmental NGOs worldwide, venture capital to environmental start-ups, sharing of best practice, recognized by many awards, B Corp	Fragmented market with global players, emerging brands, growing consumer consciousness, direct sales, transparency, focusing on genuine core values and customers committed to sustainability and minimalist style

(continued)

Table 6.1 (continued)

	Value propositions	Market segment	Cost structure and profit potential	Structure of the value chain	Position within the value network	Competitive strategy
Scott Bader	Three pillars: Business, Ecology, Humanity, avoid jeopardizing natural systems, safe, ethical and transparent chemical industry for common good, knowledge, profit sharing, circular economy, workforce development, commonwealth, charity	Production and distribution of composites such as resins, gel coatings, adhesives specialty polymers, and fireproof, smoke- and toxic- resistant materials, mainly in Europe, North America for various industries	Growing sales, profitable, but margins fluctuating and uncertain conditions due to tightening regulations, Brexit, and issues regarding safe access to raw materials, expansion in Japan, India, Australia to mitigate negative effects	Trusteeship as unique form of community ownership, corporate governance system, continuous innovation, using "The Natural Step" sustainability methodology to reduce environmental impact, develop employees, improve health and safety conditions	Leading role in its segments in innovation, technology, certified processes and products, professional awards for social and environmental sustainability performance, exemplary role in donating to local, national, and international charities in education, health care, community development, sustainable livelihoods	Strong competition with variety of competitors, innovation, customer care, long-term strategic commitment, enhancing niche market presence, close partnerships, supply and geographic expansion

	Value propositions	Market segment	Cost structure and profit potential	Structure of the value chain	Position within the value network	Competitive strategy
TerraCycle	Eliminating the concept of waste, recycling the non-recyclable, implementing eco-capitalism, circular economy, awareness raising, enhancing partners' brands and consumer loyalty, additional consultancy services (PR, social media)	Collection, recycling, reusing waste considered non-recyclable, national brand- and customer-funded waste collection programs, material sales including "Storied Plastic," regulated waste recycling	Zero or negative cost raw material due to sponsored waste collection programs, all products made of waste, increasing awareness, growing sales and profitability, improving product mix to achieve higher margins	Scientific research, product, process, business model, marketing innovations, 200 + million individual waste pickers, global brands as engaged partners, fair partnerships in logistics, plastic processing, consumer awareness raising (TV shows, online game)	Global market leader, opinion leader, pioneer in eliminating the concept of waste, solving global social and ecological problems, mobilizing brands, individuals, and communities, donating to charities selected by waste pickers, funding programs in emerging countries, over 200 business, sustainability awards	Unique service, no direct competition, strong brand, effective differentiation, close and intensifying cooperation with stakeholders, even with large waste management companies abroad

Source Author's construction

Ecologically Conscious Business Models in the Hungarian Sample

This section briefly introduces the business models of 14 well-known Hungary-based ecologically conscious business organizations along the same six dimensions as the international cases. The descriptions are based on the interviews with the businesses and information available on the companies' websites and in company documents such as mission statements, annual reports, ethical codes of conduct, sustainability reports, compliance reports, programs, and product catalogues.

Skanska Hungary

Skanska Hungary is a leading commercial property developer with a focus on project development, leasing, and facility management. The main goal of the company, as part of the Sweden-based Skanska group, is to help build a better society and generate shareholder value alongside promoting social responsibility. Through innovative and sustainable solutions, the company is involved in creating a sustainable future for all stakeholders, including employees, customers, and communities. It is committed to safety, ethical behavior, green, and community investment, as well as diversity and inclusion. Skanska's core values are caring for the lives of people, the environment, and future generations by supporting health and well-being and promoting green solutions, doing business in an ethical and transparent way, development, innovation, learning and sharing expertise, and cooperation and commitment to its customers, as summarized by András Schmidt, sustainability manager of Skanska Hungary.

The company has developed more than 200,000 square meters of commercial space for offices and retail in Hungary, and more projects are under development. It is located in Budapest, and since 2015 has also involved a construction business. Skanska Hungary is focusing on green real estate development, and promotes close cooperation through tailor-made solutions primarily for business clients.

The company has steadily grown into a medium-sized company and had annual turnover of over five million USD and around 70 employees in 2019. It has been profitable since its inception in 1987. The market outlook seems to be favorable, but depends on economic growth trends. The sensitivity of its clients to the sustainability features of buildings is still evolving, so it considers it important to keep its prices at around the market average, despite the higher costs of its social and environmental responsibility practices. However, in many cases improvements in environmental performance can lead to financial savings due to decreases in material and energy consumption.

Skanska Hungary's value chain includes property development, architectural design, construction, and project management. The Hungarian construction department is smaller than in the Polish, Czech, and Romanian sister companies, although innovation performance (such as creative interior design) is of particular importance. The company strives to minimize the negative environmental impact of the construction process and facility management through industry-leading practices like reducing energy, water, material consumption, the amount of waste, and carbon emissions.

Within its value network, in addition to social responsibility (with a focus on supporting employee well-being through occupational safety and clients via applying the "WELL" standard, helping local communities through corporate community investment, and considering future generations), the protection of the environment is of particular importance to Skanska Hungary. It is the only developer in Hungary that has been audited and certified according to the standards of ISO 14001 environmental management schemes. Its buildings are also certified in line with the LEED standard. The company also pays attention to adhering to its core values when choosing potential partners. Skanska Hungary has developed and applied a code of conduct to its own employees and suppliers. Over the years, the professional and sustainability performance of the company has been recognized by awards such as "The City of the Future Award" in the For a Greener City category in 2016, Leading Green Building Development of the Year in the "Construction and Investment Journal Award" in 2016, and the "Office of the Year" in 2016 and 2018.

Skanska Hungary is a medium-sized player in the Hungarian construction industry and faces strong competition, while the Swedish group is one of the world's leading real estate developers. The industry has recently been a key economic sector in Hungary. The company can maintain its competitive advantages by continuously developing its industry-leading environmental and work and health safety practices that go beyond strict regulatory compliance.

Nekedterem Hungary

The mission of owner-manager Eszter Molnár and her company is to provide its customers with food products from local producers in Budapest and its surroundings via a webshop, home delivery, food-box delivery, and subscription services. Its product range includes high quality, pure, local, small-scale, artisan Hungarian products. Nekedterem's goal is to minimize the length of the supply chain and transportation, use recyclable, biologically degradable packaging materials, and selectively collect the waste produced during its operation.

Nekedterem serves consumers who are searching for healthy, high-quality fresh or processed food products from Hungarian small-scale, artisan producers who prefer to make purchases online, with home delivery. Products in many cases are organically certified or guaranteed additive-free and chemical-free. Its customers are mainly individuals and families, and Nekedterem supplies corporate partners who want to provide their employees with fresh seasonal fruit.

The company offers premium products at higher than average prices. Due to its stable customer base, Nekedterem is still a micro enterprise, but it has experienced an increase in annual turnover since its inception. Its profitability is stable, and the owner is optimistic about the future due to strong customer loyalty and the growing popularity of health-conscious food consumption.

The structure of Nekedterem's value chain is simple. It involves purchasing goods from local Hungarian farmers and suppliers around Budapest. The processing of online orders, home delivery of orders, and serving consumers at the company's site (which also functions as a pick-up point) are key elements of the business. The company is continuously searching for new products and partners, monitoring existing ones, and keeping contact with its stakeholders.

Within its value network, Nekedterem maintains close contact with its stakeholders and monitors the operations and conditions of suppliers. Through this, the company has a strong desire to support the local economy and local communities. Nekedterem strives to promote environmental consciousness and minimize environmental harm during its operations. It also promotes the health of future generations by providing fresh, healthy, clean food to families. The company is strengthening its connections and relations with civil society, occasionally serving them and people in need by fundraising and donating food.

Nekedterem perceives the competition to be only moderately strong because of its unique niche in the market. Compared to the home delivery services of large supermarket chains such as Auchan, Tesco, or specialty stores, the company's service is special because it offers fresh organic, healthy products. Compared to food-box delivery schemes based on community-supported agriculture (such as that of Szatyorbolt), Nekedterem offers home delivery as a convenience service.

Réthy Fashion

Réthy Fashion's value proposition is recycling and reusing denim jeans fabric by rethinking the connection between environmental protection and fashion. The company designs and creates high quality, innovative fashion products made of denim fabric. At fashion shows and environmental events, it also engages its stakeholders with environmental awareness-raising activities, and promotes selective waste collection. Réthy Fashion is also engaged in social value creation through employing disadvantaged people. The idea is to protect the climate and fight global warming by striving toward a circular economy.

The company's market segment is designing, producing, and selling unique fashion products to individual and business customers who are interested in environmentally conscious and custom-designed clothing.

Réthy Fashion sells its products in its own showroom, via a webstore, in a sample shop, and at fairs.

Réthy Fashion was established in 2012 as a family business, but started to develop after moving to a new site with its own recycling center in 2016. It still counts as a micro enterprise, and its profitability is around the break-even point. The company's high-quality design products can cost more and reach higher prices than the market average. Based on a satisfied and growing customer base, Réthy Fashion expects to undergo steady but limited development due to the relatively low level of demand and average level of ecological consciousness of consumers in Hungary.

The structure of Réthy Fashion's value chain consists of collecting, cleaning, processing, color sorting, tailoring, and sewing denim fabric. Raw materials can include lace, empty coffee capsules, buttons, and zippers, of which uniquely designed products, uniforms, and accessories are made. The company also operates a jeans repair service, does tailoring work, and runs an upholsterers. High-quality product development, awareness-raising activities at fashion shows, and educational events are key parts of its value chain, too.

Within its value network, Réthy Fashion promotes social engagement in environmental protection, recycling, environmental education, and employment of disadvantaged people. After its inception, the company participated in the fourth NESsT-Citibank Social Enterprise Development Program because of its commitment to environmental and social responsibility. Réthy Fashion's goal is to set an example, for example, by having been a 100 per cent carbon-neutral enterprise since 2015. The company has continuously been working on raising consumer awareness. It advocates eco-fashion and recycling at various environmental events such as eco-fashion shows, eco-days, jeans waste collections, and exhibitions. In 2013, Réthy Fashion was awarded the special Ozone Green Award, which was founded by a Hungarian television channel (*Ozone Network*) for environmentally conscious viewers.

The company has faced very strong competition, even if it has only one main competitor in Hungary. This competitor competes on price, while Réthy Fashion's main competitive advantages are high quality, unique design, increasingly efficient operations, and an expanding brand

and customer base. The company expects that the ecological consciousness of consumers will increase, and more and more committed partners will find Réthy Fashion due to its strong value commitments.

Bio-Drog Berta

This small-scale, family-based company, founded by Zoltán Berta, has been engaged in organic farming for almost three decades and is committed to value creation for its local and national community. Its goal is to use the talent and skills of its owners and employees in a form of agriculture that is still not common in Hungary. Bio-Drog Berta strives to produce as many innovative products as possible, to utilize through processing the greatest proportion of plants grown on excellent agricultural land as possible, and to supply the needs of primarily Hungarian consumers.

Bio-Drog-Berta has the potential to produce, process, and trade approximately 160 kinds of organic, health-preserving, health-improving, processed plant-based products made of fruit, vegetables, cereals, seeds, herbs, spices, and flowers. Its product range includes fruit and vegetable products, flours, creams, syrups, pastes, tea, vinegar, chocolate, and aperitifs. The company's primary focus is serving Hungarian consumers of organic products through resellers or direct sales, although its products are well known in 14 European Union countries, in Switzerland, and in the United States.

The company has been investing its profits into asset and product development since its foundation in early 1990s. The goal has been to achieve the highest level of processing in order to develop the broadest possible product range. Company products have been well received, and are successful on the market. Production costs are higher than for conventional production, and the main limiting factors have been a growing labor shortage and the potential weakness of an environmentally conscious consumer base. During recent years, the annual sales of Bio-Drog Berta have significantly decreased, along with the number of employees. Profitability is sustainable at a much smaller scale, in the form of a micro-sized enterprise, and due to unfavorable industry trends, significant growth cannot be expected.

The organization's value chain originally covered a full range of organic farming activities such as production, processing, storage, and sales of products cultivated on high-quality agricultural land in Central Hungary. Production involved family farmers from the local community. Bio-Drog Berta's continuous research and development was aimed at the waste-free processing of crops. Its processing capacity has been continuously expanded during the years with increased drying capacity since 1995, a canning industry since 2000, an artisanal chocolate program since 2012, and cold-press oil production since 2014. However, due to significant labor shortages in the industry and the region, the company has faced capacity constraints for years; also, its sales activity has been limited. As a result, a considerable part of the potential product range has recently become unavailable.

Bio-Drog Berta has obtained Hungarian, American, and Swiss certification for its products. Because of the need to make up for the operational limitations of its value chain related to labor-market difficulties, different types of collaboration have been developed over the years. For instance, the company has employed prisoners and people with disabilities recruited by an NGO for several years. For its outstanding social responsibility performance, it was awarded the "KÖVET" award by the KÖVET Association for a Sustainable Economy. The company has also been an active partner of "Bátor Tábor," a foundation that supports seriously ill children and their families, for more than five years. In serving its local community, Bio-Drog Berta also established a community park called "Musical Instrument Trees" to boost tourism in the region based on the Danube river.

Regarding its competitive strategy, the company has faced very strong competition, although the complexity of its value chain, capacity for innovation, and excellent health-promoting features of its products may represent competitive advantages in the domestic market. In multiple cases, Bio-Drog Berta has suffered from unfair competition such as patent infringements by former partners, but due to its weak human resources and financial capacity, it was not able to engage in lengthy litigation processes.

Ecoizm/Zöldbolt

The mission of the founder, Adrián Zelenák, and his enterprise is to distribute sustainable and ecological household products in its brick-and-mortar stores and via e-commerce. Its products serve consumers' everyday needs, and in all cases have some significant environmental beneficial characteristics in relation to substitute products. Ecoizm is continuously monitoring product innovations and promoting environmental awareness.

In its stores and via its webshop Ecoizm sells a wide range of environmentally friendly household products, as substitutes for conventional products, to domestic and foreign individuals, retailers, and wholesale partners. Its mix includes products in the segments of beauty and health care, cleaning and washing, food staples, eco paper and stationery, home and garden, eco clothing, toys and baby products, books and DVDs, and energy-efficient products for water-, power- and heat-saving.

Ecoizm saw sharp growth after its start in 2008. It then witnessed a moderate but steady increase in sales and profitable operation as a small enterprise. Its profit margins are significantly lower in the wholesale than in the retail segment, but the potential for profit has been favorable for years.

Its value chain consists of search- and purchasing-related activities, in some cases the retail packaging of larger items, own brand packaging, serving retail and wholesale partners, a webshop operation, and after-sales services. Ecoizm also has an online magazine with fresh environmental news and provides awareness-raising services for its partners. The enterprise is continuously striving to make its office operation greener through the recycling of paper and packaging materials. Its office and stores have been powered by 100 per cent renewable energy (from a nearby wind power plant) since 2017.

Ecoizm is always searching for household products with the best characteristics in terms of environmental load, and raising its consumers' awareness. Its aims are to be a flagship player in the market, and a reference point for purchasing eco-products. The enterprise has developed its own rating system for products in different categories for much more convenient and transparent searching. It is continuously monitoring the latest innovation and product developments, and cooperates with the authorities when introducing innovations such as new packaging-free solutions in the retail sector. It has close relationships with civil society organizations such as the Association of Conscious Consumers, the Hungarian Cyclists' Club, the Hungarian Ornithological and Nature Conservation Association.

Ecoizm perceives its competitive situation to be moderately strong because its wide range product offerings, value commitments, and customer base do not fully overlap with those of its competitors and some other major Hungarian eco shops such as Zöldpolc and Ökokuckó. Consumers can thus differentiate, so these shops are able to coexist. Over the years, some of its products have appeared on the shelves of large international supermarket chains including Tesco and Drogerie Markt, and also in specialized stores (for example, washable diapers in shops for baby products). In these cases, its competitive advantage based on specific and unique products does not exist, but one of Ecoizm's main goals, to disseminate eco-products, has been achieved, which the enterprise considers much more important than improving sales figures at all costs.

ALTEO Energy

ALTEO's main value proposition is related to sustainable energy production, energy trade, and bespoke energy services that will help the company achieve its climate protection goals at an appropriate cost level and security of supply. The company is committed to promoting energy democracy, customized services, and sustainable business benefits for its customers. It strives to create solutions that are easy-to-adapt, flexible, innovative, and efficient. ALTEO aims to be an industry leader by example, and to generate long-term economic, environmental, and social value. The company believes that everyone has right to a healthy environment, to which ALTEO can contribute by adhering to the principles of operating in an ethical and transparent way, responsible corporate governance, the protection of human life and security, environmental responsibility throughout the supply chain, ensuring equal treatment, and fostering lasting, mutually beneficial partnerships.

Company market segments include the construction, operation and maintenance of power plants based on natural gas and renewable energy sources such as solar, wind, water, landfill gas, biomass, biogas power. ALTEO mainly serves large business partners by producing electricity, and retail customers primarily through natural gas trading.

General market conditions have been challenging for years due to labor-market-related supply issues and a stringent regulatory environment. Taking advantage of its favorable market segment potential, ALTEO has rapidly grown since its foundation in 2008. In 2019, annual sales reached nearly 90 million USD (increasing by almost 40 per cent at the group level). This positive trend has been supported by the successful extension of several long-term key contracts and the acquisition of guaranteed profit contracts. The number of employees has significantly increased to more than 250. ALTEO's energy trading segment is price sensitive, but in other segments the company's customers are strongly loyal. Return and profit potential is outstanding, and stock prices have been increasing year by year, while credit ratings are favorable and improving.

ALTEO's value chain includes the construction, operation, and maintenance of power plants. The company has a leading role in research and development and customer-oriented product development. Through its energy provision and trading services, ALTEO is a qualified supplier for numerous partners. In line with strong industry trends, the company is striving to develop and implement high-quality information and communication technologies specific to the energy sector. Its support functions (such as human resources, legal affairs, finance, accounting, and administration) all are based on respect for and the financial and moral recognition of employees, good working conditions, and responsible relationships. The company culture is strong and optimistic; employee turnover is well below the average for the industry and national economy. In 2017, ALTEO introduced the ALTEO Academy to organize sustainability training for employees to enhance their holistic vision.

ALTEO plays an exemplary role in its value network, striving for the position of opinion leader and benchmark actor in the industry. The company's intention is to set an example by being a highly innovative, environmentally and socially responsible player in its market. ALTEO's energy production has been "certified green" by the Hungarian Energy Office. The company has applied environmental management standards, and published award-winning sustainability reports. In 2019, it published an integrated report to present its economic, sustainability, and social impact. For years, its chief executive officer, Attila Chikán, Jr., has been an active member and president of the Business Council of Sustainable Development Hungary (BCSDH), and a member of the Hungarian Business Leaders' Forum. ALTEO has trust-based, mutually beneficial relationships with its stakeholders through providing tailor-made solutions to clients, closely cooperating with nonprofit organizations (WWF, the National Council for Sustainable Development), and following the activities of flagship organizations such as Greenpeace. The company promotes sustainability along its value chain and ecological orientation via its participation in BCSDH. ALTEO also aims to educate and motivate people to consider and live out the principles of sustainability.

ALTEO's competitive strategy is to maintain its leading position, and continue setting an example. The company has some competitive advantages and a moderately strong competitive position, for example, in relation to the largest market player E.On, due to its genuine value-based commitment and ecological consciousness. These factors are increasingly important to its customers, so ALTEO can efficiently use its market potential. The company collaborates with other market players based on the principle of reciprocity. It is also actively developing its competencies, adaptability, and learning abilities because it expects significant changes in the world.

Hajtás Pajtás

Hajtás Pajtás is a bicycle courier company that delivers mail and parcels to its customers in Budapest. Its service is based on high level of trust and reliability. Unlike the typical companies in this industry, Hajtás Pajtás operates in a transparent and law-abiding way. Its value proposition includes sustainability, environmental consciousness, striving to avoid unnecessary pollution, social responsibility, and, no less importantly, promoting bicycling activism for a more livable environment in Budapest.

Its market segment is a bicycle courier service mainly for business customers, primarily for those who are seeking a reliable and confidential service. Hajtás Pajtás has recently complemented its service portfolio with an electric truck service for packages not suitable for bicycle courier delivery.

The company's services are the highest priced ones on the market due to significant labor costs and its fully transparent, law-abiding mode of operation. The company dynamically grew after its inception in 1999 until the 2008 financial crisis. During the big downturn, Hajtás Pajtás reorganized its operations and decided to totally move away from the "grey" practices typical to the industry. Accordingly, headcount was reduced, prices increased, and all profits were reinvested into becoming economically sustainable again. The company restarted developing in new directions, including increasing package sizes, webshop deliveries, cooperating with traditional courier companies such as GLS, and enhancing trust by ensuring a high level of confidentiality. Hajtás Pajtás has increased over the years into a medium-sized company, and in 2019 had annual revenue of about 1.5 million USD, and nearly 60 employees.

Hajtás Pajtás's value chain is based on its couriers. The company strives to provide them with salaries higher than the industry average. In the case of price increases, it also pays a higher wage to couriers. Couriers are also supported through in-kind benefits such as the provision of a benefits system, bicycles, repairs and parts. Hajtás Pajtás maintains a good company atmosphere and a special culture, thus for the employees who work there the job represents a lifestyle. Based on these factors, the company has played a major role in promoting bicycling in Budapest and throughout Hungary. Beyond the core business, due to its environmental consciousness Hajtás Pajtás has always been committed to pioneering other activities, including those related to office administration, such as the selective collection of waste and empty batteries, even years before this became popular in Hungary.

The goal of the owners, László Géresi and Zoltán Tóth, and their company is to set an example by promoting ecological and social responsibility, social equality, and cycling activism. For two decades, Hajtás Pajtás has been the greatest advocate of expanding the cycling movement in Budapest and has undertaken negotiations with local governments and authorities and cooperated with them to improve conditions for bicycling in the capital. The company started and organized the biggest Hungarian cycling movement (Critical Mass), and it is the founder and committed supporter of the Hungarian Bicyclist's Club.

Hajtás Pajtás has been a pioneer of bicycle courier services in the Hungarian market, and is still the market leader. Its brand is well known and respected, despite very strong competition. Due to its social impact, all courier companies now have a bicycle courier business. The area served by bicycle couriers in Budapest is expanding and the company has started collaborating with traditional players to meet demand for all those orders that can be managed by bicycle couriers as well. Hajtás Pajtás's competitive advantage is based on its strong commitment, reliability, credibility, and a brand that has gained strength over two decades.

Pannonhalmi Abbey Winery

The company's value proposition is based on the Benedictine monks' values, derived from the Regula of Saint Benedict, marketing and sales manager Tamás Illés says. These include balance between spiritual life and physical activity, love of work, self-sustenance, education, and the dissemination of culture. Its goals are to revive the culture of viticulture and wine-making, to make the nonprofit activities—including operating social, educational, cultural institutions—of the abbey economically sustainable, and to produce their own sacramental wine. The company's core values are responsibility, sustainability, and the preservation and nurturing of values and resources for future generations.

Pannonhalmi Abbey Winery's market segment is the production of high-quality premium wine for domestic sales and exporting to commercial companies and direct consumers.

Since its foundation in 2002 and the full renewal of its grapevine plantations, the company has dynamically developed in terms of quantity and quality. Its annual turnover fluctuated at first along with seasonal changes, but then increased for years to about 1.8 million USD in 2019. The company's position has been stable in the quality wine segment, and customer loyalty is strong. Profits from operations are favorable, and after the repayment of a large portion of the initial investment loan, it became financially profitable two years ago. Regarding the state of ecological consciousness, Pannonhalmi Abbey Winery expects significant improvements and changes in consumers' attitudes in the future that will positively influence the sale of its quality products.

In its value chain, the company cultivates its vineyards and engages in viticulture, grape processing, and wine-making with the least possible environmental harm. Due to expanding sales, the number of employees has increased, and during seasonal work it typically doubles. The organizational development project of the abbey is complete, and the operation of the company group has become more transparent, due to which the company expects better synergy.

Pannonhalmi Abbey Winery evaluates its position within its value network in relation to the application of a holistic approach. Its stakeholders include the beneficiaries of the social, educational, and cultural activities of the abbey. It strives to strengthen environmental consciousness through its operations and supporting functions such as administration and transportation, thereby minimizing the environmental impact of the whole company. It has actively supported the civil society organizations established by the abbey, through which the company would like to fulfill its broader mission of integrating social and environmental responsibility.

The company faces strong competition, because in the premium market segment for wines there are many competitors in the limited Hungarian market. The export orientation is thus given special emphasis. In the premium market segment, other players are also increasingly ecologically conscious, so Pannonhalmi Abbey Winery can operate successfully by relying on its traditional values and the strong loyalty of its consumers.

NES Shoes

The most important value proposition of NES Shoes is the individual and customized design, production and distribution of handmade, tasteful, and environmentally friendly shoes in a sustainable manner. Its products are made exclusively of natural, biodegradable, vegan, recycled and/or recyclable raw materials. Since 2015, its increasingly sustainable production facility has been located in Eastern Hungary, where the factory plant is heated by biomass, gets its electricity from solar panels, and strives to use local raw materials. NES Shoes also promotes the self-expression of self-aware women and men, the spread of ecological consciousness, social and individual responsibility, and the importance of aesthetics and joy.

Its market segment is specifically the production of unique shoes and making direct sales primarily to female customers who are self-aware, wish to care for the environment, and want to express their personality through their shoes. Since 2020, alongside ongoing individual orders, a limited series of sophisticated yet affordable shoes have been available in brick-and-mortar stores in Budapest as part of an expanded product range.

In the years after the inception of this micro-sized enterprise in 2008, annual sales fluctuated and profitability remained around the break-even point as performance was based solely on the individual effort and engagement of the owner-manager, Andrea Szilágyi. Costs have been higher than the market average due to the tailor-made products with strong ecological commitment. NES Shoes has recently joined forces with a manufacturer through which changes have been made to the offerings, and the product range has been extended to a limited series of shoes. The company predicts that domestic purchasing power is now sufficient to support growth, but consumer awareness is still developing. The aim of the company is to strengthen serial production while maintaining a personalized service and improving profitability.

NES Shoes' value chain consists of customized and serial design, production and sales. It has had no inventory until recently, only making new collections every three months in advance of exhibitions that could be purchased at its show room. In 2020, this model was completed with a limited serious of sophisticated shoes to be sold in brick-and-mortar stores in Budapest. The value chain also includes high-quality personal customer management, a lifetime repair warranty for every product, and continuous research and development for monitoring and testing ecological raw materials such as "mushroom leather." NES Shoes also nurtures personal, fair, and caring relationship with employees at the manufacturing plant.

The company typically sells directly to customers and resellers, with whom it has personal relationships. The ecological aspects of its operation are particularly important, so the sources of raw materials and circumstances of production are carefully considered and selected. NES Shoes also strives to minimize the need for transport and to enhance the proportion of pre- and post-consumer recycling in its operations. Its civil society relations and collaboration are of significant importance, and the company promotes and supports artistic, educational activities. The designer-owner and her brand are well known in the special market segment for their value commitments, which reputation the designer has also used to increase customer awareness.

Due to the special product range of customized environmentally friendly shoes and the global geographic fragmentation of its competitors, NES Shoes has not really perceived strong competition so far. In general, Hungarian customers are still less environmentally conscious than in richer countries such as those of Northern Europe. Ecological consciousness is slowly evolving in Hungary, and customers typically seek out NES Shoes because of the products' aesthetic features, not due to their minimal environmental impact.

Béres Pharmaceuticals

Béres's most important value proposition is natural health preservation by using a unique trace element supplement, "Béres Drops," and other natural products that strengthen the immune system. Its operations are based on the principles of human-centeredness, supporting people in need, and acknowledging and promoting education, culture, and science. Béres also has a subsidiary that is engaged in environmentally friendly viticulture and wine-making. Its core values include righteousness, reliability, predictability, social-, national-, and environmental responsibility, perseverance, diligence, compassion and commitment, most of the latter based on the founder family's deeply felt Christian values. Béres aims to produce high-quality products and operate a successful, transparent, and efficient organization imbued with team spirit.

The company's products are made of natural ingredients and are designed for health-conscious consumers who are actively seeking to prevent illness or are living with special needs. Its main markets are Hungary, Russia, and Eastern Europe. Béres is one of the best known Hungarian brands, and the company is a market leader in several product segments such as immune-system strengthening products, complex multivitamin, mineral and trace element products, and vitamin C and complex vitamin D supplements.

The predecessor of the company was established in the late 1980s based on an invention of the late József Béres Sr. known as "Béres Drops," and has organically grown from a small family business into a large company with annual revenue of about 45 million USD, and is still owned and managed by the Béres family. It predominantly makes domestic sales, but exports are dynamically expanding. Indirect costs are a large part of its cost structure, but their proportion is decreasing. Béres has succeeded in making production more efficient, so its profitability has increased. Its profit margins are below the average of international competitors, but for the company this is not the focus, but rather behaving ethically with all of its stakeholders and promoting their well-being, while remaining sufficiently profitable.

Key factors in Béres's value chain are intense, successful product innovation, the licensing of new products, and the protection of industrial property rights. During recent years, the company has successful expanded its factory and warehouse in Szolnok, Eastern Hungary, thereby creating new work places. Its logistical capacity has also been developed, and strategic alliances built with its main sales channel, pharmacies. The company's contract manufacturing business has significantly increased and several successful products made in collaboration with competitors are now sold outside Hungary. Béres's outstanding marketing and communication performance has been recognized with numerous awards. Its human-centered approach to human resource management is manifest in an attractive and supportive working environment.

Considering Béres's position within its value network, the following facts can be highlighted. The company is committed to using a code of ethics and behaving fairly to a wide range of stakeholders, from employees to the natural environment. The Béres Foundation was established to support people in need, education, culture, and science through financial and in-kind donations. Béres Winery supports the development of the Tokaj wine region, its traditions, and wine culture. Béres strives to retain employees and build respectful, positive relationships with its consumers, partners, and the authorities; it has even cooperated with several of its competitors. Through its environmental policy, Béres aims to create a safe working environment, to reduce pollution and material consumption, to provide training, and to motivate its employees to develop an environmental consciousness.

In the industry in which it operates, regulation is very strict, and competition with big international manufacturers is strong but fair. However, Béres also has to compete with dubious Far Eastern producers in terms of cost and price competition. Continuous product innovation, a high-quality management system rolled out along the whole value chain, and strict compliance with the law are key success factors, besides Béres's strong value commitment that differentiates the company and helps maintain a loyal consumer base and the organization's organic development.

Kör Architect Studio

The company's value proposition includes designing ecological and sustainable buildings, providing education, developing the wider industry, and continuously striving to implement an ecological approach. Kör Architect Studio is committed to Rudolf Steiner's anthroposophy and the idea of a self-governing society, which represents an alternative approach to the prevailing socio-economic system. The principles of this concept are freedom of spiritual life, direct democracy, and a solidarity economy; moreover, the healthier functioning of the economy based on an alternative economics that is not built on the principle of profit and the exploitation of natural and human resources. Core values are cooperation, preferring human-scale solutions, and harmony between humanity and the natural environment.

Kör Architect Studio's market segment is the architectural design of ecological and sustainable buildings like autonomous houses and resilient houses. This is complemented by educational and industrial development services and awareness-raising activities. The company has no permanent, long-term partners, unlike the situation in some segments of the Hungarian construction industry.

The company is a micro-sized enterprise whose annual revenue and economic situation fluctuates depending on the number of orders. It has successfully maintained its business operations so far, but it appears that the future is impossible to forecast. In general, market conditions in the construction industry now favor big players with integrated operations and significant lobbying capacity. Although the company does not have permanent partners, conscious customers who have similar value commitments may find it, and other designers recommend the company when they are faced with special demands concerning ecological design. Satisfied and loyal customers also recommend it to others. Overall, ecological consciousness is still rewarded because some customers specifically choose the company because of its commitment and attitude.

Kör Architect Studio's value chain is short. It is a micro enterprise that works with trusted partners in architectural design in accordance with the organic social concept of anthroposophy. It has its own product development process, the results of which are the concepts of the autonomous house, the resilient house, and bio toilets. It strives to make its office operations more environmentally friendly, for instance, through the use of solar cells. However, the success of this goal will depend on future resources. The owner-manager's activities in higher education, professional training, and talks and writing about awareness raising also play an important role in the company's value chain.

Within its value network, Kör Architect Studio pays particular attention to the stakeholders of its operations in accordance with an ecological approach. It closely cooperates with its partners, and potential customers and partners can find the company even in the absence of a company website. Its goal is to set an example and to maintain committed relationships with social organizations. The owner-manager, Attila Ertsey, participated in the establishment of a green party, and has been the leader of the Nádasdy Academy, which holds annual ecological and artistic symposiums about facilitating a paradigm shift in the socio-economic system.

The company has faced very strong competition in the architectural design market in general, but the ten to twenty actors in the eco-design segment tend to coexist and cooperate. Through strong commitment to ecological and sustainable building design, Kör Architect Studio strives to create a network of self-governing, collaborative, and human-scale companies through which the healthier, organic operation of companies can prevail, instead of a situation of competition and "overgrowth."

Pipacs Bakery

Pipacs Bakery produces organically certified bread. Its main value propositions are ecological values, connection to nature, the protection of life and health, human-centeredness, and the material and moral appreciation of employees. The company respects all members and communities within its value chain. It strives to avoid night shifts, in sharp contrast to other bakeries. Its relationships with partners are based on trust and mutual responsibility over the long term, owner-manager Ádám Fülöp expresses.

The company's market segment is producing organic bread in an artisan bakery, primarily for health-conscious and environmentally aware individual consumers. Pipacs Bakery has only a few distributor partners with limited sales volumes. It operates no night shifts, so the product range is narrow and focuses on organic bread and a few kinds of pastries. In its shop, Pipacs sells raw materials for bread making and some staple food products made by its partners such as cheese, butter, jam, honey, and sausages, which are mainly organically certified.

Pipacs Bakery has grown rapidly since its foundation in 2014, both in terms of production volumes and sales. The company has been reinvesting its profits into machinery and human resource development for years. It pays better salaries than the industry average, and its organically certified raw materials are much more expensive than non-certified ones, so its products are more costly than conventional ones. Customer loyalty to Pipacs Bakery has been strong since the beginning. In many cases, it is not environmental consciousness but health issues that drive its clients to buy organic products.

With organic bread baking, the value chain starts with the purchase of high quality, certified raw materials, and the quality of flour is the key factor. Only organic raw materials from organic farms are used by Pipacs Bakery, which uses flours from Hungarian mills plus one Hungarian farmer, while only some additional raw materials are sourced from overseas for which there is no local alternative. Flour is ground by selected, trustworthy Hungarian mills with which Pipacs Bakery has long-term relationships. The company sells its products at an organic market, in its own shop, and via a few resellers. Pipacs Bakery has been maintaining salaries at a more favorable level than the industry average and does not use night shifts to avoid violating its own strict value commitment to human-centeredness.

Pipacs Bakery was the first bakery in Hungary not to use night shifts, and only a few have followed its example so far. However, owing to this practice the company is not as affected by labor shortages because employees are more engaged and loyal. Its focus is on direct consumers, because Pipacs Bakery has not been able to supply larger quantities of products to reseller partners due to the unconventional work shifts. The company wants to set an example, promote artisanal organic bread, and prioritize direct human relationships with partners. An important element of its value network is promoting the products of its key partners.

The company perceives competition as moderate, and even strives to cooperate with industry competitors on the basis of shared values. It consciously pursues a strategy of non-competition, mutual support, and learning from other players. Its commitment to organic production is its strongest value, but customer loyalty may be due to the high quality, healthy products it offers rather than the organic certification. Nevertheless, these circumstances do not change the depth of Pipacs Bakery's commitments, as the company believes in making long-term changes in a positive direction, because there is no other way to create a livable future.

Pendits Vineyards and Winery

Pendits' main value proposition is following the principles and values of biodynamic farming and winemaking as a philosophy of life. Through this spiritual approach based on anthroposophy, the company seeks to live and work in harmony with nature, acknowledging the organic unity of man, plants, animals, and terroir. Pendits takes into account the impact of natural cycles in its operation and believes that the economy is an organism that should have the ability to be self-sustaining and autonomous. By building on regional values, products, and relationships, Pendits's goals are to produce a clean and healthy product of excellent quality that is associated with social responsibility and the conservation of the integrity of terroir, to develop sustainably, and to strengthen and utilize environmental, cultural, and local community values, as well as engage in innovative research, and support family farms.

The company's market segment is ecological, biodynamic farming, viticulture, and winemaking, and producing biodynamic and organically certified products for some major partners such as merchants and restaurants, as well as direct consumers.

Pendits is a micro-sized family enterprise that was established in 1991. It employs one permanent employee and seasonal workers, besides the two owners. Its economic situation fluctuates depending on the demands of the main partners. Various trends and difficulties associated with the wine market cause significant challenges from year to year. Pendits has also been suffering from labor shortages. The company believes that organic products do not necessarily have to be more expensive than conventional ones, but the consumption of organic products in Hungary is not yet widespread. However, due to improving living standards and purchasing power and a gradual increase in consumer awareness, this market segment has significant development potential in Hungary. Pendits can also build its development on its loyal customer base.

The company's value chain includes viticulture, winemaking, and trade. Innovation is also a key element. For instance, Pendits has been researching how to use covering vegetation among rows of vines to improve soil characteristics and increase biodiversity. It also has studied how to manage manual labor shortages in the region, and thereby increase economic viability. Most of its employees do not share Pendits's ecological commitment, but respect the owners' genuine commitment, fair attitude, and persistent activity.

Pendits was the first certified biodynamic wine estate in the traditional Hungarian Tokaj-Hegyalja wine region, being certified since 2011. It operates according to the strict regulations defined in European Union wine law, and the international trademark of Demeter International. The company is the only Hungarian member of the international biodynamic association established by Nicolas Joly, a leading organization in the biodynamic market segment. Pendits has excellent personal and professional relationships with the Bioculture Association, Biokontroll Hungary certification organizations, and the Hungarian Research Institute of Organic Agriculture. It continuously supports regional and local communities and intends to represent an example. It also participates in youth education, and awareness-raising activity. The owner-manager, Márta Wille-Baumkauff, is president of the Hungarian Association of Independent Winegrowers (Vindependent), and strives to help shape favorable regulation for the industry through long-term cooperation with the Hungarian authorities.

In Hungary, there are very few biodynamic wineries, and those that exist are typically small enterprises. The size of the area on which organic farming is practiced is growing, but there is not yet significant domestic demand for the associated products. Pendits faces strong price competition because the company competes with conventional wine producers. However, through its special technology and products, Pendits can differentiate itself from the market average and build its development on its value commitments that represent a competitive advantage.

MagNet Bank

MagNet Hungarian Community Bank is a commercial bank that was founded as a savings cooperative in 1995. It became a triple-bottom-line focused, values-based community bank that strives to promote sustainability and environmental and social responsibility a decade ago. This kind of organization is also known as an ethical or sustainable bank. Respect and trust, consciousness, innovation, transparency, and human-centeredness are key elements of MagNet Bank's value proposition, deputy chief executive officer Gábor Pozsonyi explained.

MagNet Bank works within the market segment of commercial banks. It does not provide some services, such as securities account management or credit cards, to its customers for historical, business, and moral reasons. Its main customers are individuals and business enterprises, and MagNet Bank is one of the most important banking partners of nonprofit organizations in Hungary.

MagNet Bank has developed organically through some minor acquisitions into a company with about 20 million USD annual turnover. It has lower than industry average profitability, but income is more stable, and the bank has never made a loss in its entire history, including during the 2008 financial crisis. Its values-based practices have proved to be resilient due to a more favorable credit portfolio grounded on a customer base with a higher than average willingness to cooperate and repay loans.

In its value chain, MagNet Bank focuses on banking services such as account management, loans, deposits, receivables management, and factoring for retail, corporate, and nonprofit customers. Supporting Hungarian civil organizations and communities is of particular importance to the company.

MagNet Bank is a member of the international organization Global Alliance for Banking on Values due to its values-based approach related to ethical and sustainability principles. The company has been a supporter of the long-term social, environmental and economic development and cultural life of its stakeholder communities. It provides community banking products such as a Community Donation Program through which MagNet Bank donates 10 per cent of its annual profit to nonprofit organizations selected by customers. The company also has community deposits and loans and a Supportive Bank Card program, Pay as You Like account management, and an Individual Donation Program. In the course of credit scoring, MagNet Bank applies positive screening measures to projects that have a beneficial impact on the environment and society. The company supports civic events and community-building activities through providing space in its MagNet Community House.

Competition has been very strong in the retail and small business banking sector in Hungary, but MagNet Bank's values-based functioning successfully differentiates the company from conventional banks. Social and environmental responsibility, credibility, transparency based on its value commitments, and a loyal clientele are MagNet Bank's main competitive advantages.

Table 6.2 describes the main characteristics of the Hungary-based ecologically conscious business models.

To conclude, the business models of the businesses in the Hungarian sample are based on the various value commitments of the representatives of the enterprises (founders, owners, and managers). The market segments of their operations and the structure of their value chains are characterized by great variety. Most of them operate at a higher cost level and/or lower but more stable level of profitability (due to their more committed customer base) compared to the market average of their competitors who have no ecological consciousness, or only a lower level. Micro-sized enterprises face a more challenging economic situation as they struggle with financing, human-resource-related issues including labor shortages, and deficiencies in general business knowledge such as in marketing, sales, and finance. In terms of their position within the value network, most of them have a smaller environmental load than the market average and a strong social responsibility orientation. They pay special attention to their stakeholders (as defined in a broad sense, usually starting with human relationships and expanding to local communities and future generations). More than two-thirds of the respondents stated that setting an example, having a progressive approach, or pioneering or fulfilling the role of opinion-leader are central elements of their operation. The development and promotion of value-oriented, ethical business practices are among the basic goals of most

Table 6.2 Main characteristics of ecologically conscious business models in the Hungarian sample

	Value propositions	Market segment	Cost structure and profit potential	Structure of the value chain	Position within the value network	Competitive strategy
Skanska Hungary	Building for a better society with social responsibility and generating shareholder value	Commercial property development, project management, leasing, facility management, construction	Steady growth to medium size, positive profitability, influenced by economic trends, cost savings	Design, construction, project management, innovation, minimizing negative impacts	Strong social responsibility focus and environmental protection, certification, awards	Very strong competition in a key sector, continuously developing environmental, work, safety practices
Nekedterem Hungary	Sale of healthy, high-quality local food via webshop, home delivery	Fresh/processed food from local, small-scale, artisanal producers, home delivery	Higher costs and prices, micro-sized but improving trend, sales and profits	Purchasing food, products, processing orders, delivery, monitoring, updating	Close contact with stakeholders, supporting local economy, communities	Moderate competition, unique position between supermarkets and box deliveries

(continued)

Table 6.2 (continued)

	Value propositions	Market segment	Cost structure and profit potential	Structure of the value chain	Position within the value network	Competitive strategy
Réthy Fashion	Recycling, reusing jeans in new fashion products, awareness raising	Design, unique fashion products for ecologically conscious customers	Micro enterprise at break-even, with steady but limited growth potential	Collecting raw materials, unique product design, repair, awareness raising	Carbon neutral, promotes social engagement, environmental education, awards	Very strong competition on price, advantages of quality, design, brand
Bio-Drog Berta	Organic farming, value creation for local, national community, innovative products and processes	Organic health-improving processed plant-based products, primarily for Hungarian organic-consumers	Micro-sized, significant decrease in sales, so far sustainable profit, negative industry trends	Potential for full range of organic farming, significant processing capacity, labor shortage in production	Domestic and international organic certification, supporting NGOs, local community, awards	Very strong competition, patent infringements, innovative, healthy products as competitive advantage

	Value propositions	Market segment	Cost structure and profit potential	Structure of the value chain	Position within the value network	Competitive strategy
Ecoizm /Zöldbolt	Distribution of innovative, eco-household products, awareness raising	Wide range of eco-household products for individuals and resellers	Sharp then moderate and steady increase in sales, positive profit potential	Purchasing, packaging, selling, awareness raising, using renewable electricity	Monitoring latest innovation, cooperating with authorities, NGOs	Medium strength competition, differentiation, spread of eco-products
ALTEO Energy	Sustainable energy production, trade and customized service	Construction and operation of power plants using natural gas and renewable energy	Continuous growth in annual revenues, profits, improving stock prices	Leading role in R&D, digitization, loyal stakeholders, strong co.culture	Exemplary role, opinion leader, active cooperation with NGOs	Maintain leading position based on genuine value commitments

(continued)

Table 6.2 (continued)

	Value propositions	Market segment	Cost structure and profit potential	Structure of the value chain	Position within the value network	Competitive strategy
Hajtás Pajtás	Bicycle courier, trust and reliability, transparency, sustainability, activism for a livable capital	Reliable, confidential, bicycle courier service mainly for businesses, electric truck delivery possible	High labor costs, medium-sized company, increasing sales for years depends on general market trends	Couriers are key, providing support to them, special culture, cycling activism in Budapest and the country	Setting an example, promoting ecological, social responsibility, bicycling activism, commitment	Pioneer, market leader in environment of very strong competition, cooperation, reliability and brand reputation
Pannonhalmi Abbey Winery	Reviving winemaking, sustainability based on Benedictine values	Production of high-quality white and red wine for commercial and direct customers	Small company with dynamic development, net profit, growing demand	Viticulture, winemaking, growing workforce, synergies in the company group	Holistic, broad stakeholder definition, environmental, social consciousness	Strong competitors are also eco-conscious, values, consumer loyalty is key

	Value propositions	Market segment	Cost structure and profit potential	Structure of the value chain	Position within the value network	Competitive strategy
NES Shoes	Customized design, increasingly sustainable production, self- and eco-consciousness	Individual orders of unique shoes, limited series, direct sales, stores in Budapest	Fluctuating performance in sales, break-even profit, micro-sized, expansion into serial production	Customized and serial design, production, sales, customer care, lifetime warranty, innovation	Ecological, social commitments, personal relationships, good reputation, awareness raising	Less strong competition due to special product, fragmented global competitors, aesthetics is key
Béres Pharmaceuticals	Health preservation, natural products, social, environmental responsibility, Christian values	Natural immune system, vitamin, mineral, trace element products in Hungary and Eastern Europe	Organic growth into a large family enterprise, margins below those of competitors, focus on sufficiency	Product innovation, licensing, patents are key, factory expansion, strategic alliances, many awards	Fair, long-term relationships with wide range of stakeholders, donations, local development	Strong competition, product innovation, quality management, compliance key, value-based differentiation

(continued)

Table 6.2 (continued)

	Value propositions	Market segment	Cost structure and profit potential	Structure of the value chain	Position within the value network	Competitive strategy
Kör Architect Studio	Ecological architectural design based on anthroposophy, education	Architectural design of autonomous, resilient houses, development	Micro-sized, fluctuating revenues, profitability, based on specific demands	Product development, working with partner designers, education, writing	Close cooperation with stakeholders, setting example, promoting paradigm shift	Fierce competition in gen eral, collaboration in eco-design, creating a network
Pipacs Bakery	Production of organic bread, ecological values, trust, human-centeredness	Organic, artisanal bread, a few pastry and food products, for individuals with specific needs	Rapid growing but still micro enterprise, higher costs, stable customer base	High quality, organic raw materials, long-term cooperation, no night shifts	Setting an example, promoting artisanal products, direct relationships	Moderate competition, striving for collaboration, strong value commitments
Pendits Vineyards and Winery	Biodynamic winemaking, holistic approach, social responsibility	Ecological, biodynamic, organic-certified farming, viticulture, winemaking	Micro-sized family company, labor shortages, loyal customers	Viticulture, winemaking, trade and innovation, labor shortages	Leader, advocate of biodynamic practices and regional values, awareness raising	Strong competition with conventional wine producers, differentiation

	Value propositions	Market segment	Cost structure and profit potential	Structure of the value chain	Position within the value network	Competitive strategy
MagNet Bank	Community and impact bank based on sustainability, transparency	Commercial bank mainly for individuals, NGOs, no securities, credit cards	Organic development, lower but more stable profitability than average	Core banking services for retail, corporate, NGOs, support for communities	Member of GABV, supporting development of stakeholder communities	Very strong competition, successful differentiation, loyal customers

Source Author's construction

of them. In general, these organizations are in a strong or very strong competitive position. If they consider the competition to be less challenging, this is clearly attributable to their competitive advantage due to their special attributes that originate in their ecological consciousness or other value commitments. Such competitive advantages include having a strong brand, a loyal customer base, superior quality products, or being innovative, adaptive, and resilient. Almost two-thirds of the sample companies emphasized that they tend to seek out mutually beneficial forms of cooperation and knowledge sharing, rather than look to compete. Their flexibility and self-sustaining capabilities are strong and they rarely receive subsidies and nor do they usually require them, as they are willing and able to prosper on their own.

Summary

This chapter has presented the business models of ecologically conscious business organizations in an international and Hungarian sample. Their common attributes, compared to the market average, are less environmental impact, greater social responsibility, and the employment of a wider definition of and special attention to a wide range of stakeholders. Additionally, the companies under analysis seek to set an example and lead the markets in which they operate. They may also be required to operate with higher costs and/or lower but more stable levels of profitability, and often face strong competition. However, in this fierce competition, the competitive advantages derived from the material benefits obtained through their genuine value commitments (as confirmed by Cornell economist Robert Frank [2004]) support their long-term survival, pursuit of cooperation, knowledge sharing, and resiliency.

The business models of Hungary-based organizations are similar to those of the leading ecologically conscious international businesses in terms of value propositions and cost structure in most cases. The market segments and the structure of value chains may nevertheless vary greatly, representing the multifarious external and internal operating environments of the individual companies. There are also remarkable differences regarding the size of the international enterprises, which are significantly bigger than the Hungarian ones. The potential for profit of the companies in the international sample is greater, as they operate in a global competitive environment. The smallest Hungarian organizations typically face a more challenging economic situation because they struggle with finance- and human-resource-related challenges and deficiencies in general business knowledge, such as marketing, sales, finance, or human resource management.

Naturally, some of the differences identified above arise due to sampling bias, because in the international sample only world-renowned companies were studied, but—because of our local knowledge—even very small businesses were examined in the Hungarian sample.

The results of the empirical research were also compared to those found in the literature. The main findings of Parrish (2010) in relation to the differences between sustainable enterprises and conventional businesses were confirmed. The objective and raison d'être of successful sustainable enterprises is to preserve and strengthen the quality of human and natural resources over the longest possible time. Sustainable enterprises do not solely pursue a strategy of cost-effectiveness, but rather strive to increase the benefits and synergies of their activities. They harmonize their objectives, seeking satisfactory results from different goals simultaneously, and do not just aim to maximize the value of a single set of goals.

The characteristics of the ecologically conscious business organizations in the sample are also similar to those identified in the most sustainable business models, or "truly sustainable businesses," as Dyllick and Muff (2015) describe them. These businesses go beyond making an effort to minimize negative impacts and seek to understand how to maximize positive impact in relation to critical social and ecological issues. Such enterprises forge solutions to the most pressing sustainability challenges into business opportunities, and try to exert an influence throughout their entire sector or beyond it. This is done through increasing their transparency, sharing examples of good practice, building cooperation with non-economic actors, and striving to change the rules of the game.

In several cases, the businesses described above can be considered "entrepreneurs inspired by nature," based on Hofstra (2015). These enterprises have a different worldview and innovate products and services that help regenerate natural services, re-connecting people with nature. They recognize that humankind is a part of nature, and very much depends on it. Resources are limited, and sustainable businesses are required to solve real ecological problems in parallel with meeting human needs and generating economic value. The main principles of successful nature-inspired businesses are very similar to those that the ecologically conscious businesses in the sample adhere to. They take into account the different interests of business, society, and nature. They achieve long-term economic efficiency combined with taking an ethical perspective and being ecologically effective. They discover but do not exploit nature, and they generate business value in a broad sense, including economic, ecological, moral, social, and spiritual value.

Gast and her co-authors (2017) define ecological entrepreneurship as the process of identifying, evaluating, and implementing business opportunities that minimize the environmental impact of an enterprise, and operating for the benefit of local communities and society as a whole. As the authors argue, intrinsic motivation, personal values, and volunteering is of paramount importance in terms of commitment to sustainability. Ecological enterprises do not primarily pursue economic goals, but seek to change people's mindsets and society as a whole, and to create value for the environment and society. Operating in an ecologically sustainable way involves redesigning business practices and networking. The role of networks and cooperating with stakeholders is extremely important, as individual enterprises alone have less chance of influencing public policies.

Most of these characteristics are revealed in all of the businesses under analysis.

In conclusion, future research directions are defined that partially address the limitations of the findings, and support the further study, identification, and promotion of ecologically sustainable economic activities. The relevance of the present results can be tested by repeating the research on the same samples, or on extended samples. A variety of significant issues related to ecological consciousness in a business context could not be focused on in this book, but such issues—as the following questions indicate—may be studied in the future. What is the context of ecologically conscious business?—with particular attention to the differences between inclusive and extractive institutional systems and social systems (Acemoglu and Robinson 2012). What environmentally beneficial impact may ecologically conscious business functioning potentially have? Does drawing on the best practices of ecologically conscious businesses allow specific recommendations to be made in relation to the ecological turn of the present economic system? How can a spiritual value orientation in a business organization foster this ecological turn, and how can the evolution of consciousness and spirituality in business be supported? We have examined ecologically conscious businesses, but the extensive literature about sustainable and ecologically conscious consumption has not been addressed. It would be worthwhile studying how an ecological consciousness and value orientation may appear and take effect in both supply-side and demand-side economies.

References

Acemoglu, D., & Robinson, J. A. (2012). *Why Nations Fail: The Origins of Power, Prosperity, and Poverty*. New York: Crown Business.

Alves, B. (2020). *Cosmetics Industry in Brazil—Statistics & Facts*. https://www.statistacom/topics/5424/cosmetics-industry-in-brazil/#dossierSummary. Accessed 15 July 2020.

ASSOCHAM – Ernst & Young. (2018). *The Indian Organic Market: A New Paradigm in Agriculture*. https://www.ey.com/Publication/vwLUAssets/ey-the-indian-organic-market-report-online-version-21-march-2018/$File/ey-the-indian-organic-market-report-online-version-21-march-2018.pdf. Accessed 30 June 2018.

AVPN – Asian Venture Philanthropy Network. (2016). *Green Monday Movement—One Mission, Many Ventures*. https://avpn.asia/case-study/portfolio-management-green-monday-movement-one-mission-many-ventures/. Accessed 14 June 2020.

Bhasin, K. (2011, Aug 25). *PHOTOS: Inside TerraCycle's Incredible 99% Recycled Office*. https://www.businessinsider.com/terracycle-office-tour-2011-8. Accessed 10 June 2020.

B Lab. (2020a). *B Impact Report: Natura Cosméticos SA*. https://bcorporation.net/directory/natura-cosmeticos-sa. Accessed 8 June 2020.

B Lab. (2020b). *B Impact Report: Organic India USA*. https://bcorporation.net/directory/organic-india-usa. Accessed 8 June 2020.

B Lab. (2020c). *B Impact Report: Patagonia, Inc*. https://bcorporation.net/directory/patagonia-inc. Accessed 9 June 2020.

B Lab. (2020d). *B Impact Report: The Body Shop International*. https://bcorporation.net/directory/the-body-shop-international. Accessed 8 June 2020.

Business Wire. (2020). *Analysis on New Product Launches in Covid-19 Related Markets. Outdoor Apparel Market 2020–2024: Technavio*. https://www.businesswire.com/news/home/20200501005038/en/Analysis-New-Product-Launches-Covid-19-Related-Markets-Outdoor. Accessed 9 June 2020.

Chen, C. (2018, January 26). *Retail May Be Sinking, but Outdoor Apparel Is Killing It*. TheStreet. https://www.thestreet.com/story/14463219/1/retail-may-be-sinking-but-outdoor-apparel-is-killing-it.html. Accessed 9 June 2020.

Chesbrough, H., & Rosenbloom, R. S. (2002). The Role of the Business Model in Capturing Value from Innovation: Evidence from Xerox Corporation's Technology Spin-off Companies. *Industrial and Corporate Change, 11*(3), 529–555. https://doi.org/10.1093/icc/11.3.529.

Di Ciancia, C. (2017, December 29). *Houdini's Trick: Adventure Without Impact. A Sportsware Brand of Clothes to Wear with a Clear Conscience*. Welum. https://www.welum.com/article/houdini-sportswear-trick-maximum-experience-zero-impact-2/. Accessed 16 June 2020.

Dyllick, T., & Muff, K. (2015). Clarifying the Meaning of Sustainable Business: Introducing a Typology from Business-as-Usual to True Business Sustainability. *Organization & Environment, 29*(2), 156–174. https://doi.org/10.1177/1086026615575176.

Eliances. (2017, October 17). *Tom Szaky Founder Terracycle Eco-Capitalism King Over 20 Countries*. http://eliancer.com/tom-szaky-founder-terracycle-eco-capitalism-king-over-20-countries. Accessed 10 June 2020.

Fast Company. (2018). *The World's Most Innovative Companies 2018*. https://wwwfastcompany.com/most-innovative-companies/2018. Accessed 9 June 2020.

Fast Company. (2020). *Most Innovative Companies: Patagonia*. https://wwwfastcompany.com/company/patagonia. Accessed 9 June 2020.

Frank, R. H. (2004). *What Price the Moral High Ground? Ethical Dilemmas in Competitive Environments*. Princeton: Princeton University Press.

Friedman, V. (2017, July 27). A Call to Activism for Outdoor Apparel Makers. *The New York Times*. https://www.nytimes.com/2017/07/27/fashion/bears-ears-patagonia-rei-adidas-activism.html. Accessed 7 May 2018.

Gaille, B. (2018, August 4). *21 Outdoor Apparel Industry Statistics, Trends & Analysis*. https://brandongaille.com/21-outdoor-apparel-industry-statistics-trends-analysis/. Accessed 7 June 2020.

Gast, J., Gundolf, K., & Cesinger, B. (2017). Doing Business in a Green Way: A Systemic Review of the Ecological Sustainability Entrepreneurship Literature and Future Research Directions. *Journal of Cleaner Production, 147*, 44–56. https://doi.org/10.1016/j.jclepro.2017.01.065.

Gelles, D. (2018, May 5). Patagonia v. Trump. *The New York Times*. https://www.nytimes.com/2018/05/05/business/patagonia-trump-bears-ears.html. Accessed 7 May 2018.

Gingerich, E. F. R. (2016). Case Studies: Spirituality and Sustainability. Interface Global (Ray C. Anderson, Atlanta, GA, USA). In S. Dhirman, & J. Marques, J. (Eds.), *Spirituality and Sustainability: New Horizons and Exemplary Approaches* (pp. 169–171). Switzerland: Springer International Publishing. https://doi.org/10.1007/978-3-319-34235-1_11.

GlobeNewswire. (2019). *Global Outdoor Clothing Market Will Reach to USD 19.45 Billion By 2026*. Zion Market Research. https://www.globenewswire.com/news-release/2019/07/11/1881331/0/en/Global-Outdoor-Clothing-Market-Will-Reach-to-USD-19-45-Billion-By-2026-Zion-Market-Research.html. Accessed 9 June 2020.

GlobeScan. (2019). *The 2019 GlobeScan-Sustainability Leaders Survey*. Report. https://globescan.com/wp-content/uploads/2019/07/GlobeScan-SustainAbility-Leaders-Survey-2019-Report.pdf. Accessed 7 June 2020.

Grand View Research. (2020). *Flooring Market Size, Share & Trends Analysis Report By Product (Soft Coverings, Resilient, Non-Resilient), By Application (Residential, Non-residential), By Region, And Segment Forecast, 2020–2027*. https://www.grandviewresearch.com/industry-analysis/flooring-market-analysis/methodology. Accessed 7 June 2020.

Green Monday. (2020). https://greenmonday.org/en/. Accessed 6 June 2020.

Hackett, J. (2019, August 14). *Flexitarian (Semi-Vegetarian) Diet Definition*. The Spruce Eats. https://www.thespruceeats.com/what-is-a-flexitarian-3376803. Accessed 6 June 2020.

Hawken, P. (1993). *The Ecology of Commerce: A Declaration of Sustainability*. New York: HarperBusiness.

Hofstra, N. (2015). Entrepreneurship Inspired by Nature. In L. Zsolnai (Ed.), *The Spiritual Dimension of Business Ethics and Sustainability Management* (pp. 159–166). New York: Springer. https://doi.org/10.1007/978-3-319-11677-8_13.

Houdini. (2018). *Planetary Boundaries Assessment 2018. This Is Houdini.* https://api.houdinisportswear.com/storage/2A69199BFCBA925CC9260D61F41301EA566C760FB9A727B5DABB2C330C13D1BC/08df8496f36f49f0bb821fdeafdd775e/pdf/media/e5eec5e201b242e9a2aa14aba9c3b696/Houdini_Planetary_Boundaries_Assessment_2018.pdf. Accessed 6 June 2020.

Houdini. (2020). https://www.houdinisportswear.com/en/. Accessed 6 June 2020.

IFOAM – International Federation of Organic Agriculture Movements. (2017). *19th Organic World Congress—Awards*. https://owc.ifoam.bio/2017/awards. Accessed 8 June 2020.

Interface. (2019). *Annual Report 2019*. https://s22.q4cdn.com/139673446/files/doc_financials/2019/ar/tile20191229_10k_web.pdf. Accessed 7 June 2020.

Interface. (2020a). https://www.interface.com/US/en-US/homepage. Accessed 7 June 2020.

Interface. (2020b, May 8). *Investor Presentation.* https://s22.q4cdn.com/139673446/files/doc_presentations/2020/05/Investor-Presentation-05.08.2020-FINAL.pdf. Accessed 7 June 2020.

Jacob, A. (2012, August 28). Scott Bader—A Long Term Commitment to Composites. *Reinforced Plastics Magazine*. https://www.materialstoday.com/composite-industry/features/scott-bader-a-long-term-commitment-to-composites/. Accessed 9 June 2020.

Jans, G. (2017, June 19). Outdoor Sector Shows Good Performance: ISPO, "There is High Growth". https://www.ispo.com/en/markets/id_79708040/good-figures-for-the-outdoor-sector-high-growth-.html. Accessed 9 June 2020.

Jones, G., & de Pinho, R. R. (2006, August). *Natura: Global Beauty Made in Brazil.* Harvard Business School Case 807-029 (Revised October 2012). https://edisciplinas.usp.br/pluginfile.php/…/807029-PDF-ENG.pdf. Accessed 25 June 2018.

Krarup, M., Kiørobe, N., & Sramkova, H. (2015). *Moving Towards a Circular Economy: Successful Nordic Business Models*. Copenhagen: Nordic Council of Ministers.

Lampikoski, T. (2012). Green, Innovative, and Profitable: A Case Study of Managerial Capabilities at Interface Inc. *Technology Innovation Management Review, 2*(11), 4–12. https://timreview.ca/article/624. Accessed 11 June 2020.

Largest Companies. (2020). http://www.largestcompanies.com/company/Houdini-Sportswear-AB-227636. Accessed 7 June 2020.

Mannion, L. (2018, May 24). *Saving the Planet…One Dumpling at a Time.* Thomson Reuters Foundation. https://www.reuters.com/article/us-hongkong-food-environment/saving-the-planet-one-dumpling-at-a-time-idUSKCN1IP2VN. Accessed 14 June 2020.

Melo, A. (2018, Abril 16). Natura ultrapassa Unilever e lidera mercado de beleza no Brasil. Valor. http://www.valor.com.br/empresas/5456961/natura-ultrapassa-unilever-e-lidera-mercado-de-beleza-no-brasil. Accessed 25 June 2018.

Natura. (2020a). https://www.naturabrasil.fr/en-us/. Accessed 8 June 2020.

Natura. (2020b). https://www.naturabrasil.com/. Accessed 8 June 2020.

Natura. (2020c). *Natura 2019* (Annual Report). https://static.rede.natura.net/html/home//br_07/relatorio-anual/natura_annual_report_2019.pdf. Accessed 8 June 2020.

Natura & Co. (2020). *Creating the Best Beauty Group for the World* (2019 Report). https://naturaeco.com/report_2019_en.pdf. Accessed 8 June 2020.

Organic India. (2017). *Sustainability Report 2016/2017*. https://organicindia.com.au/wp-content/uploads/2017/08/Ebook-Sustainability-Report-2017-Final-Digital.pdf. Accessed 7 June 2020.

Organic India. (2020a). https://www.organicindia.com/. Accessed 8 June 2020.

Organic India. (2020b). https://organicindiausa.com/. Accessed 8 June 2020.

Parrish, B. D. (2010). Sustainability-Driven Entrepreneurship: Principles of Organization Design. *Journal of Business Venturing, 25*(5), 510–523. https://doi.org/10.1016/j.jbusvent.2009.05.005.

Parvati Magazine. (2017, April 17). Community: TerraCycle, with Tom Szaky. *Parvati Magazine.* http://parvatimagazine.com/2017/04/community-terracycle-tom-szaky/. Accessed 10 June 2020.

Patagonia. (2018). *Annual Benefit Corporation Report. Fiscal Year 2017*. https://www.patagonia.com/static/on/demandware.static/-/Library-Sites-PatagoniaShared/default/dw824fac0f/PDF-US/2017-BCORP-pages_022218.pdf. Accessed 9 June 2020.

Patagonia. (2020). http://eu.patagonia.com/hu/en/home/. Accessed 9 June 2020.

Patagonia Provisions. (2020). https://www.patagoniaprovisions.com/pages/our-ambassadors. Accessed 9 June 2020.

PR Newswire. (2020, May 6). *TerraCycle US Reports 2019 Year-End Financial and Operational Results*. https://www.prnewswire.com/news-releases/terracycle-us-reports-2019-year-end-financial-and-operational-results-301053497.html. Accessed 10 June 2020.

Scott Bader. (2018). *Annual Report 2017*. http://www.scottbader.com/wp-content/uploads/Scott-Bader-Annual-Report-2017.pdf. Accessed 27 June 2018.

Scott Bader. (2019). *Annual Report 2018*. https://www.scottbader.com/wp-content/uploads/Annual-Report-2018.pdf. Accessed 9 June 2020.

Scott Bader. (2020). https://www.scottbader.com/. Accessed 9 June 2020.

Shahbandeh, M. (2020). *Breakdown of the Cosmetic Market Worldwide 2011–2019, by Product Category*. https://www.statista.com/statistics/243967/breakdown-of-the-cosmetic-market-worldwide-by-product-category/. Accessed 10 June 2020.

Srivastav, T. (2018, May 2). *Organic India's CEO on Organic Product Popularity and Why They Don't Advertise on TV*. The Drum+. https://www.thedrum.com/news/2018/05/02/organic-indias-founder-organic-product-popularity-and-why-they-dont-advertise-tv. Accessed 8 June 2020.

Statista. (2019). *Sports & Outdoor Segment Relevant Market Data. Highlights Worldwide*. https://www.statista.com/statistics/979475/outdoor-clothing-market-value-forecast-worldwide/. Accessed 9 June 2020.

Sustainable Growth Associates. (2018). *References*. https://www.sg-associates.eu/references/. Accessed 29 June 2018.

S&P Global. (2020). *The Sustainability Yearbook 2020*. https://www.spglobal.com/esg/csa/yearbook/. Accessed 8 June 2020.

Technavio. (2020). *Top 10 Cosmetics Companies in the World 2020*. https://blogtechnavio.com/blog/top-10-cosmetics-companies. Accessed 8 June 2020.

TerraCycle. (2018). https://www.terracycle.com/en-US/. Accessed 5 July 2018.

TerraCycle. (2020a). https://www.terracycle.com/en-US/. Accessed 10 June 2020.

TerraCycle. (2020b). *Offering Circular Dated January 27, 2020*. TerraCycle US Inc. https://www.sec.gov/Archives/edgar/data/1714781/000110465920007210/tm205941d1_253g2.htm. Accessed 10 June 2020.

The Economic Times. (2017). Organic India Eyes Rs 500 Crore Turnover by FY20 End. https://economictimes.indiatimes.com/industry/cons-products/fmcg/organic-india-eyes-rs-500-crore-turnover-by-fy20-end/articleshow/62240529.cms. Accessed 8 June 2020.

The Natural Step. (2014). *Case Study: Interface*. https://thenaturalstep.org/project/interface/. Accessed 9 June 2020.

The Natural Step. (2020). *Approach*. https://thenaturalstep.org/approach/. Accessed 9 June 2020.

Tin Shed Ventures. (2020). http://www.tinshedventures.com/. Accessed 9 June 2020.

Vaccaro, A. (2009, March 24). *10 Tips from an Eco-Capitalist: Tom Szaky Shares TerraCycles' Secrets to Success*. GreenBiz. https://www.greenbiz.com/blog//03/24/10-tips-eco-capitalist-tom-szaky-shares-terracycles-secrets-success. Accessed 9 June 2020.

Yusof, H. (2020, May 29). David Yeung, CEO & Co-Founder of Green Monday. *The Business Times* 2020, https://www.sgsme.sg/news/david-yeung-ceo-co-founder-green-Monday. Accessed 6 June 2020.

Zimberoff, L. (2017, June 12). *This Guy Is Trying to Break Hong Kong's Meat Addiction*. Bloomberg. https://www.bloomberg.com/news/articles/2017-06-12/this-guy-is-trying-to-cure-hong-kong-s-meat-addiction. Accessed 7 June 2020.

Part IV

Conclusions

This book has addressed the problematic of ecological consciousness in business organizations through studying the theoretical concepts, value orientation, and business models of ecologically conscious businesses. The role of an ecological consciousness has become increasingly important as the ecological degradation of the Earth and the role of business in causing ecological harm has become more obvious. It is also well known that the values of economic actors influence their business decisions. A large body of scientific literature has thus investigated the value orientations of businesses. However, the topic of ecological consciousness has been much less deeply studied in this context, and there are hardly any examples of research about the relationship between value orientations and ecological consciousness in business.

To fill this gap, the present book has gone beyond previous studies to investigate the value orientations of ecologically conscious business organizations through the application of qualitative methodology, and analyzed the value commitments and business models of exemplary ecologically conscious businesses from all over the world.

7
The Future of Ecologically Conscious Business

This chapter explores the current global context of ecologically conscious business and makes some conclusions about the future of business.

In a seminal book, *The Entropy Law and the Economic Process*, published in 1971, Nicholas Georgescu-Roegen argues that physical reality influences economic reality, and natural resources are irreversibly degraded when the economy exploits them. The Earth has a carrying capacity that limits the sustainability of human populations and material consumption (Georgescu-Roegen 1971). Recent concepts such as the Great Acceleration, Planetary Boundaries, and the Anthropocene reinforce the claim that Earth system processes have environmental boundaries, and human activities since the Industrial Revolution have been responsible for the global environmental changes of our times. Defining and respecting a "safe operating space for humanity" at all levels of Earth system functioning is a prerequisite for achieving sustainability (Steffen and Broadgate et al. 2015; Steffen and Richardson et al. 2015).

At present, humanity does not fulfill the requirements of sustainability. Humankind has been in a state of ecological overshoot since the early 1970s, and now uses as many ecological resources as could be sustainably produced by 1.6 Earths. The ecological footprint is a measure that

A. Ócsai, *Ecologically Conscious Organizations*, Palgrave Studies in Sustainable Business In Association with Future Earth,
https://doi.org/10.1007/978-3-030-60918-4_7

compares the resource demand of individuals, populations, governments or businesses, and activities (such as consumption, production, exporting and importing) to the resources the planet can sustainably supply. It quantifies, usually in units of global hectares, what area of biologically productive land and water would be required to produce all the resources the object of measurement consumes, and to absorb the waste it generates. In 2020, due to coronavirus-induced lockdowns around the world, Earth Overshoot Day (the day when humanity's demand for ecological resources and services exceeds the amount Earth can regenerate in a year), was August 22, more than three weeks later than a year before. This reflects a reduction in humanity's footprint of almost ten percent, mostly owing to the decrease in wood harvesting and CO2 emissions from fossil fuel combustion. Efforts to respond to the global health crisis have demonstrated that acting swiftly and improving ecological resource consumption trends is possible when people put health above all else, collaborate in the pursuit of shared goals, and consider the consequences of their decisions at all levels (Global Footprint Network 2020). Can economies and business organizations also meet these criteria?

Mainstream economics is in conflict with the potential solutions that are required to reach a state of "one-planet compatibility." It does not recognize the biophysical limits of ecosystems on which the economy depends, and it considers technology to be the ultimate solution to resource constraint problems. The mainstream economic approach tends to focus only on markets, and to ignore externalities (Costanza 2010). Modern economic activities are based on individualistic and materialistic values, have a focus on maximizing short-term profit or utility, and promote infinite economic growth. They do not acknowledge the intrinsic value of nature, but use living beings as mere natural resources, threaten the integrity and diversity of natural ecosystems, destroy the autonomy and culture of local communities, and decrease future generations' prospects for a decent life (Zsolnai 2015; Shrivastava et al. 2019).

The late London Business School professor Sumantra Ghoshal criticized mainstream management ideology and its orientation toward competitiveness. Companies strive to increase their market share and power to maximize profits, so their ultimate goal is to make markets as imperfect as possible. According to this understanding, social value creation is not part of business organizations' set of core values, but only an add-on element at most (Birkinshaw and Piramal 2005; Tencati et al. 2009). Rushing after productivity in order to increase profitability and shareholder value is often counterproductive for businesses themselves. An analysis of trends in the business sector in the United States in the early 2000s showed that what appeared as productivity gains actually ruined many companies. Tendencies such as extreme power centralization, cooking the books, cashing in goodwill that had been cultivated for years, trashing brands, drastic downsizing and cost cutting, exploiting employees, and neglecting environmental harm ultimately undermined the long-term health of the business enterprises concerned (Mintzberg 2007). Regrettably, short-term shareholder value maximization and competitiveness, self-interest and aggression, and an exclusive focus on financial performance negatively affect stakeholders and ultimately business itself (Tencati et al. 2009).

In contrast to mainstream economic thinking, ecological economics, a transdisciplinary field that emerged from the work of Georgescu-Roegen and other scholars in the 1980s, strives to understand how the economy is embedded in the natural ecosystems that support human existence. It recognizes the carrying capacity of the Earth and the limits and constraints that the natural environment creates, and shows that the economy cannot grow indefinitely in a finite environment. Nature, society, and the economy are interconnected in dynamic unity. Humans should act as responsible and caring members of the community of life and respect the intrinsic value of natural beings. Taking a holistic and organic perspective and considering intergenerational equity and the issue of sustainable development play an important role in this (Daly and Farley 2004; Costanza 2010; Brown and Timmerman 2015; Capra and Jakobsen 2017). Ecological economics also claims that if the economy can reach and be maintained at a sustainable scale, with fair distribution and efficient allocation, well-being can be improved without economic growth. Just as in nature when a field fills up with early successional plants that coexist and cooperate, so the economy should also go through a transition from a phase of growth to a steady state, in which, instead of cut-throat competition, more collaborative, alliance-building, stable kinds of relationships prevail (Costanza, 2010). Nevertheless, the propositions of ecological economics have mostly remained at the academic level and are not reflected in business practices (Shrivastava et al. 2019).

Recently, the concept of the circular economy has emerged. This is based on an organic worldview based on the unity of economy, nature, and society, solidarity, sustainability, respect for pluralistic values, and transparent cooperation. It strives for change at structural and individual levels in terms of values, consumption, and lifestyle habits. Circularity means that production, distribution, consumption, and recycling take place in a cyclical way, not through linear processes. Instead of one-off consumption events, the circular economy promotes products with extended lifetimes, and supports waste reduction through the recycling, upcycling, and reuse of materials, commodity efficiency, and local-level solutions (Ims and Jakobsen 2006; European Commission 2015, 2018; Jakobsen 2017). The principles of the circular economy have started to spread throughout the world economy, and have been applied in several ecologically conscious business models that are described in the empirical research contained in this book, such as in the operations of Houdini, Interface, Natura, Scott Bader, and TerraCycle. However, the future development of the concept and its success at contributing to a sustainable future depend on how much it is applied to boost competitiveness and sustainable growth (for example, the explicit goals of many business organizations, and the target of the European Union's development agenda). Transitioning to a steady state economy with the primary goal of respecting planetary boundaries seems to require a different approach.

Business leaders are familiar with the meaning of the term VUCA (volatility, uncertainty, complexity, and ambiguity) nowadays. The US Army War College introduced the notion in the late 1980s, and the acronym itself gained general recognition after the September 11, 2001 attacks (Lawrence 2013; US Army Heritage and Education Center 2019). Strategic business management has also adopted the term and has been using it to describe the way that a volatile, uncertain, complex, and ambiguous business environment is becoming the new normal due to consecutive financial, economic, and geopolitical crises. Risks have been continuously increasing, and not only in a business context. In the epoch of the Anthropocene, human activities are dramatically influencing the trajectory of the Earth System toward a "Hothouse Earth" pathway that is likely to cause serious disruption to ecosystems, societies, and economies. To steer the Earth System onto a "Stabilized Earth" trajectory, deep transformation and a fundamental reorientation of human values, equity, behavior, institutions, culture, science, technologies, and economies are vital (Steffen et al. 2018; Shrivastava et al. 2019, 2020). Some transformations have been initiated but much more needs to be done to preserve humanity's chance of a livable future.

Mainstream economics and the market economy in their current form have not been able to overcome their shortcomings; for instance, by acknowledging biophysical limits, or internalizing market externalities. Ecological economists suggest that governments, quasi-government institutions, and community institutions at local, regional, and global levels, such as watershed trusts, global atmospheric trusts, or ocean trusts, may be able to fix markets (Costanza 2010)—at least theoretically. The majority of states seem to be unwilling to move beyond their short-term economic interests and collaborate to create comprehensive and coercive international environmental agreements due to their weak political, economic, and social commitments to sustainability. While the successful and effective implementation and enforcement of such international regulations and a real start to the green transformation of the global economy have been awaited for decades, the voluntary environmental assessments, reporting frameworks, and environmental and social labelling schemes applied by business, civic, and professional organizations have proliferated. Such self-regulatory initiatives include, inter alia, the Forest Stewardship Council, Fair Trade, the Marine Stewardship Council, Rainforest Alliance, and ISO 14001. However, the outcome of the voluntary environmental programs of business organizations can be shallow, contradictory, and serve as tools for greenwashing, without leading to measurable improvements in environmental performance. Thus, private and voluntary environmental regulations and standard setting by business organizations cannot be an alternative to comprehensive and legally binding international environmental regulation (Fekete 2015).

The number of socially and environmentally oriented businesses such as B-corporations and social enterprises has been steadily increasing, but the majority of business organizations, corporations, and unincorporated businesses still use the natural environment and humans in an instrumental way to achieve their own business goals, thereby furthering ecological and social degradation (Shrivastava et al. 2019).

In terms of translating ethics, social, and environmental responsibility to the organizational level, the discipline of business ethics has more than three decades of history. It has developed concepts, normative models, and organizational solutions, provided evidence, and created a deeper understanding of the social role of business. However, business ethics has failed to contribute effectively to solving the social, ethical, and environmental problems caused by business organizations. The reason for this is that it has been unable to realize that some of the features that are inherent to mainstream business prevent business enterprises, and primarily global corporations, from becoming genuinely ethical organizations. The instrumental and opportunistic use of ethics to make business gains, the moral disengagement strategies of business executives, a legal and financial institutional setting that dilutes responsibility, the superficial and contingent results of voluntary compliance, a lack of market mechanisms for rewarding responsible behavior, and weak stakeholder activism have hindered business ethics from meeting its stated goal of fostering the ethical behavior of businesses. Business ethics should aspire to generate an open and critical approach toward the basic assumptions of current management practices and their underlying theoretical concepts. The transformation of business is much needed. To this end, moving away from the corporate model via fostering a collaborative logic, more efficient management accountability, more strongly empowered non-governmental organizations, political commitment and leadership, and the international regulation of business that protects and promotes basic human rights, the well-being of people, and sustaining natural ecosystems are potential solutions (Boda and Zsolnai 2016; Boda 2019).

Business practitioners should consider and face up to the great challenge of humanity's survival and the future of the planet. Sustainable change is crucially needed through changing existing business systems and enterprises, and creating new ones in order to reduce the negative externalities caused by companies and contribute to solving social and environmental problems. Although some sustainable changes and much incremental change have been achieved, the vast majority of sustainable change initiatives fail. The conceptual and practical challenges of engaging with unfamiliar and complex problems, evaluating these problems via previously unused methods, developing and applying brand new solutions, motivating internal and external stakeholders to change their mindsets and habits and improving their skills can make implementing changes difficult. In general, five major obstacles can be identified that may impede sustainable change: (i) an ambiguity of objectives, (ii) a narrow frame of reference based on a focus on shareholder value maximization and a lack of systemic thinking about sustainability problems, (iii) the adversarial external perspective and lack of understanding and cooperation of external stakeholders who are also directly affected by changes, (iv) the functional isolation of the issue and change management teams and organizational inertia, (v) performance standards that are unsuited to assessing the complex creation of value related to sustainable change. Behind these obstacles to sustainability change is the mainstream paradigm of business that is disembedded from the social, planetary, and ethical context. To overcome the obstacles to sustainable change, a new paradigm is required which promotes sustainability at all levels and brings into being a resilient and humane economy that serves the common good (Wallis 2020).

A new economic paradigm is needed which promotes sustainability at all levels and creates a resilient and humane economy that serves the common good. Ecological consciousness in its broadest sense embraces the well-being of all living beings, and can be the cornerstone of this new paradigm. What kinds of economic and business initiatives and practices can we see now that may be promising in relation to the new and emerging business paradigm?

Current economic systems use Gross Domestic Product (GDP) as an indicator of development, thus encouraging the pursuit of infinite material growth. Acknowledging that human well-being depends on the well-being of the living Earth, and that a focus on one-dimensional GDP growth has led to escalating social and ecological ills and imperils the human future, in 2017 the governments of Scotland, Costa Rica, Slovenia, and New Zealand created an organization to promote well-being as the goal of development. Since then, numerous organizations, networks, individuals, academics, and businesses have joined the initiative (Costanza et al. 2018; Korten 2020b). The vision of a "wellbeing economy" is based on principles of prioritizing long-term human well-being, ecological stability, and environmental justice, protecting environmental standards, developing green infrastructure, satisfying basic needs, and ensuring a decent living for everyone, fairly distributing resources, and engaging in transparent and inclusive democratic processes at all levels, as well as prioritizing social and ecological goals in all business ventures, as well as cooperation and the public control of money. The city of Amsterdam and countries like New Zealand, Iceland, and Scotland are already implementing some of the principles of wellbeing economics and many more experiments such as renewable energy developments, ecovillages, Transition Towns, and regenerative agriculture projects are happening around the world (Costanza et al. 2018; Wellbeing Economy Alliance 2020).

The Club of Rome, through its Reframing Economics project, is also working to support the shift away from mainstream economics and policy making toward a philosophy of "beyond GDP," which considers the well-being of people and the planet and strives to reverse ecosystem, climate- and social tipping points of vital importance. Through the Emerging New Civilization Initiative, the Club of Rome's fundamental goal is to develop a new paradigm for the greater Earth Community. Based on ancient wisdom, African Ubuntu philosophy, Buddhist and other indigenous knowledge systems, its core values are promoting human dignity, promoting the understanding that human beings are inherently relational, respect for nature, and preserving the commons for future generations. The awareness of the need for a paradigm shift is a manifestation of developing human consciousness and the understanding that people have to reflect on who they are as humans and what values should determine their relationships with each other and nature (Club of Rome 2020).

The concept of "Ecological Civilization" acknowledges that the future of humanity depends on a successful transition to a state where humans can live in a balanced and harmonious relationship with Earth's living systems, and every person's needs for health and happiness are met. The current structure of civilization is designed to dominate nature. Capitalism inherently exploits and destroys nature, the biosphere, and human civilization. To reconcile humanity with nature, the system should be based on a long-term approach, cooperation, and production aimed at satisfying needs, not generating profit. A successful transition should include the transition of governance from transnational corporations to national governments, from competition to cooperation, and from GDP growth to an economy in which everyone's spiritual and material needs are fulfilled while respecting planetary limits. Economic performance should be measured according to the health of the biosphere, local ecosystems, communities, and individuals (Korten 2020a).

"Diverse economies" scholarship draws attention to the fact that, while thinking of how to fundamentally transform society and build more resilient economies based on the need for a paradigm change away from the mainstream capitalist economy, one should consider the "iceberg" of diverse community economies. Capitalist economic practices such as waged labor, the production of commodities for exchange in markets, and capitalist businesses are "above the waterline," thus make up only a smaller part of the whole iceberg. Below the waterline are many other practices, including economic ones (such as cooperatives, informal loans, and in-kind payments), social ones (such as housework, family, and childcare), and ecological (photosynthesis, composting, and metabolic processes) ones. The systemic framing of such diverse economies has led to the development of an inventory of economic activities arranged into five types, including enterprise, labor, transactions, property, and finance, containing dozens of items in each type. Representing this economic heterogeneity can help to undermine the power of a capital-centric worldview and realize the diversity of economic practices. The approach thus supports the identification of a variety of economic pathways for transitioning toward sustainable community economies (Gibson-Graham and Dombroski 2020).

According to the concept of the "collaborative enterprise," a change of paradigm is also needed. Business should consider ecological and social boundaries and embed themselves in natural and social systems through creating long-term, mutually beneficial relationships with every stakeholder. The basis of the sustainable future of the collaborative enterprise is value creation that is shared throughout the entire value network (Tencati and Zsolnai 2010). Such a radical renewal of business models is key to the future of business organizations. The most important goal is to maintain consistency with the flourishing of life on Earth, including human, nonhuman, and future life. To this end, progressive business models should be able to embrace sustainable, circular, frugal approaches and practices, pursue different and sometimes even opposing goals simultaneously, apply systemic thinking and coordinate activities harmoniously, and efficiently balance environmental, social, and economic dimensions. They should be stakeholder oriented and be led from the top by visionary, committed leaders and teams. Progressive businesses are exceptional compared to mainstream businesses. However, they can be considered as only the first step in a long and difficult journey to transform business enterprises into organizations that fit the reality of the Anthropocene (O'Higgins and Zsolnai 2018).

From this analysis of several concepts and initiatives, we see that in order to meet the requirements of the ecological and social reality of the Anthropocene, business organizations should develop radically new solutions, extraordinary innovations, and unusual business models. Important inspiration for this may be ecological consciousness. Driven by an ecological consciousness, businesses can reconsider and change their underlying assumptions, core values, raison d'être, and definitions of success. From where can businesses gain such inspiration and creativity, and the persistence to cope with such an enormous challenge?

Ian I. Mitroff has developed a model that analyzes four dimensions of any problem, defined as scientific/technical, interpersonal/social, systemic/ecological, and spiritual/existential. In the mainstream business world, the scientific/technical perspective is the dominant viewpoint, and leads to a preference for technical solutions to every problem. The interpersonal/social perspective considers problems from a social, group, or community point of view. The systemic/ecological perspective analyzes the long-term consequences and local, regional, and global impacts of problem solutions. The spiritual/existential perspective serves to promote respect for the dignity, beliefs, and feelings of individuals, and the consideration of existential issues such as the meaning of life, or the purpose of one's life (Mitroff 1998; Ims and Zsolnai 2009). Through using this model, businesses can obtain deeper insight and understanding of their own situations. The process also supports critical thinking, the re-evaluation of basic assumptions, out-of-the-box thinking, and creativity.

Spirituality is the search for the meaning of life—in various sociocultural forms—that connects people with every living being and with God or Ultimate Reality (European SPES Institute 2020). It can contribute to a deeper understanding of different decision-making situations and systems, the creation of new categories, and the overcoming of existing paradigms (Zsolnai 2014). Spirituality can be the background and intrinsic motivational basis for economic actors to behave ethically, serve the common good, and measure their success multidimensionally (Zsolnai 2015). Through spiritual-based leadership, spirituality as the internal source of wisdom can help direct the actions of leaders, and this consciousness will be reflected in their decisions in the external business world (Pruzan 2011, 2015). Spirituality can lead to a qualitative change in leaders, and through them also in organizations, ultimately affecting every stakeholder of an organization (Lozano and Ribera 2004).

What can we say about the ecologically conscious business organizations studied in the empirical research described in this book? Are they exemplars of future businesses in the face of the new ecological reality?

All of the internationally well-known global corporations, medium-sized companies with a regional reach, and small-scale local lifestyle businesses in the samples are genuinely committed to ecological values and ecologically conscious functioning. They all have their own initiatives for reducing or eliminating environmental harm and improving their social performance, even considering the needs of future generations in several cases. They are taking important steps in the long journey of transforming economic activities into sustainable ones, but they cannot magically make themselves carbon neutral or carbon negative in an instant. Furthermore, their endeavors are increasingly challenging as company size increases. However, they are also very far from following a mainstream business approach, and are moving in a good direction. Ecologically conscious business models, and the exemplary people behind them, can play a significant role with regard to sustaining the future of humankind and the Earth. Their noble goals and innovative practices give us hope, inspire people, and help and invite others to become more conscious and to work creatively for the betterment of the world.

Not only do ecological impacts and "real world" consequences really matter, but it is also critical that people do authentic things without craving the fruits of their action. In other words, to create a livable future, and to achieve our ecological and ethical goals, we should act with genuine commitment, and "with non-attachment and for God's sake only" (Huxley 1947, p. 312). As psychologist Stanislav Grof argues, the obstacles that stand in the way of the transformation of the future of the planet for the better are located deeply inside the human personality, and reflect the level of evolution of the consciousness of humanity. Untamed forces and absurd, violent, and greedy elements of human nature prevent the reorientation of our concern for ecological priorities. The global crisis is thus of a psychospiritual nature, and a radical inner transformation of humanity that increases emotional maturity and spiritual awareness appears to be a prerequisite for reinforcing ethical values, displaying sensitivity toward others, accepting voluntary simplicity, and developing an ecological consciousness. A hopeful solution is—as Grof (1998, p. 220) suggests—"systemic and deep inner work with inspired action in the external world [...], if it were practiced on a sufficiently large scale."

References

Birkinshaw, J., & Piramal, G. (eds.) (2005). *Sumantry Ghoshal on Management: A Force for Good*. Harlow: Prentice Hall.

Boda, Z. (2019). Business Ethics as Critical Thinking: Moral Motivations and the Limits of Ethics. In J. B. Ciulla & T. K. Scharding (Eds.), *Ethical Business Leadership in Troubling Times* (pp. 41–59). Cheltenham – Northampton: Edward Elgar. https://doi.org/10.4337/9781789903058.00011.

Boda, Z., & Zsolnai, L. (2016). The Failure of Business Ethics. *Society and Business Review, 11*(1), 93–104. https://doi.org/10.1108/SBR-11-2015-0066.

Brown, P. G., & Timmermann, P. (eds.) (2015). *Ecological Economics for the Anthropocene: An Emerging Paradigm.* New York: Columbia University Press. https://doi.org/10.7312/brow17342.

Capra, F., & Jakobsen, O. D. (2017). A Conceptual Framework for Ecological Economics Based on Systemic Principles of Life. *International Journal of Social Economics, 44*(6), 831–844. https://doi.org/10.1108/IJSE-05-2016-0136.

Club of Rome. (2020). http://www.clubofrome.org/. Accessed 20 July 2020.

Costanza, R. (2010). What is Ecological Economics? Interview by Ted O'Callahan on May 11, 2010, Yale Insights. Ideas from the Yale School of Management. https://insights.som.yale.edu/insights/what-is-ecological-economics. Accessed 20 July 2020.

Costanza, R., Fioramonti, L., Kubiszewski, I., Henry, L., Lovins, H., McGlade, J., Mortensen, L. F., Philipsen, D., Pickett, K., Ragnarsdóttir, K. V., Roberts, D., Sutton, P., Trebeck, K., Wallis, S., Ward, J., Weatherhead, M., & Wilkinson, R. (2018). Toward a Sustainable Wellbeing Economy. The Solutions Journal, Vol. 9, No. 2, April 2018, https://www.thesolutionsjournal.com/article/toward-sustainable-wellbeing-economy/. Accessed 20 July 2020.

Daly, H. E., & Farley, J. (2004). *Ecological Economics: Principles and Applications.* London: Island Press.

European Commission. (2015). Closing the Loop: Commission Adopts Ambitious New Circular Economy Package to Boost Competitiveness, Create Jobs and Generate Sustainable Growth. Press release, Brussels, 2 December 2015, http://europa.eu/rapid/press-release_IP-15–6203_en.htm. Accessed 27 March 2020.

European Commission. (2018). Circular Economy. Implementation of the Circular Economy Action Plan. 2018 Circular Economy Package. http://ec.europa.eu/environment/circular-economy/index_en.htm. Accessed 27 March 2020.

European SPES Institute. (2020). Definition of spirituality. http://www.eurospes.org/content/our-mission-spiritual-based-humanism. Accessed 20 July 2020.

Fekete, L. (2015). Regulatory Roadblocks to Environmental Sustainability. In B. Fryzel (Ed.), *The True Value of CSR* (pp. 211–230). London: Palgrave Macmillan. https://doi.org/10.1057/9781137433206_13.

Georgescu-Roegen, N. (1971). *The Entropy Law and the Economic Process*. Cambridge: Harvard University Press.

Gibson-Graham, J. K., & Dombroski, K. (2020). Introduction to The Handbook of Diverse Economies: Inventory as Ethical Intervention. In J. K. Gibson-Graham & K. Dombroski (Eds.), *The Handbook of Diverse Economies* (pp. 1–24). Cheltenham – Northampton: Edward Elgar. https://doi.org/10.4337/9781788119962.00008.

Global Footprint Network. (2020). https://www.footprintnetwork.org/. Accessed 20 July 2020.

Grof, S. (1998). *The Cosmic Game: Explorations of the Frontiers of Human Consciousness*. Albany: State University of New York Press.

Huxley, A. (1947). *The Perennial Philosophy*. London: Chatto & Windus. https://archive.org/download/perennialphilosp035505mbp/perennialphilosp035505mbp.pdf. Accessed 20 July 2020.

Ims, K. J., & Jakobsen, O. D. (2006). Cooperation and Competition in the Context of Organic and Mechanic Worldviews—A Theoretical and Case Based Discussion. *Journal of Business Ethics, 66*(1), 19–32. https://doi.org/10.1007/s10551-006-9055-z.

Ims, K. J., & Zsolnai, L. (2009). Holistic Problem Solving. In L. Zsolnai & A. Tencati (Eds.), *The Future International Manager* (pp. 116–129). London: Palgrave Macmillan. https://doi.org/10.1057/9780230274068_7.

Jakobsen, O. (2017). *Transformative Ecological Economics: Process Philosophy, Ideology and Utopia*. London – New York: Routledge. https://doi.org/10.4324/9781315205434.

Korten, D. C. (2020a). Ecological Civilization: The Vision. https://davidkorten.org/home/ecological-civilization/. Accessed 20 July 2020.

Korten, D. C. (2020b). Wellbeing versus GDP: The Challenge and Opportunity of Human Development in the 21st Century. International Science Council, May 16, 2020. https://council.science/human-development/latest-contributions/wellbeing-versus-gdp-the-challenge-and-opportunity-of-human-development-in-the-21st-century/. Accessed 20 July 2020.

Lawrence, K. (2013). Developing Leaders in a VUCA Environment. UNC Executive Development, UNC Kenan-Flagler Business School. https://www.emergingrnleader.com/wp-content/uploads/2013/02/developing-leaders-in-a-vuca-environment.pdf. Accessed 20 July 2020.

Lozano, J. M., & Ribera, R. (2004). A New Chance for Management, A New Challenge for Spirituality. In L. Zsolnai (Ed.), *Spirituality and Ethics in Management* (pp. 175–185). Boston, Dordrecht, London: Kluwer Academic Publishers. https://doi.org/10.1007/1-4020-2365-0_15.

Mintzberg, H. (2007). *How Productivity Killed American Enterprise*. https://mintzberg.org/sites/default/files/article/download/productivity2008.pdf. Accessed 20 July 2020.

Mitroff, I. I. (1998). *Smart Thinking for Crazy Times. The Art of Solving the Right Problems*. San Francisco: Berrett-Koehler.

O'Higgins, E., & Zsolnai, L. (2018). Future of Business. In E. O'Higgins & L. Zsolnai (Eds.), *Progressive Business Models: Creating Sustainable and Pro-social Enterprise* (pp. 289–303). London: Palgrave Macmillan. https://doi.org/10.1007/978-3-319-58804-9_13.

Pruzan, P. (2011). Spirituality as the Basis for Leadership. In L. Bouckaert & L. Zsolnai (Eds.), *The Palgrave Handbook of Spirituality and Business* (pp. 287–295). London: Palgrave. https://doi.org/10.1057/9780230321458_35.

Pruzan, P. (2015). Further Reflections on Spirituality and Spiritual-based Leadership. In L. Zsolnai (Ed.), *The Spiritual Dimension of Business Ethics and Sustainability Management* (pp. 191–198). New York: Springer. https://doi.org/10.1007/978-3-319-11677-8_19.

Shrivastava, P., Stafford Smith, M., O'Brien, K., & Zsolnai, L. (2020). Perspective: Transforming Sustainability Science to Generative Positive Social and Environmental Change Globally. *One Earth*, 2(4), 329–340. https://doi.org/10.1016/j.oneear.2020.04.010.

Shrivastava, P., Zsolnai, L., Wasieleski, D., Stafford-Smith, M., Walker, T., Weber, O., Krosinsky, C., & Oram, D. (2019). Finance and Management for the Anthropocene. *Organization & Environment, 32*(1), 26–40. https://doi.org/10.1177/1086026619831451.

Steffen, W., Broadgate, W., Deutsch, L., Gaffney, O., & Ludwig, C. (2015). The Trajectory of the Anthropocene: The Great Acceleration. *The Anthropocene Review, 2,* 81–98. https://doi.org/10.1177/2053019614564785.

Steffen, W., Richardson, K., Rockström, J., Cornell, S. E., Fetzer, I., Bennett, E. M., Biggs, R., Carpenter, S. R., de Vries, W., de Wit, C. A., Folke, C., Gerten, D., Heinke, J., Mace, G. M., Persson, L. M., Ramanathan, V., Reyers, B., & Sörlin, S. (2015). Planetary Boundaries: Guiding human development on a changing planet. Science 347: 6223, 1259855, pp. 1–10. https://doi.org/10.1126/science.1259855.

Steffen, W., Rockström, J., Richardson, K., Lenton, T.M., Folke, C., Liverman, D., Summerhayes, C.P., Barnosky, A.D., Cornell, S.E., Crucifix, M., Donges, J.F., Fetzer, I., Lade, S.J., Scheffer, M., Winkelmann, R., & Schellnhuber, H.J. (2018). Trajectories of the Earth System in the Anthropocene. *Proceedings of the National Academy of Sciences* Aug 2018, *115* (33), 8252–8259. https://doi.org/10.1073/pnas.1810141115.

Tencati, A., Perrini, F., Hofstra, N., & Zsolnai, L. (2009). Engaging in Progressive Entrepreneurship. In L. Zsolnai & A. Tencati (Eds.), *The Future International Manager* (pp. 153–171). London: Palgrave Macmillan. https://doi.org/10.1057/9780230274068_9.

Tencati, A., & Zsolnai, L. (eds.) (2010). *The Collaborative Enterprise: Creating Values for a Sustainable World*. Bern: Peter Lang. https://doi.org/10.3726/978-3-0353-0005-5.

U.S. Army Heritage and Education Center. (2019). Who First Originated the Term VUCA (Volatility, Uncertainty, Complexity, Ambiguity)? https://usawc.libanswers.com/friendly.php?slug=faq/84869. Accessed 20 July 2020.

Wallis, J. (2020). Obstacles to Sustainable Change in Business Practice. In L. Zsolnai & M. Thompson (Eds.), *Responsible Research for Better Business: Creating Useful and Credible Knowledge for Business and Society* (pp. 211–233). London: Palgrave Macmillan. https://doi.org/10.1007/978-3-030-37810-3_10.

Wellbeing Economy Alliance. (2020). https://wellbeingeconomy.org/. Accessed 20 July 2020.

Zsolnai, L. (2014). Ethics Needs Spirituality. In L. Zsolnai (Ed.), *Beyond Self. Ethical and Spiritual Dimensions of Economics* (pp. 79–83). Bern: Peter Lang. https://doi.org/10.3726/978-3-0353-0596-8/20.

Zsolnai, L. (2015). Spirituality, Ethics and Sustainability. In L. Zsolnai (Ed.), *The Spiritual Dimension of Business Ethics and Sustainability* Management (pp. 3–11). New York: Springer.https://doi.org/10.1007/978-3-319-11677-8_1.

Index

A. Ócsai, *Ecologically Conscious Organizations*, Palgrave Studies in Sustainable Business In Association with Future Earth,
https://doi.org/10.1007/978-3-030-60918-4

The manufacturer's authorised representative in the EU is Springer Nature Customer Service Centre GmbH, Europaplatz 3, 69115 Heidelberg, Germany. If you have any concerns regarding our products, please contact ProductSafety@springernature.com

Printed and bound by CPI Group (UK) Ltd, Croydon, CR0 4YY

06/10/2026

02228468-0002